Colloquial
Bengali

The Colloquial Series
Series Adviser: Gary King

The following languages are available in the Colloquial series:

Afrikaans	German	Romanian
Albanian	Greek	Russian
Amharic	Gujarati	Scottish Gaelic
Arabic (Levantine)	Hebrew	Serbian
Arabic of Egypt	Hindi	Slovak
Arabic of the Gulf	Hungarian	Slovene
Basque	Icelandic	Somali
Bengali	Indonesian	Spanish
Breton	Irish	Spanish of Latin
Bulgarian	Italian	America
Burmese	Japanese	Swahili
Cambodian	Kazakh	Swedish
Cantonese	Korean	Tamil
Catalan	Latvian	Thai
Chinese (Mandarin)	Lithuanian	Tibetan
Croatian	Malay	Turkish
Czech	Mongolian	Ukrainian
Danish	Norwegian	Urdu
Dutch	Panjabi	Vietnamese
English	Persian	Welsh
Estonian	Polish	Yiddish
Finnish	Portuguese	Yoruba
Frencht	Portuguese of Brazil	Zulu (forthcoming)

COLLOQUIAL 2s series: *The Next Step in Language Learning*

Chinese	German	Russian
Dutch	Italian	Spanish
French	Portuguese of Brazil	Spanish of Latin America

Colloquials are now supported by FREE AUDIO available online. All audio tracks referenced within the text are free to stream or download from www.routledge.com/cw/colloquials. If you experience any difficulties accessing the audio on the companion website, or still wish to purchase a CD, please contact our customer services team through www.routledge.com/info/contact.

Colloquial
Bengali

The Complete Course for Beginners

Mithun B. Nasrin and
W.A.M. van der Wurff

LONDON AND NEW YORK

First published 2009
by Routledge
2 Park Square, Milton Park, Abingdon, Oxon OX14 4RN

Simultaneously published in the USA and Canada
by Routledge
711 Third Avenue, New York, NY 10017

*Routledge is an imprint of the Taylor & Francis Group,
an informa business*

© 2009 Mithun B. Nasrin and W.A.M. van der Wurff

Typeset in Times by Graphicraft Limited, Hong Kong

All rights reserved. No part of this book may be reprinted
or reproduced or utilised in any form or by any electronic,
mechanical, or other means, now known or hereafter invented,
including photocopying and recording, or in any information
storage or retrieval system, without permission in writing
from the publishers.

British Library Cataloguing in Publication Data
A catalogue record for this book is available from the
British Library

Library of Congress Cataloging-in-Publication Data
Nasrin, Mithun B.
   Colloquial Bengali / Mithun B. Nasrin and W.A.M. van der Wurff.
    p. cm. – (The colloquial series)
   Includes index.
   1. Bengali language – Spoken Bengali. 2. Bengali language – Textbooks
for foreign speakers – English.
   I. Nasrin, Mithun B. II. Title.
   PK1663.N38 2008
   491.4′4–dc22   2008014997

ISBN13: 978-1-138-95007-8 (pbk)

Contents

Introduction   1

The sounds of Bengali   9

The Bengali script   18

1 আপনার নাম কি?   27
   apnar nam ki?
   What's your name?

2 এরা কি আপনার মামাতো ভাই?   39
   era ki apnar mamato bhai?
   Are these your cousins?

3 ওনার কয়টা বাড়ী আছে?   50
   onar kOeTa baRi ache?
   How many houses does he have?

4 কালীমন্দিরটা কোন দিকে?   61
   kalimondirTa kon dike?
   In what direction is the temple of Kali?

5 আপনি কি কি দেখেছেন?   73
   apni ki ki dekhechen?
   What have you seen?

6 আপনি কি খাবেন?   87
   apni ki khaben?
   What would you like to eat?

7 আপনি কি রান্না করছেন?   97
   apni ki ranna korchen?
   What are you cooking?

8	দেখাবো? dækhabo? Shall I show it to you?	108
9	এই চেকটা কি এখানে ক্যাশ করে নিতে পারি? ei cekTa ki ekhane kæsh kore nite pari? Can I cash this cheque here?	120
10	এখানে কেউ থাকে না? ekhane keu thake na? Doesn't anyone live here?	131
11	তারপরে কি হল? tarpOre ki holo? What happened next?	144
12	আপনারা স্কুলে কি কি পড়তেন? apnara skule ki ki poRten? What did you study at school?	156
13	জমি হাল দেওয়ার জন্য কি ব্যবহার করেন? jomi hal dewar jonno ki bæbohar kOren? What do you use for ploughing the land?	168
14	ফ্লাইট দশটায় ছাড়লে ক'টায় রিপোর্ট করতে হবে? flaiT dOshTae chaRle kOTae riporT korte hObe? If the flight leaves at ten, at what time should I check in?	180
15	নববর্ষে আর কী কী করা হয়? nObobOrshe ar ki ki kOra hOe? What else is done on New Year's Day?	191

Transliterations of Bengali-script texts	203
Bengali script – summary	212
Numbers	216
Bengali grammar – summary	221
Translation of reading texts	231
Key to exercises	234
Bengali–English glossary	257
Index	279

Introduction

The Bengali language (Audio 1:1-6)

This book provides you with an introduction to Bengali, the language of Bangladesh and the state of West Bengal in India. It may be the case that you want to learn this language for purely practical reasons, because you need to communicate with native speakers of Bengali, in Bengal or elsewhere. Or perhaps you have become interested in Bengali language, culture and literature through seeing films by Satyajit Ray (pronounced **shOttojit rae** in Bengali), the director who was awarded a Lifetime Achievement Oscar in 1992, or through hearing about the poems and stories of Tagore, winner of the 1913 Nobel Prize for literature (Tagore's Bengali name is actually Rabindranath Thakur, pronounced **robindronath Thakur**).

Whatever your motivation for learning Bengali, we obviously need to begin with the basics. Let's therefore start with a simple sentence (the earphones symbol indicates that this material appears on the audio accompanying this book; listen to it to hear how this sentence is pronounced):

ami   bangla   jani   na
(I   Bengali   know   not – i.e. I don't know Bengali)

As you can see, where English puts the verb or verbs ('don't know') immediately after the subject ('I'), Bengali usually puts the verb towards or at the end of the sentence. Also note that the word **na** 'not' immediately follows the word to which it refers, i.e. **jani**. This is different from English, but once you know it, there is nothing difficult about it. In fact, if we tell you that the Bengali word for 'am learning' is **shikhchi**, you may also be able to say the following useful sentence in Bengali:

I'm learning Bengali.

Listen to the audio to check whether you have got it right.

You may also have guessed the sentence that you will be able to utter truthfully once you have worked your way through this book:

ami bangla jani
(I   Bengali   know   – i.e. I know Bengali)

From these examples, you will have gathered that, in Bengali itself (and nowadays also sometimes in English), the language is called **bangla**. The word of course also crops up in the name for the region where it is spoken, i.e. Bengal, and in the name Bangladesh, which very appropriately means 'Bangla Country' (hence its variant spelling, Bangla Desh).

This brings us to the matter of words or vocabulary. It cannot be denied that mastering Bengali vocabulary, like learning the vocabulary of any language, will take a real effort on your part. However, there are two facts about Bengali that will go some way toward easing the task of vocabulary acquisition.

Two helpful facts about Bengali

The first helpful fact is that English and Bengali belong to the same linguistic group, called the Indo-European family of languages. This

Introduction

means that both English and Bengali (and many other languages spoken in Europe and the southern and western parts of Asia) are descendants of one and the same language, which was spoken some six thousand years ago. In the course of time, the dialects of this language have grown apart to such an extent that they are now completely different languages. Nevertheless, the distant kinship means that, here and there, recognisable similarities still exist between English and Bengali.

Thus, the Bengali word **jani** in the sentences given above is related to the English word 'know': in spelling, you can see the consonants **j-n** corresponding to 'k-n' (in English, of course, the 'k' in 'know' is not pronounced any more, making the relatedness of the two words somewhat hard to detect). And as you probably realised, the Bengali word **na** is the same as English 'no(t)'. Other examples are **nam** ('name'), **aT** ('eight'), **dãt** ('tooth'), **dOrja** ('door') and **gOrom** ('warm'). It is true that the number of similar-sounding words like this is not large, yet they are very useful in the early stages of learning the language: they will help you realise that you are not groping your way around in completely unknown territory – there are some objects that you can already recognise.

So can you guess which of the following Bengali words corresponds to which English one?

pOth	naked
lOmba	up(per)
dui	bind
tritio	nose
næ̃ngta	mouth
bãdha	third
nak	long
upore	path
mukh	two

A second fact about Bengali is even more helpful: dozens if not hundreds of Bengali words will look very familiar to you because they are loanwords adopted from English into Bengali. This happened during the long period of close contact between the two languages when nearly the whole of the South Asian subcontinent was under British rule. As a result, it is not too difficult to guess the meanings of the following words, all of which are part and parcel of everyday Bengali:

ce-ar, **Tebil**, **kap**, **peleT**, **gelash**, **ofish/opis/apis**

Again, you should listen to the audio to hear how these English words sound when pronounced in Bengali. As the last example shows, there are sometimes various pronunciations in use for such loanwords.

The borrowing of words from English into Bengali is still taking place today. English is spoken as a second or third language by many Bengalis and some of them like to pepper their Bengali with English words, phrases or even complete sentences. Although perhaps we shouldn't be saying this, if at any point you're searching for a Bengali word but don't know or remember it, you could try simply using the English word. As long as you embed it properly into the Bengali grammatical structure, chances are you will be understood. You might, for example, try the following sentence whenever you get tired of saying 'I don't know Bengali':

ami inglish jani

Of course, it is better still to use the Bengali word, **ingreji** (actually, this is just a more thoroughly Bengalified version of the same word) and say:

ami ingreji jani

Varieties of Bengali

Before we describe the set-up and aims of this book and plunge right into the Bengali language, there are a couple of other things that you should know about the different types of Bengali that you may encounter. First, like all other languages, Bengali has various regional dialects, which diverge to a greater or lesser degree from each other and from what is considered by speakers of Bengali themselves to be 'proper' Bengali. As a learner of the language, you are probably best off steering clear of regional dialects and aiming for 'proper' Bengali, i.e. the Bengali that is spoken by educated speakers and that does not evoke negative reactions from other speakers. This is the Bengali that you will find in this book.

However, 'proper' Bengali itself comes in two types, since there is a standard Bengali in the West (i.e. in the Indian state of West Bengal, where the majority of the *c.* 70 million speakers of the language are Hindu) and a different standard Bengali in the East (i.e. in Bangladesh, where most of the *c.* 130 million speakers are Muslim). Each of these two standards evokes mildly negative reactions from the other group, with the Western standard sounding over-refined to

Introduction

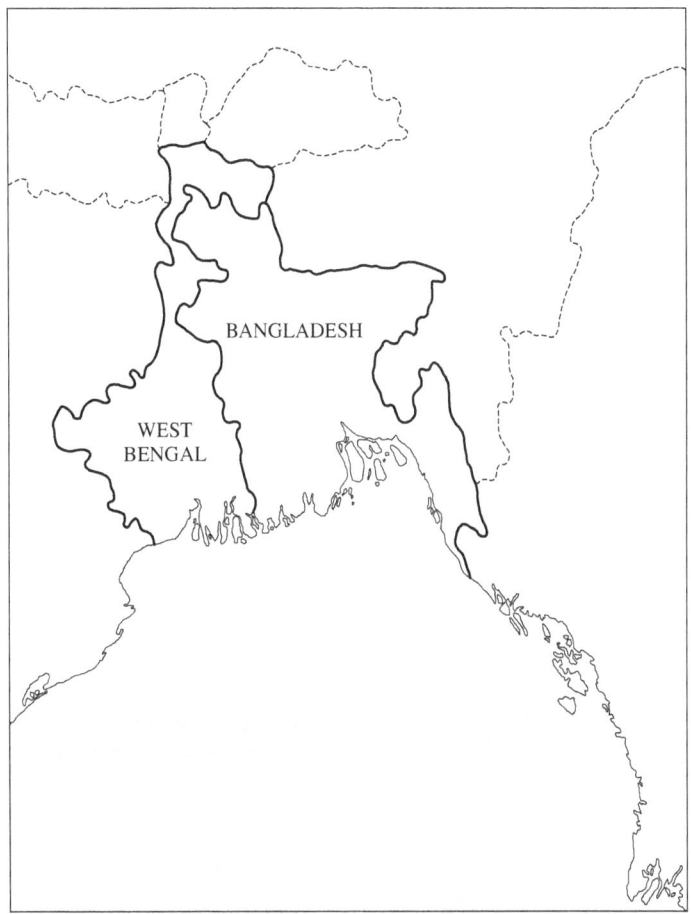

Bengal–Bangladesh and the Indian state of West Bengal

some Eastern ears, and the Eastern standard sounding rural or backward to some Western ears (we hope we are offending nobody by these characterisations – as you will discover, all types of Bengali actually sound extremely pleasing and mellifluous). The differences between the two varieties are not enormous, but they can be found in all areas of the language: pronunciation, vocabulary and grammar (in particular, word endings). We will in all cases note such differences, using the labels 'Eastern' and 'Western' (or simply 'E' and 'W'). Note that the W-forms are also often used by Hindus living in Bangladesh.

Another division is that between written and spoken Bengali. You will have noted that the Bengali words and sentences given so far have all been in the Roman alphabet. But we can assure you: Bengali has a script all its own, developed from the same source as the *devanagari* writing system of Sanskrit, the ancient language of Northern India. As you will find out further on in this book, the Bengali script requires some effort to master but (like Bengali pronunciation and grammar) it is not shockingly difficult, and it does a good job at representing clearly and unambiguously most of the sounds of the language. To give you a little taste of what is ahead, we give here the sentence 'I am learning Bengali' in Bengali script. (The script reads from left to right.) Do you remember how it is pronounced?

আমি বাংলা শিখছি

Finally, when you know enough Bengali to tackle literary texts written roughly before the middle of the last century, you will encounter there a type of Bengali that shows many old-fashioned word forms and heavy use of Sanskrit words. This elevated and slightly artificial variety of the language is called **shadhu bhasha**, i.e. 'pure language'. It is important because it is used in some of the writings by Rabindranath Thakur and other great authors of 19th- and early 20th-century Bengali literature. In the same period, texts were also written in a less stylised variety of Bengali; this is often called **colti** (or **colito**) **bhasha**, i.e. 'current language', since it was closer to the ordinary spoken language. Present-day writing in Bengali is mostly in either the Western or Eastern standard, depending on where the author comes from. It is not unusual, however, to find Bangladeshi texts that include some Western forms.

Learning colloquial Bengali with this book

So you want to learn Bengali. You have just discovered that you can already recognise some Bengali words. You have also learned to say **ami bangla jani na** and **ami bangla jani**. How will this book help you to move from the first sentence to the second one?

It will do so by offering you a large amount of colloquial Bengali as it would be used by ordinary speakers and writers of various types and in various situations. The material has been carefully graded, so that what is simplest and most useful for a learner comes first, and what is more difficult or specialised comes later. In the first four units, all the material is immediately followed by an English translation and in the later units, lists of vocabulary are given, so that the meaning of any dialogue or text will always be clear. The audio, which forms an essential part of the book, allows you to hear what the material in this book would actually sound like, enabling you to develop a 'feel' for the spoken language and its pronunciation. In addition, the audio contains various types of exercises. Care has been taken to present all this material in a context that is as natural as possible, so that it provides you with a model of the colloquial Bengali that you will encounter (and that you are aiming to produce) across a range of everyday settings and situations.

Besides the Bengali-language material, together with translations, this book also contains explanations of the rules (and exceptions) of Bengali grammar. However, the focus is always on grammar in use: particular points are explained in the context of the Bengali dialogues or written texts and the emphasis lies on what you can do with the various grammatical forms. This is also reflected in the nature of the exercises in the book, which invite you to understand or do things in Bengali rather than produce isolated forms. A key to the exercises is provided at the back of the book, as is a summary of the main grammatical patterns and a glossary.

Practice makes perfect

Since only practice makes perfect, we would advise you to regularly repeat the material that you have learned. If anyone should try to read this book from cover to cover in one go, in order to be done with it quickly, we see little prospect of them learning much or enjoying the learning experience. A language guide simply cannot be read like a detective novel. So to prevent this book from ending up on your bookshelf with you none the wiser for it, you will need to take your time over each unit and to regularly go through earlier units again. This does not have to take the form of doing the same things in the same way again and again. Instead, you could turn to an earlier text and listen to it with the book closed; you could try to memorise parts of texts; if you have a microphone you could read out certain portions and make a recording of yourself speaking Bengali; you could devise your own questions or exercises to supplement those in the book; you could copy texts and pin them on the wall next to your bed; and you could change dialogues by making a speaker older or younger, or by shifting certain events from the past into the present or future and vice versa, or by replacing the mention of single objects or people by several objects or people (all of these changes will affect the grammatical forms to be used).

For further practice, try to enlist the help of a native speaker of Bengali. Or go online: the Internet makes available a certain amount of spoken Bengali, with endless possibilities for repetition. For instance, at the time of writing this book, news broadcasts in Bengali are available at:

- <http://www.voa.gov/stream/bangla.html> and
- <http://www.bbc.co.uk/bengali/radio/aod/bengali_promo.shtml>.

In the early stages of learning, such material could be used for the purpose of becoming familiar with the sound of the language, while at later stages, it should be possible to identify specific words or phrases and eventually work out the meaning of complete sentences. When it comes to written Bengali on the Internet, there is a much greater wealth of material. Whichever way you choose to use it (and we provide some concrete suggestions in later units of this book), it will reinforce the central message of this book: colloquial Bengali is something to be explored and enjoyed. We hope we have whetted your appetite for it.

What you can do when you have worked through this book

When you have worked through the material in this book, you will know enough Bengali to do the following things:

- describe and talk about present situations and activities
- describe and talk about situations and events in the past
- describe and talk about wishes, commands, expectations and possibilities relating to the future
- describe relations of various kinds between things, people and events
- express and ask about a wide range of feelings and opinions
- report what other people have said or thought

The topics about which you will be able to communicate in Bengali include matters as diverse as family relationships, jobs, travel, food, money, the seasons, agriculture, schools and air travel. In addition, you will be able to read simple texts on these topics. You will also have gained some experience in reading more difficult texts, and be ready to continue improving your knowledge and understanding of Bengali on your own.

The sounds of Bengali

Although the pronunciation and script of Bengali are not extremely difficult, they are both new to you, so we will start in this section by just describing the pronunciation of Bengali. To represent the sounds of the language, we will use a system of transliteration which (with one exception) employs the ordinary letters of the Roman alphabet. But in the following section, we will also introduce the Bengali writing system and will start using it in selected texts from Unit 2 onwards. The amount of Bengali script will gradually increase as you move further on. However, a transliteration of all Bengali-script texts is given at the back of the book, which also has a Bengali–English glossary with each Bengali word given in transliteration.

But let's first consider the sounds of Bengali, beginning with the vowels. In each case, we give a description of the sound quality, with reference to an identical or very similar sound in English or another European language, followed by some example words. Since describing sound quality on paper is notoriously difficult, it is essential that you should listen to the audio, on which each of the following sounds and words containing them can be heard.

Vowel sounds (Audio 1:7)

Transliteration	Quality	Example words
a	as in French *oh! là là!* or Italian *mamma mia*	**ma** mother **baba** father
i	as in French *petit*; similar to English 'see', but without a final 'y' glide	**ki** what **didi** elder sister
u	as in French *coup*; similar to English 'shoe' but without final 'w' glide	**mul** root **dur** far

Transliteration	Quality	Example words
e	as in French *chez*; similar to English 'pay', but without final 'y' glide	**ke** who **desh** country
æ	as in English 'back', 'mat'	**bæla** time period **æk** one
o	as in French *beau*; similar to English 'go', but without final 'w' glide	**tomar** your **bon** sister
O	as in English 'pot'	**kOl** watertap **kOra** to do

Now try to pronounce all seven vowels in sequence.

    a   i   u   e   æ   o   O

You can also pronounce seven meaningful words in this way but to do so, you must first learn to pronounce the Bengali consononant **kh**. It is similar to the initial sound heard in English 'cool', 'coat' and 'cash-and-carry', which have a 'k'-sound followed by a puff of breath or aspiration. But the aspiration in Bengali **kh** is stronger than in English, resulting in something that may sound like a 'k' followed by the *ch* heard in broad Scottish *loch* or German *acht*, *Nacht*.

If you can make this sound **kh** (and there'll be plenty more practice, because there are several sounds in Bengali with such aspiration), you can say the following seven words:

khal	canal	**khæla**	to play
khil	bolt (of door)	**khola**	open
khuli	skull	**khOl**	deceitful
khelap	defaulting		

All the vowels of Bengali also occur with slightly nasalised pronunciation, which we shall indicate with a tilde (~) written over the vowel letter. Some examples are:

bã	left(hand)
ũcu	high
hæ̃	yes

The effect is as if there is an unpronounced 'n' or 'm' following the vowel in question. At an earlier stage of the language, there was indeed such a nasal consonant in most of these words. Eastern Bengali often keeps the nasal consonant or drops it altogether without any trace being left (so you may hear **bam** and **ucu** in Bangladesh).

The sounds of Bengali

Bengali also has several diphthongs, which consist of a unit of two vowels, the second one being **u**, **o**, **i** or **e**. The main Bengali diphthongs are:  **(Audio 1:8)**

Transliteration	Quality	Example words
ai	as in English 'my tie'	**khai** I eat **nai** there isn't (Eastern)
ae	similar to **ai** but the second part is more open than **i** (aim for an **e**-sound)	**khae** s/he eats **pae** s/he gets
au	as in English 'loud' and 'down-and-out'	**lau** gourd **kau** sour peach
ao	similar to **au** but the second vowel sounds like **o** rather than **u**	**khao** you eat **nao** (small) boat
ei	as in English 'say' when pronounced with an emphatic final 'y' glide	**shei** that **nei** there isn't
oi	the vowel **o** immediately followed by a 'y' sound	**boi** book **koi** I say
Oe	the vowel **O** followed by **e**; the sound differs from **oi** in being much more open	**shOmOe** time **nOe** nine
ou	the vowel **o** followed by an emphatic final 'w' sound	**bou** bride **couddo** fourteen

In some words, two identical vowels follow each other. We use a hyphen to make this clear: **ce-e** 'than', **me-e** 'girl/daughter'. They are sometimes pronounced with a light **y** sound in the middle: **ceye**, **meye**.

Consonant sounds (Audio 1:9)

In the example words given so far, you have already seen and heard a fair number of the consonants of Bengali. In giving a full list, it is convenient to present them in groups of four of five, since their differences and similarities are brought out most clearly in that way. We start with the group of velar sounds:

k	as in English 'keen' and 'kind', but WITHOUT any aspiration	**keu** someone **akash** sky

kh	as in English 'keen' and 'kind', but with strong aspiration (sometimes sounding like 'k' followed by *ch* of Sottish *loch*)	**kham** envelope **ekhane** here
g	as in English 'go' and 'dig'	**gal** cheek **rag** anger
gh	like **g** but followed by aspiration	**ghOr** room **aghat** a blow
ng	as in English 'king' and 'song'	**rOng** colour **anggul** finger/toe

(Audio 1:10) These are all called velar sounds because, in pronouncing them, the tongue touches the back of the roof of the mouth (i.e. the velum). Pay special attention to the difference between the pair **k** and **g**, without any following aspiration, and the pair **kh** and **gh**, followed by strong aspiration. At the end of a word, aspiration is less forceful: **nOkh** 'nail' (W **nokh**) and **megh** 'cloud' may sound as if they end in **k** and **g**, especially in fast speech.

The dental sounds are made with the tip of the tongue touching the back of the upper teeth:

t	like English 'two' and 'ten' but with the tip of the tongue more to the front, and WITHOUT following aspiration	**tin** three **shat** seven
th	**t** followed by aspiration	**thutni** chin **matha** head
d	like English 'do' and 'deed' but with the tip of the tongue more to the front	**dui** two **nodi** river
dh	**d** followed by aspiration	**dhan** paddy, rice **dodhi** yoghurt
n	as in English 'no' and 'nine'	**nun** salt (Western) **kan** ear

(Audio 1:11)

(Audio 1:12) Again it is important to make a clear contrast between the aspirated consonants of this group (**th** and **dh**) and the non-aspirated ones (**t** and **d**). At the end of a word, as in **pOth** 'path' and **kãdh** 'shoulder', aspiration is less strong. When the sound **n** is immediately followed by a dental consonant, as in **cinta** 'thought' or **bOndho** 'closed', the **n** itself is also dental (i.e. the tip of the toungue touches the back of the upper teeth, in anticipation of the following consonant). When followed by a vowel or coming at the end of a word, Bengali **n** is just like English 'n'.

(Audio 1:13) The next group (for which we use capital **T** and **D**, to distinguish them from the dental sounds **t** and **d**) is called retroflex. In

The sounds of Bengali 13

pronouncing these retroflex consonants, the tip of the tongue does not touch the teeth but is pulled back a little to touch the ridge of the gums. The effect is that of English 't' or 'd' in words like 'try' and 'dry': if you say these English words in slow motion and stop just before reaching the sound 'r', you have hit the Bengali retroflex sounds **T** and **D** spot on. To an English ear, the Bengali retroflex consonants may sound very similar to the dental ones, but in Bengali they are as different as 't' and 'th' are in English (where 'tin' is not at all the same as 'thin'). So try to distinguish these Bengali dental and retroflex pairs from the beginning, even if it is difficult.

T	as English 't' in 'try' and 'tree', but WITHOUT aspiration	**Taka** taka, money **aT** eight
Th	T followed by aspiration	**Thikana** address **ciThi** letter
D	as English 'd' in 'dry' and 'drum'	**Dan** right(hand) **ThanDa** cold
Dh	D followed by aspiration	**Dheu** wave **Dhaka** Dhaka

Again, the contrasts **T** – **Th** and **D** – **Dh** need to be carefully made.
The following group is called palatal, since the front of the tongue touches the palate when pronouncing these sounds: **(Audio 1:14)**

c	as in English 'chin' and 'choose', but without much lip-rounding	**car** four **pãc** five
ch	c followed by aspiration; in Eastern Bengali, it often sounds like English 's' in 'see', or 'ts' in 'lots'	**chele** boy, son **kichu** something
j	as in English 'jam' and 'jar'; in Eastern Bengali, it may sound like English 'z' in 'zest', often with a light 'd' before it	**jOl** water **kobji** wrist
jh	j followed by aspiration	**jhal** hot, spicy **majhi** boatman

The labial sounds (i.e. lip sounds) of Bengali are:

p	as in English 'pin' and 'pool' but WITHOUT any aspiration	**pa** foot **kOpal** forehead
f	similar to English 'fin' and 'fool', but with the lower lip nearly touching the upper lip rather than the upper teeth	**fOl** fruit **laf** jump
b	as in English 'bye-bye' and 'blue'	**biman** aeroplane **khObor** news

(Audio 1:15)

bh	b followed by aspiration	bhalo	good
		gobhir	deep
m	as in English 'my' and 'mummy'	tumi	you
		am	mango

The older pronunciation of **f** was the sound **p** followed by aspiration; this can still be heard, especially in West Bengal. The sound **bh** has a common variant which is a sort of 'v'-sound as in English 'very' and 'over', but with the lower lip nearly touching the upper lip rather than the upper teeth.

(Audio 1:16) This leaves a few consonants that do not fit neatly into a group. First, Bengali also has the sounds **l** and **h**, which are easy to pronounce because they are just like English 'l' and 'h'. But be sure to make the Bengali **l** always clear – it should sound like the first 'l' (not the second 'l') in English 'little'. Examples are:

lal	red	hat	hand
alu	potato	bibaho	marriage

Next, there is the frequent sound **sh**, which is very similar to English 'sh' as in 'shoeshine' and 'rush', except that Bengali **sh** has no lip rounding. When **sh** is followed by dental **t** or **th** in the same word, it is pronounced more like English 's' as in 'sister'; we will use the symbol **s** to represent this sound. It also occurs in loanwords from English and Arabic. Some examples of **sh** and **s** are:

shal	year	stri	wife
dOsh	ten	sinema	cinema; film
asha	to come	naser	Naser (Muslim name)
aste	coming		

As we saw above, the sound **s** is also used in Eastern Bengali as a possible pronunciation of **ch**, resulting in pronunciations such as **sele** and **kisu** (for Western Bengali **chele** 'boy' and **kichu** 'something'). In this book, we will represent such words with the symbol **ch** – but remember that there can be a difference in pronunciation of these words between East and West Bengal.

(Audio 1:17) Bengali **r** is somewhat different from English 'r': it is a trilled sound, which is similar to the *r* in the broad Scottish pronunciation of *Mary* and *Aberdeen* and to the *r* in Spanish (*Rio Grande* or *hombre*). Some words with **r** are:

rakha	amar	bhru
to put	my	eyebrow

The sounds of Bengali

Bengali has a second 'r'-sound, for which we use capital **R**. It is a retroflex sound, made by curling back the tip of the tongue and producing a short trilled or flapped 'r'. The effect is somewhat similar to that of a strong American 'r', so you could begin by aiming for that sound. Some words with **R** are:

baRi	**taRa-taRi**	**Dhæ̃Rosh**
house	quickly	lady's finger

You have now seen and heard all the consonants of Bengali. There is just one more fact about them that you need to know: some words have long or double consonants. This is the case in words such as:

(Audio 1:18)

bollo	s/he said	**abba**	father (Eastern)
amma	mother (Eastern)	**bhaggo**	fortune

In the first two words, an extra-long **l** or **m** sound will be heard. The third and fourth word may sound as if someone has trouble pronouncing them and, as it were, gets stuck on the sound **b** or **g** for a moment before managing to finish them.

Practice

It is high time for some practice now, to familiarise you with all these sounds, to sharpen your ear for the distinctions among them, and to get you started on pronouncing them in the best Bengali that you can muster at this moment. Do not forget also to do the exercises on the audio.

Exercise 1

Here are some pairs of words that differ only in one single sound. First read them out, taking care to indeed distinguish them properly. Then, for each pair, make a short sentence in which you correct someone who has mispronounced them. For the first pair, your sentence would be:

na, '**am**' na: '**ham**'! ('No, not **am**: **ham**!').

1	**am**	mango		**ham**	measles
2	**jal**	net		**jhal**	hot, spicy
3	**Dal**	branch		**Dhal**	slope
4	**shaRi**	sari (worn by women)		**shari**	line, queue
5	**kOl**	watertap		**khOl**	deceitful

6	**hat**	hand		**haT**	market
7	**Thik**	right, OK		**Tik**	tick
8	**bhat**	(cooked) rice		**bat**	rheumatism
9	**cai**	I want		**chai**	ashes
10	**cai**	I want		**cae**	s/he wants
11	**bolo**	say (it)!		**bollo**	s/he said
12	**Daka**	to call		**Dhaka**	Dhaka

Exercise 2 (Audio 1:19)

Included among the example words given earlier in this section to illustrate the Bengali sounds are all the numerals from one to ten (except for **chOe** 'six'). Find them, make a list of them, pronounce them slowly and carefully a couple of times, and then learn the sequence by heart.

Exercise 3

Count down from ten to one. Also learn this sequence by heart.

Exercise 4 (Audio 1:21)

Also included among the example words given above are several names of body parts. Find them, make a list, and learn them by heart.

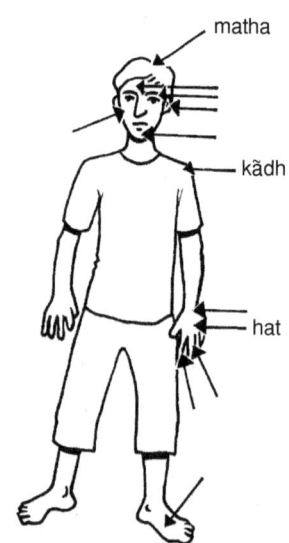

The sounds of Bengali **17**

Then point at your hand, and say: **amar hat** 'my hand'. Also do this for the other parts of your body that you can name in Bengali. Then repeat this, but now using the words **Dan** 'right' and **bã** 'left' where appropriate. Start with: **amar Dan hat** 'my right hand'.

Exercise 5 (Audio 1:22)

You have invited a Bengali-speaking friend to a family party, and want to introduce your family to him/her. Do this by identifying each of your family members in turn, starting with: **amar ma** 'my mother'. You can also find other words for relatives in this chapter – make a list and learn them.

Exercise 6

Using the example words given above, you can make several word pairs. Find the Bengali words for the following pairs. The first one has been done for you. After doing this, learn them by heart. Then make sentences in which you correct someone who mixes up the two words, as follows: **na, ekhane na, okhane** ('No; not here; there'). Also reverse the order: **na, okhane na, ekhane**.

here – there   **ekhane – okhane**   warm (remember
someone – something   this one?) – cold
who? – what?   open – closed
my – your   letter – envelope
son – daughter   cloud – sky
brother (**bhai**) – sister   river – boat
mother – father   right – left
mother – father (Eastern)   yes – no
hand – foot

The Bengali script

Now that you have become familiar with the sounds of Bengali, the next logical step is to start learning the Bengali writing system. Since we give all the material also in transliteration, you could decide to leave the script for later, and move on to Unit 1 from here. However, we would advise you to tackle the script as well now. Learning it is an essential part of learning the language.

Whether you tackle it now or later, it will take time to get used to the 50 or so symbols that the script has (not counting the so-called 'conjunct' consonants), so it is best to go slowly in the beginning and spread out the learning task over time. In this section, you will learn about the principles of the script, the shapes of the most common vowel letters, and a few of the consonant letters. The other letters will be introduced gradually over the course of the units that follow.

(Audio 1:23) Bengali is written from left to right and the lines follow each other from top to bottom. A difference from English is that the Bengali letters are written not on the line, but BELOW the line: each letter as it were hangs down from a line rather than standing on one as in English. You can see this in the following example, which contains the phrase meaning 'my mother', in Bengali printed script and in transliteration.

Bengali print:	আ ম া র	ম া
transliteration:	a m a r	m a

In this and many other cases, the Bengali script works in a way similar to the alphabet, where one letter usually represents one sound. You can see the letter ম for the sound **m**, appearing in both **amar** and **ma**, and the final letter র in **amar**. But you can also see that the two '**a**'s in **amar** are written differently. This difference is due to the following property of vowel letters in Bengali:

The Bengali script

> **Vowel letters in Bengali have two shapes**
> - one shape is used when the vowel follows a consonant in the same word
> - the other shape is used elsewhere (i.e. if the vowel comes at the beginning of a word or follows another vowel)

For the sound **a**, the two shapes are:

া (following a consonant)   মা **ma** mother
আ (elsewhere)   আম **am** mango

For the vowel **i**, the symbols are:

ি (following a consonant)   মিল **mil** similarity
ই (elsewhere)   ইমাম **imam** Muslim clergyman

Note that the ি seen in মিল **mil** represents the sound **i** pronounced after a consonant (i.e. after **m**), but it is WRITTEN BEFORE the consonant letter. The spelling of the word **mil** also shows you another consonant letter, ল for **l**.

Some vowel letters are WRITTEN BELOW the consonant which, in pronunciation, they actually follow – this is the case for the sound **u**.

ু (following a consonant)   মুখ **mukh** mouth, face
উ (elsewhere)   উমা **uma** Uma (Hindu goddess, wife of Shiva)

In the example word মুখ you can see a further consonant letter: খ for **kh**.

The vowel sound **o** is different again. When following a consonant in pronunciation, it takes the form of two strokes WRITTEN AROUND this consonant letter.

ো (following a consonant)   কোল **kol** lap
ও (elsewhere)   ওর **or** his/her

The word কোল contains another new consonant letter: ক for **k**.

Exercise 1

Here is a summary of the Bengali letters you have seen so far. For each, write down what sound it represents. The first one has been done for you.

	Vowels							
Bengali letter	আ	া	ই	ি	উ	ু	ও	ো
Sound	a	___	___	___	___	___	___	___

	Consonants				
Bengali letter	ক	খ	ম	ল	র
Sound	___	___	___	___	___

Exercise 2 (Audio 1:24)

Using the list you have made in Exercise 1, now read each of the following. You will recognise most words from the previous section.

(a) খাল   খিল   খুলি   খোলা
(b) আমি   আমার   আমার মা   আমার মুখ
(c) আম   লাউ   লাল আলু
(d) আমি   খাই   আমি আম খাই

Here are four more consonants letters, with example words:

p প পা **pa** foot   পুকুর **pukur** pond
b ব বালি **bali** sand   খাবো **khabo** I will eat
t ত তুমি **tumi** you   রাত **rat** night
n ন আনার **anar** pomegranate খান **khan** Khan (Muslim surname)

Exercise 3

Match each of the Bengali items in column I with one of the English translations in column II.

I	II
1 আমার বোন	a mother (and) father
2 আমার পা	b your mouth
3 তোমার বোন	c my foot
4 তোমার মুখ	d your sister
5 ওর মুখ	e mother (and) father
6 ওর বোন	f his sister
7 মা বাবা	g my sister
8 আম্মা আব্বা	h his mouth

Were you able to work out the pronunciation of the last Bengali item? (This is something that we'll come back to in Unit 6.) And do you remember what the difference is between the last two Bengali items?

The Bengali script

The vowel letter in Bengali which requires most attention is the letter representing the sound **O**. When it doesn't follow a consonant, it has a clear shape (it looks like a shortened version of আ), but when following a consonant, it is NOT WRITTEN AT ALL.

O / (following a   কল **kOl** watertap   মরা **mOra** to die
consonant)
O অ (elsewhere)   অমিল **Omil** difference   অমর **OmOr** immortal

This means that a consonant on its own can represent a sequence of that consonant followed by the sound **O**; such an **O** sound is often called an 'inherent' **O**. In fact, consonants written in isolation (ক, খ, ম, র etc.) are referred to as **kO**, **khO**, **mO**, **rO** etc., i.e. the consonant followed by inherent **O**. **(Audio 1:25)**

There is a complication involving the letter অ and the inherent vowel sound coming after a consonant. In some words, this is not the sound **O** but **o**. Two examples are:

অতি **oti** (too) much   কবি **kobi** poet

You have already seen that there is a separate letter for the sound **o**, so in principle these words could (and perhaps should) be written with that letter. They would then look as follows:

ওতি **oti**   কোবি **kobi**

For some words containing the sound **o**, both spellings exist (e.g. the second syllable of খাবো / খাব **khabo** 'I will eat') but for the large majority the spelling is fixed. The two words given above, for example, always take the form অতি and কবি, with the pronunciation being **o**.

Another complication is that, if a consonant is written without a vowel letter following it, it can also stand for simply the consonant sound. In the word আমরা **amra** 'we', for example, the **m** is directly followed by the sound **r**, without any **O** or **o** in between, while in the word অমর **OmOr** 'immortal' there is an inherent **O** sound after the letter ম but not after the letter র. This is a systematic ambiguity of the Bengali script.

There are two devices in Bengali spelling that are sometimes used to resolve this ambiguity. First, if a word has two consonants following each other and there is no inherent vowel after the first one, this is often signalled by giving the second consonant (or sometimes the whole combination) a special shape. Two examples are the words **broto** 'vow' and **proti** 'each'. To make clear that the sound **r** in these words immediately follows the **b/p**, the **r** is written not in its usual shape of র but in the shape of a little squiggle below the letter ব or প.

ব্রত **broto** vow   প্রতি **proti** each

Whenever the **r** does take its usual shape (i.e. র), your best guess is that there is an inherent vowel before it. Examples are: **bOrat** 'good luck' and **pOra** 'to put on (clothes)'.

বরাত **bOrat** good luck   পরা **pOra** to put on

This leaves the ambiguity of word-final consonants. The spelling does not tell you whether they are followed by an inherent vowel (**O** or **o**) or not. The words ব্রত and বরাত, for example, both end in the letter ত in spelling, but **broto** has a final vowel in pronunciation, while **bOrat** does not. To solve this problem, a special sign can be used: the **hOshonto**, which is a small stroke written below a consonant to indicate the absence of an inherent vowel. If this **hOshonto** was used, some of the words given above would look as follows:

বরাত্   অমিল্   অমর্   আম্   খান্

(Audio 1:26)

Unfortunately, in actual practice, the **hOshonto** is seldom written (except in 'repeating' words such as তক্‌তক্‌ **tOktOk** 'sparkling clean'). This is because Bengali writing is geared to native speakers of the language, who know the exact pronunciations of words anyway, so that the spelling does not need to be precise in every single detail (if you find this strange, think of the English words 'thought', 'though', 'cough', and 'rough' and then try to figure out how systematic their spelling is). But for a learner of Bengali, these ambiguities of the Bengali script are clearly troublesome. In this book, we will therefore give a transliteration of each new word that is first introduced in Bengali spelling, so that the pronunciation is always clearly shown. If you need to check later, you can turn to the Bengali–English glossary at the back of the book, which gives all the words in transliteration.

Exercise 4

Below are two lists: the first contains words in Bengali script, the second contains their transliterations, but in scrambled order. Match them.

1 ১ তারা   a **map** size
2 ২ কান   b **likhi** I write
3 ৩ বালা   c **kan** (you know this one!)
4 ৪ কপাল   d **probOl** strong

The Bengali script

5 ৫ বোমা e **bollo** s/he said
6 ৬ মাপ f **boma** bomb
7 ৭ প্রবল g **kOpal** (you know this one too)
8 ৮ লিখি h **tara** star
9 ৯ কালো i **bala** bracelet
10 ১০ বললো j **kalo** black

As you may have guessed, after the Arabic numbers marking the items in Exercise 4, we have also given the numbers in Bengali script. Learn these Bengali numbers. Do you remember how they are pronounced? Can you also count down from 10 to 1 in Bengali? And can you pronounce the following figures:

৯, ২, ৮, ৬, ৮, ৪, ৬, ৩, ৯, ১, ৫, ৩, ৪, ৮, ৫, ৬, ৫

Do not continue until you can do all this with ease.

A final ambiguity of the Bengali script lies in the spelling of the two vowel sounds **e** and **æ**, as in **tel** 'oil' and **khæla** 'to play' or **ekhane** 'here' and **æk** 'one'. These two different sounds are represented by the same Bengali letter:

ে (following a consonant)   তেল **tel** oil   খেলা **khæla** to play
এ (elsewhere)   এখানে **ekhane** here   এক **æk** one

Note that the sound **e/æ** following a consonant sound is represented by a letter that is actually put BEFORE the consonant in writing – we have seen the same thing for the letter ি as in কি **ki** 'what'.

The ambiguity of ে and এ in Bengali writing (is it pronounced **e** or **æ**?) is of course solved in the transliteration system that we use. As a general guideline, you may also want to remember that there are more words with the sound **e** than with **æ**, so that the pronunciation **e** is more often the right one. The reason for this, and for the lack of differentiation of **e** and **æ** in spelling, is that the sound **æ** is relatively new in Bengali: a few hundred years ago, it simply didn't exist.

If it is really necessary to show in Bengali script that the sound **æ** is meant, this can be done, though the device used for it is somewhat complicated. To show you how it works, you first need to learn the letter ্য (usually called **jO-fOla**). This letter can be written after a consonant letter to indicate that the consonant is pronounced long:

অন্য **onno** other

A combination of this **jO-fOla** with the letters া and এ is sometimes used to write words containing the sound **æ**. Look carefully how this is done:

(Audio 1:27)

্যা (following a consonant) ম্যাপ **mæp** map, ব্যাখ্যা **bækkha** explanation

এ্যা (elsewhere) এ্যানি **æni** Annie

As you can see from the examples, this device is used for the short 'a' sound of English words borrowed into Bengali. But there are also native Bengali words that are written with it. In the example ব্যাখ্যা, note that the first **jO-fOla** has the function, together with the following letter া, of representing the sound **æ** but the second **jO-fOla** indicates that the preceding consonant খ is to be pronounced long or double. Finally, you may want to remember that some words with the sound **æ** are written with only a **jO-fOla**: ব্যথা **bætha** 'pain' (the থ stands for **th**).

These, then, are the basic rules of the Bengali writing system. You may feel a little overwhelmed by them at this point, but this feeling should soon subside. Whenever you read Bengali, you are going to see the same principles in action again and again, in word after word, and they will eventually become second nature to you in reading Bengali. All Bengali-script texts are also given in transliteration in the Appendix, so you can always check there.

Exercise 5 (Audio 1:28)

Below is a shopping list that you have been given. You know most of the words. Write them down in transliteration so that, when in the market, you can say quickly what you want. (But perhaps delay actually going to the market until you have studied Unit 8, where you'll learn how to express amounts.)

আনার নুন
লাউ আপেল
আম কপি cabbage (it has **o**)
লালসূআলু মুলা root, radish
তেল কলা banana (it has **O**)

Exercise 6 (Audio 1:29)

Below, several people say what they want to eat. Note the use of the vertical stroke at the end of each sentence – it is called **dāRi** and

The Bengali script **25**

represents a full stop. Finish the last line (in transliteration) and write down in English what everybody wants.

তোমার বাবা: আমি আনার খাবো (= I will/want to eat pomegranate) ।
তোমার মা: আমি আনার খাবো না। আমি আম খাবো।
এ্যানি: আমি আপেল খাবো।
তোমার বোন: আমি আনার খাবো না। আমি আম খাবো না। আমি কলা খাবো।
তুমি: _____ ।

Exercise 7 (Audio 1:30)

Read out the following pairs of words. Some clues are given by the use of **hOshonto** and by the transliteration of the inherent vowels.

1 বর্ **O** bridegroom   বউ bride
2 নেবো **e** I will take   নেবে s/he will take
3 এরা **e** these people   ওরা **o** those people
4 বক্‌বক্‌ **O O** chattering   প্যান্‌-প্যান্‌ whining
5 প্রেম্‌ **e** love   প্রেত্‌ **e** spirit, ghost
6 আলু potato   আলো light
7 আইন্‌ law   উকিল্‌ lawyer
8 বই **o** book   কই **o** where?
9 আকার্‌ shape   ব্যাপার্‌ matter

Summary of this section

Vowel sound	Spelling after consonant	Spelling elsewhere	Examples
a	া	আ	মা, আম
i	ি	ই	মিল, ইমাম
u	ু	উ	মুলা, উমা
O	not written	অ	করা, অমিল
o	ে া or not written	ও or অ	কোল, কবি, ওর, অতি
e	ে	এ	তেল, এখানে
æ	ে (or য্া/্যা)	এ (or এ্যা)	খেলা, ম্যাপ, ব্যথা (থ=th) এক, এ্যানি

Consonant sound	Spelling	Example
k	ক	করা
kh	খ	খাই
p	প	পা
b	ব	বোন
m	ম	মা
t	ত	তোমার
n	ন	তিন
l	ল	লাল
r	র	আমার
	্ (after consonant)	প্রতি

Special sign	Name	Meaning	Example
্য	jO-fOla	preceding consonant is long	অন্য
্	hOshonto	preceding consonant is not followed by inherent vowel	তক্তক্
।	dāRi	full stop	আমি আম খাবো।

Numbers 1–10

১ ২ ৩ ৪ ৫ ৬ ৭ ৮ ৯ ১০

1 আপনার নাম কি?
apnar nam ki?

What's your name?

In this unit you will learn about:

- addressing, greeting and leave-taking
- giving and asking for personal information
- names of countries
- some further Bengali letters

Dialogue 1 (Audio 1:33)

Jenny is taking a Bengali language class. In the school, she sees Dipu, a Bangladeshi man who is taking an English class there. With Dipu is a man whom Jenny doesn't know.

dipu: slamalaikum jeni, tumi kæmon acho?
jeni: walaikum-salam, dada, ami bhalo achi. apni kæmon achen?
dipu: bhalo. e holo amar bondhu.
jeni: slamalaikum.
Tunu: walaikumsalam. bah! apni to besh bhalo bangla janen. apnar nam ki?
jeni: amar nam jeni. ekhane bangla shikhchi. apnar nam ki?
dipu: or nam Tunu, she amar ækjOn bhalo bondhu.
jeni: accha. dada, amar klash shuru hoe jacche. ami ækhon jai. khoda-hafez, dipuda. khoda-hafez, Tunuda. abar dækha hObe.
Tunu: khoda-hafez.
dipu: khoda-hafez, jeni.

DIPU:	Salam, Jenny, how are you?
JENNY:	Salam, elder brother, I'm fine. How are you?
DIPU:	Fine. This is my friend.
JENNY:	Salam.
TUNU:	Salam. Well, well, you really know Bengali quite well. What's your name?
JENNY:	My name is Jenny. I'm learning Bengali here. What's your name?
DIPU:	His name is Tunu. He's a good friend of mine.
JENNY:	I see. Elder brother, my class is starting. I'm going now. Goodbye, Dipu. Goodbye, Tunu. We'll meet again.
TUNU:	Goodbye.
DIPU:	Goodbye, Jenny.

Vocabulary

slamalaikum	hello (Muslim greeting)	or nam	his/her name
kæmon	how	she	he
acho	you are	ækjOn	a/an
bhalo	good	accha	OK/all right/I see
e	this	shuru hoe jacche	is starting
holo	is	ækhon	now
bondhu	friend	jai	I go
bah	well, well!	khoda-hafez	goodbye (Muslim leave-taking)
to	really, indeed, actually	abar	again
besh	quite	dækha hObe	we'll meet

Addressing people (Audio 1:34–35)

In Dialogue 1, two words are used corresponding to English 'you': the polite pronoun **apni** (আপনি) and the familiar pronoun **tumi** (তুমি). Both mean 'you', but they are used differently:

    apni: to people that are older, higher in rank, or with whom you have no special relationship

    tumi: to people that you know and that are the same age or younger, or that are lower in rank

Apparently Dipu knows Jenny well, since he uses **tumi** to her. He must be older than Jenny, since she uses **apni** to him. She also doesn't use his first name, since that would not be polite. In such a case, Bengali resorts to the use of kinship terms, like **dada** or **bhaiya** (Eastern) for a somewhat older male (both words mean 'elder brother'), **didi** or **apa** (E) for a somewhat older female ('elder sister'), and terms like **kaka** or **caca** (E) ('uncle') and **kaki** or **caci** (E) ('aunt') or **kaki-ma** or **caci-ma** (E) ('aunt-mother') for people who are obviously older. The words **dada**, **didi** and **apa** are sometimes combined with the first name, yielding polite-familiar forms like **dipu dada**, **jeni didi**, or **jeni apa** (E). The first two can be shortened to **dipuda** and **jenidi**.

The distinction between **tumi** and **apni** is also important for the grammar of the verb, since they get different endings. The forms for the verb 'to be' are:

    tumi kæmon acho?   How are you? (literally: FAMILIAR
                                   you how are?)
    apni kæmon achen?   How are you?   POLITE

Dialogue 1 also has the verb ending going with **ami** (আমি) 'I':

    ami bhalo achi   I am fine (lit.: I good am).

Possessive and plural forms

The possessive forms of **tumi** and **apni** are:

tomar তোমার your	**tomar klash** your class	FAMILIAR POSSESSIVE
apnar আপনার your	**apnar bondhu** your friend	POLITE POSSESSIVE

The words **tumi** and **apni** also have plural forms, which must be used when addressing more than one person:

tomra তোমরা	**tomra kæmon acho?** ('how are you (plural)?')	FAMILIAR PLURAL
apnara আপনারা	**apnara kæmon achen?** ('how are you (plural)?')	POLITE PLURAL

Although **tomra** and **apnara** are plural, the verb forms are the same as in the singular. This is a general rule in Bengali: verb forms for singular and plural are always the same. So if we remind you that the word for 'we' is **amra** আমরা, can you say, 'We are fine'?

The intimate pronoun

There is one more pronoun meaning 'you': **tui** তুই, the intimate pronoun. It is used to very good friends, young children and servants, but also to address God. Since it can express close friendship but also convey contempt, it must be handled with care. To express a close relationship, the use of **tumi** usually suffices.

The corresponding verb form, possessive and plural of **tui** are:

tui kæmon achish?	how are you?	INTIMATE
tor bondhu	your friend	INTIMATE POSSESSIVE
tora kæmon achish?	how are you (plural)?	INTIMATE PLURAL

Exercise 1 (Audio 1:36)

Read the following mini-dialogue.

– slamalaikum, kaki, apni bhalo achen?
– hæ̃, bhalo achi. tumi kæmon acho, bahar?
– ami bhalo. e holo amar skuler bondhu.
– accha. tomar nam ki?
– amar nam shonTu, kaki.
– ei shonTu, klash shuru hoe jacche. amra jai, kaki-ma.
– accha. khoda-hafez.

Unit 1: *What's your name?* 31

1 How many speakers are there?
2 What are their names and, roughly, their ages?

Making simple sentences

There are two points to remember about making simple sentences:
* the verb usually comes at the end (though it can be followed by **na** 'not')
* the verb 'to be' is often left out in sentences of the type 'I am here' or 'he is my friend'.

Some examples illustrating these two principles:

amra Dhakae thaki	We live in Dhaka
ami am khabo na	I won't eat mango
amar boi ekhane	My book is here
ami bangladeshi	I am Bangladeshi

Exercise 2

For this exercise, you need a pen (**kOlom** কলম), a book (**boi** বই), a notebook (**khata** খাতা), an envelope (**kham** খাম), a cup (**kap** কাপ), a saucer (**piric**), a pencil (**pensil**), a pair of scissors (**kāci** or **keci** (E)), a newspaper (**khOborer kagoj**) and a key (**cabi**). After learning the words for these objects, put some of them at the far end of the table, leaving others close by. Then say in Bengali where each object is, e.g. **amar boi ekhane**, **amar kāci okhane**, and so on. Next, move some objects around and say where they are now. Repeat several times.

Exercise 3

Now imagine that the objects of Exercise 2 belong to your younger brother Shontu. Tell Shontu where his pen, book, etc. are (e.g. **shonTu, tomar boi ekhane, tomar kOlom okhane**).
Then do the same thing, but imagine the objects are your father's (so say **baba, apnar khata ekhane, apnar kap okhane**, etc.).

Making questions

In Bengali questions, the verb remains in its normal position at the end of the sentence. Furthermore, question words (e.g. **ki** 'what', kothae 'where', kæno 'why') do not have to come at the beginning of the question. Look at the following examples.

apni kothae thaken?	Where do you live? (lit.: you where live?)
tumi ki khabe?	What do you want to eat? (lit.: you what will-eat?)
or saikel kothae?	Where is his bicycle? (lit.: his bicycle where?)

But watch out with the word **ki**. In the example above it means 'what'. However, in questions which require the answer 'yes' or 'no' (e.g. 'Are you learning Bengali?'), **ki** has another meaning – all it does is signal that the sentence is a question. This word **ki** is often placed after the first word or word group of the question sentence. It is unstressed.

tumi ki bangla shikhcho?	Are you learning Bengali?
tumi ki hindi jano?	Do you know Hindi?
apni ki kolkatae thaken?	Do you live in Kolkata (Calcutta)?
apnar me-e ki ekhane?	Is your daughter here?

But since questions, just like in English, also have special question intonation, the question marker **ki** can be left out, e.g. **apnar me-e ekhane?** 'Is your daughter here?'

Exercise 4

You are at a Bengali function, where you meet several people. Ask them the following questions. Where appropriate, first say **ækTa prosno korte pari?** 'Can I ask a question?' (literally: a question do I-can?)

1 (to your Bengali teacher) – Is your daughter here?
2 (to a fellow student who is older than you) – How are you?
3 (to a young boy) – Do you know Bengali?
4 (to one of the musicians) – What is your name?
5 (to a good friend) – Shall we eat some mango?
6 (to a person that you've just met) – Where do you live?

Dialogue 2 (Audio 1:37)

*Mark is sitting in a Bengali restaurant in London. He talks with the owner (**malik**) about what kinds of people like Bengali food (everybody, it turns out!).*

mark: nOmoshkar.
malik: nOmoshkar. are! apni bangla janen?

Unit 1: *What's your name?*

mark: ji, Olpo ekTu jani. ami bangali khabar khub bhalobashi.
malik: accha. Oneke-i bangali khabar pOchondo kOre.
mark: ei resTurenTe ki onno desher lok o ashe? naki shudhu briTish ar bangalira ashe?
malik: shOb desher lok ashe. takie dekhun – ekhane ækjOn pakistani bhOddrolok boshe achen, okhane ækjoRa markin dOmpoti, duijOn coinik mohila, o ækjOn mishorio chattro. tachaRa-o Onek bharotio lok ashe.
mark: tai to dekhchi. apnar resTurenTer khabar mone hOe khub bhalo.
malik: ta Thik. apnar nishcOe-i khide pe-eche. apni ki khaben, bolun.

MARK: *Hello.*
OWNER: *Hello. My, my! You know Bengali?*
MARK: *Yes, I know a little bit. I like Bengali food very much.*
OWNER: *Good. Many people like Bengali food.*
MARK: *Do people from other countries also come to this restaurant? Or do only British and Bengali people come here?*
OWNER: *People from all countries come here. Look – here, a Pakistani gentleman is sitting, there an American couple, two Chinese ladies, and an Egyptian student. Also, many Indian people come here.*
MARK: *I see, indeed. The food in your restaurant is very good, I guess.*
OWNER: *That's right. You must be hungry. Tell me, what would you like to eat?*

Vocabulary

nOmoshkar	hello	ashe	he/they come(s)
are!	my, my!; my goodness!	naki	or
ji	yes (polite form; E)	shudhu	only
Olpo ekTu	a little	ar	and
khabar	food	shOb	all
khub	very, very much	takie dekhun	look
bhalobashi	I love	bhOddrolok	gentleman
Oneke-i	many people	boshe achen	is sitting, is seated
pOchondo kOre	he/they like(s)	ækjoRa	a(n), a pair
		dOmpoti	couple
lok	person, people	mohila	lady
o	also	chattro	student

tachaRa(-o)	besides	ta	that		
Onek	many	Thik	right		
tai	that	nishcOe-i	certainly, surely		
dekhchi	I see, it seems	apnar khide pe-eche	you are hungry		
mone hOe	it seems, I think	bolun	say! (polite form)		

Vocabulary: greetings and leave-takings

The general word for saying 'hello' (and also 'goodbye') in Bengali used to be **nOmoshkar**. It is still used widely by Hindus, Buddhists and Christians. But among Muslims, the Arabic form **slamalaikum** (or its longer form, **as-salam-alaikum**) is now usual. The proper reply to it is **walaikum-salam**. For leave-taking, both parties use **khoda-hafez** (or **allah-hafez**).

Bengalis appreciate it if you use the form that they would normally use. An informal greeting that does not show religious affiliation is **adab**, which is used for leave-taking as well.

Vocabulary: nationalities

Some names of nationalities and countries are:

	Nationality	Country	Language(s)
Bangladeshi	bangladeshi	bangladesh	bangla
Indian	bharotio	bharot	bangla, hindi, tamil, etc.
Burmese	bormi	barma	bormi
Pakistani	pakistani	pakistan	urdu, panjabi, shindhi, etc.
Iranian	parshi	parOssho	farshi
Egyptian	mishorio	mishOr	arbi
Chinese	cina/coinik	cin	cina
English	ingrej	bilat	ingreji
British	briTish	jukto-rajjo (UK)	ingreji
French	fOrashi	frans	fOrashi
American	markin	jukto-rastro (US)	ingreji

The word **bangali** ('Bengali') does not express a nationality but a cultural identity, shared by all speakers of **bangla** in **bangladesh** and **poshcim bangla** ('West Bengal') in **bharot**. After the name of a language, the word **bhasha** 'language' is often added: **bangla bhasha**, **bormi bhasha** etc. ('the Bengali/Burmese etc. language'). To say

Unit 1: *What's your name?*

'Indians', 'Pakistanis' etc., **-ra** is added after the name of the nationality: **bharotiora, pakistanira,** etc.

Exercise 5

Make a card for each nationality/country given above, writing the English words on one side and the Bengali ones on the other. Learn the terms. Then shuffle the cards and pick out two with the English text facing you. Suppose you have picked out 'Indian' and 'French'. Then say in Bengali:

> **nOmoskhkar. ækTa prosno korte pari? ami bharotio. ami Olpo ekTu fOrashi bhasha jani. apni ki fOrashi?**
> ('Hello. May I ask a question? I am Indian. I know a little French. Are you French?')

Or suppose you have picked out 'Chinese' and 'Egyptian'. Then say:

> **nOmoskhkar. ækTa prosno korte pari? ami coinik. ami Olpo ekTu arbi bhasha jani. apni ki mishorio?**
> ('Hello. May I ask a question? I am Chinese. I know a little Arabic. Are you Egyptian?')

Go through the cards several times in this way.

Dialogue 3 (Audio 1:38)

Jenny is applying for a visa for Bangladesh. An officer at the Bangladesh High Commission in London writes down some basic data about her.

kaunselor:	apnar nam ki?
jeni:	amar nam jeni smith.
kaunselor:	apni kon desher nagorik?
jeni:	ami briTish.
kaunselor:	apnar Thikana bOlen.
jeni:	ami lOnDone thaki, ægaro nOmbor, niu feTar len, i si car pi, car i i.
kaunselor:	apnar fon nOmbor bOlen.
jeni:	amar fon nOmbor shunno dui shunno- dui chOe sat pãc nOe aT shat æk.
kaunselor:	apni ki kaj kOren?
jeni:	ami ækjOn shebika. ækTa hashpatale kaj kori.
kaunselor:	accha. ami shOb likhechi. apni okhane boshe ekTu Opekkha kOren.

OFFICER: *What is your name?*
JENNY: *My name is Jenny Smith.*
OFFICER: *Of which country are you a citizen?*
JENNY: *I'm British.*
OFFICER: *Please say your address.*
JENNY: *I live in London; number 11, New Fetter Lane, EC4P 4EE.*
OFFICER: *Please say your phone number.*
JENNY: *My phone number is ০২০ - ২৬৭৫৯৮৭১. [so what is it?]*
OFFICER: *What work do you do?*
JENNY: *I'm a nurse. I work in a hospital.*
OFFICER: *OK. I've written everything down. Please sit there and wait for a while.*

Vocabulary

(bhisa) kaunselor	visa officer	**ki kaj**	what (kind of) work
kon	which	**kOren**	you do (polite form)
nagorik	citizen	**shebika**	nurse
bOlen (E)	say!	**kaj kOra**	to work
= **bolun**	(polite form)	**likhechi**	I've written
thaki	I live	**ekTu**	a little, a bit
ægaro	eleven	**Opekkha kOra**	to wait
shunno	zero		

Exercise 6

Choose an appropriate answer to each question.

1 **apni kothae thaken?**
   (a) **amar nam robi.**
   (b) **ami bilate thaki.**
2 **apni ki ekhane kaj kOren?**
   (a) **na, ami ekhane bangla shikhchi.**
   (b) **niscOe-i, ami bharote thaki.**
3 **apnar bondhu ki bormi?**
   (a) **na, she parshi.**
   (b) **hæ̃, ami markin.**
4 **apni ki khaben?**
   (a) **ami ækTa kOla khabo.**
   (b) **ami ækTa hashpatale kaj kori.**

Unit 1: *What's your name?*

5 apnara kæmon achen?
   (a) ami bhalo achi.
   (b) amra bhalo achi.
6 tomar ma kothae, shonTu?
   (a) ami shOb likhechi.
   (b) amar ma ekhane.

Learn by heart the appropriate answer to each question. Then ask yourself the question and give the answer.

Bengali script: more consonants and vowels

Learn the following five consonants:

c	চ	চার car four	নাচ	nac dance
ch	ছ	ছেলে chele boy	আছি	achi I am
T	ট	আট aT eight	একটা	ækTa a(n)
d	দ	দুই dui two	দাদা	dada elder brother
bh	ভ	ভালো bhalo good	গভীর	gobhir deep

Do you remember the squiggly spelling of **r**? It indicates **r** pronounced after a consonant (e.g. প্রচুর **procur** a lot of). Another symbol is used when **r** comes immediately before a consonant. It consists of a small stroke written above the consonant:

কর্তা **kOrta** boss   মার্কিন **markin** American

You have already learnt symbols for the vowels **i** and **u**. They are sometimes called the 'short' letters for **i/u**. But in some words, these same sounds are written differently, with the so-called 'long' letters for **i** or **u**:

i ী (following a consonant)   নীল **nil** blue
i ঈ (elsewhere)   ঈদ **id** Eid (the Muslim festival)

u ূ (following a consonant)   মূল্য **mullo** price, value
u উ (elsewhere)   উর্বর **urbOr** fertile

Whether a word has the 'long' or 'short' spelling for the vowel **i/u** depends on the word in question. Clearly, this is a point where Bengali spelling could do with some simplification (but, again, comparison with English spellings like 'peek', 'peak' and 'pique' suggests that the variability in Bengali is still limited).

Exercise 7

What do the following mean?

1 চাচী।
2 এখানে।
3 বর্মীরা।
4 তোমার দাদা।
5 আপনার ছেলে।
6 একটা নেপালী বই।
7 আপনারা কেমন আছেন?
8 আমরা খুব ভালো আছি।
9 তোমার দিদি কি এখানে?
10 না। আমার দিদি এখন ভারতে।

2 এরা কি আপনার মামাতো ভাই?
era ki apnar mamato bhai?

Are these your cousins?

In this unit you will learn how to:

- talk about relatives and other people
- express existence
- recognise some further Bengali letters

Dialogue 1 (Audio 1:40)

Shumon is showing Deepa some family snapshots.

dipa: era kara?
shumon: onara amar mama o mami.
dipa: o era ki apnar mamato bhai?
shumon: na. eiTa amar khalato bhai ar oiTa tar bondhu. ei chobiTa dillite tola. tara shObai chuTite dilli giechilo.
dipa: ar oi chobite kara?
shumon: ora amar choTo bhai o bon. ar ei me-e duiTa amar fupato bon.
dipa: ei moTa cheleTa ke?
shumon: o amar choTo kakar chele. she khub beshi khae, tai amra take nam diechi 'khadok'.
dipa: oke dekhe mone hOe ækTa belun.
shumon: mOjar kOtha. ami take bolbo.

DEEPA: *Who are these people?*
SHUMON: *They are my mother's brother and his wife.*
DEEPA: *And are these your mother's brother's sons?*
SHUMON: *No. This is my mother's sister's son and that is his friend. This photo was taken in Delhi. They had all gone to Delhi on holiday.*
DEEPA: *And who is in that photo?*
SHUMON: *They are my younger brother and sister. And these two girls are my father's sister's daughters.*
DEEPA: *Who is this fat boy?*
SHUMON: *He is the son of my youngest paternal uncle. He eats a lot – therefore we have given him the name 'Fatso'.*
DEEPA: *Seeing him, he looks like a balloon.*
SHUMON: *That's funny. I'll tell him.*

Vocabulary

ke	who (singular)	**chuTi**	holiday
kara	who (plural)	**choTo**	little, young
onara	they (polite form)	**moTa**	fat
ei/eiTa	this	**khub beshi**	a lot
oi/oiTa	that	**diechi**	(we) have given
chobi	picture	**khadok**	'eater', fatso
dilli	Delhi	**dekhe**	having seen
tola	taken	**mOjar kOtha**	a funny thing to say
shObai	all of them, everyone	**bolbo**	(I) will tell

Vocabulary point: family

Bengali has many quite precise terms for family relations. For example, **mami** means not just 'aunt', but 'wife of brother of mother' (she is married to your **mama**, i.e. your mother's brother). And the children of your **mama** and **mami** are not just your 'cousins', but your **mamato bhai** and **mamato bon** (though, like all cousins and indeed others of your age group, they can also be referred to as simply **bhai** and **bon**).

For every relation it is often specified whether they are **bORo** ('older'; literally 'big') or **choTo** ('younger'; literally 'small'). An older male cousin, for example, can be called **bORo bhai** or also **dada** (the single-word term for 'elder brother'). To refer to the second eldest, the word **mejo** is used, as in **mejo bhai** (or **mejda**).

Unit 2: *Are these your cousins?*

You have already encountered some basic family terms. Below, we give some more. For some of them, Eastern and Western Bengali have different words.

father's brother	**kaka, caca** (E)
wife of father's brother	**kaki(ma), caci(amma)** (E)
their children	**kakato bhai** and **bon, cacato bhai** and **bon** (E)
father's sister	**pishi(ma)** (W), **fupu** (E)
husband of father's sister	**pishe(mOshae)** (W), **fupa** (E)
their children	**pistuto bhai** and **bon** (W), **fupato bhai** and **bon** (E)
mother's brother	**mama**
wife of mother's brother	**mami(ma)**
their children	**mamato bhai** and **bon**
mother's sister	**mashi(ma)** (W), **khala(-amma)** (E)
husband of mother's sister	**mesho(mOshae)** (W), **khalu** (E)
their children	**mastuto bhai** and **bon** (W), **khalato bhai** and **bon** (E)
sister's son	**bhagne**
sister's daughter	**bhagni**
husband	**shami**
wife	**stri**
child	**bacca**

```
┌─────┬─────┬─────┐              ┌─────┬─────┐
kaka x kaki  pishi x pishe  baba x ma    mama x mami   mashi x mesho
caca   caci  fupu    fupa   abba   amma                khala   khalu
(E)    (E)   (E)     (E)    (E)    (E)                 (E)     (E)
                                    │
                                   ami
```

A Bengali family tree

Exercise 1 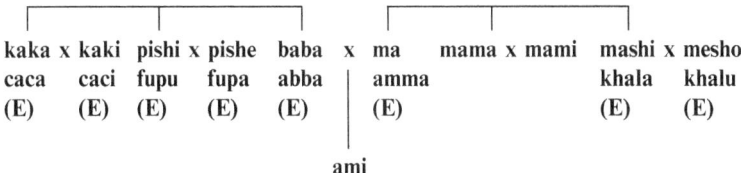 (Audio 1:42)

Bijoy and Kumkum are trying to dazzle each other with their very international families. How many of Bijoy's relations live abroad (= **bideshe**)? And Kumkum's?

bijOe: apni kothae thaken?
kumkum: ami, amar shami o baccara shObai kanaDae thaki.

bijOe: tai na ki (= *is that so*)? amar bORo fupu o fupa o okhane thaken.
kumkum: amra shObai bideshe thaki. bORo caca o caci thaken niu zilænDe, choTo mama thaken spene, mejo khala o khalu thaken mishOre.
bijOe: shotti (= *really*)! amar mamato bhai o fupato bon kaerote thake. ar bhagne o bhagni thake jukto-rastre. ami o amar stri thaki inglænDe.

Exercise 2

Write down the names of your sisters, brothers, uncles, aunts and cousins. For each, make a Bengali sentence identifying them. For example, if your younger sister is called Susan (**suzen**) and your mother's elder brother is called uncle Ben (**ankel ben**) make the following sentences about them:

suzen amar choTo bon   Susan is my younger sister.
ankel ben amar bORo mama   Uncle Ben is my mother's elder brother.

Exercise 3

Can you read the following? Which words refer to male relatives? And which to female ones?

1 ছেলে
2 বাবা
3 খালা
4 আপা
5 চাচাতো বোন
6 মামি
7 চাচি
8 ছোট বোন
9 কাকী
10 খালু

Grammar point: personal pronouns

In a sentence like 'He gave me his phone number', there are three personal pronouns: 'he', 'me' and 'his'. The word 'he' is the subject of the sentence (the person carrying out the action), so the subject form 'he' is used. The word 'me' is the object (the person affected in some way by the action), so it has the object form. And 'his' is the possessive form.

Bengali pronouns also have this system: they have a subject form, a possessive form and an object form. Here is a list of them, in the singular and plural:

Unit 2: *Are these your cousins?*

	Subject	Possessive	Object
sing. 'I'	ami	amar	amake
'you' (familiar)	tumi	tomar	tomake
'you' (polite)	apni	apnar	apnake
'you' (intimate)	tui	tor	toke
'he/she' (close by)	e	er	eke
'he/she' (far off)	o	or	oke
'he/she' (other)	she	tar	take
plur. 'we'	amra	amader	amader
'you' (familiar)	tomra	tomader	tomader
'you' (polite)	apnara	apnader	apnader
'you' (intimate)	tora	toder	toder
'they' (close by)	era	eder	eder
'they' (far off)	ora	oder	oder
'they' (other)	tara	tader	tader

You have already seen many of the forms for 'you' in Unit 1. The forms for 'he/she' have a number of distinctive properties:

- There are no separate forms for masculine ('he') and feminine ('she').
- Instead, different forms are used to identify a person who is close by (**e** 'this one') or further off (**o** 'that one').
- There is also a form (labelled 'other' above) that is used to refer to somebody who has already been identified. Examples are **she** and **take** in:

> shonTu: tumi ki 'shOrbonam' shObdoTa jano, bahar?
> Do you know the word 'pronoun', Bahar?
> bahar: na, ami jani na. kintu shumi bhalo bækOron jane.
> No, I don't know. But Shumi knows grammar well.
> she ekhane. ami take jiggesh korchi.
> She is here. I will ask her.

The forms **o/or/oke** and their plurals are also sometimes used in this function. But in E. Bengali, this use does not sound respectful.

Some further example sentences with different personal pronouns are:

> era tomake pOchondo kOre na.
> They ('these ones') don't like you.

> apnader baRi kothae?
> Where is your (plural) home?

o amake tar fon nOmbor dieche.
He has given me his phone number.

amader kaki amaderke khub bhalobashen.
Our aunt [which one?] loves us a lot.

Note the use of **amaderke** in the last sentence: the plural objective forms sometimes get an extra -**ke** added to them.

Exercise 4

Transcribe the following **shOrbonam** (pronouns):

এরা   আপনার   ওকে   তুই   তাকে   ও   আপনারা   একে   তোমাকে

Then use them to fill in the blanks:

1 ami _____ bhalobashi.
2 _____ ki apnar chele-me-e?
3 _____ stri kothae?
4 amar stri okhane. ami ki _____ Dakbo?
5 _____ ki apnar mamato bhai?
6 ami _____ pOchondo kori kintu _____ pOchondo kori na.
7 _____ kæmon achish?
8 _____ kæmon achen?

Exercise 5

Answer the following questions. Use the clues given.

1 eTa (= this) ki tor saikel? (hæ̃, . . .)
2 tomar fupato bhai kothae thake? (. . . lOnDone . . .)
3 shonTu ki hindi jane? (na, she . . . kintu . . . bangla . . .)
4 tumi ki amake bhalobasho na? (na, . . . bhalobashi na)
5 tomar bondhu ki kOla pOchondo kOre? (na, she . . . kintu . . . am . . .)
6 tumi ki tar mamato bhai? (na, ami . . . khalato . . . ; amar ma tar . . . o tar ma amar . . .).

Dialogue 2 (Audio 1:45)

Arif is hungry. Why does this make his sister Sultana upset?

Unit 2: *Are these your cousins?*

arif:	didi, khawar kichu ache?
sultana:	hæ̃, ache. kOla ache.
arif:	na, nei. kalke ami kOlagulo khe-e felechi.
sultana:	tai na ki? frije bhat-mach ache.
arif:	na. kono bhat-mach nei. ami shOb khe-e felechi.
sultana:	khabar Tebile ruTi alu-bhãji ache. jao, khao.
arif:	na didi, ami oshOb eimattro khe-e felechi.
sultana:	shOb kichu khe-e felecho? chi chi! tumi æto peTuk!
ARIF:	*Sister, is there anything to eat?*
SULTANA:	*Yes, there is. There are some bananas.*
ARIF:	*No, there isn't. I ate up the bananas yesterday.*
SULTANA:	*Is that so? In the fridge, there is rice and fish.*
ARIF:	*No, there isn't any rice and fish. I've eaten it all up.*
SULTANA:	*On the dinner table there is roti and fried potato. Go and eat that.*
ARIF:	*No sister, I have eaten all that just now.*
SULTANA:	*You have eaten everything? Shame on you! You are so gluttonous!*

shOb kichu khe-e felecho?

Vocabulary

khawar kichu	something to eat	**tai na ki?**	is that so?
kalke	yesterday	**bhat-mach**	rice and fish
khe-e felechi	(I) have eaten up	**khabar Tebil**	dinner table

ruTi alu-bhāji	roti and potato fry	shOb kichu	everything
jao	go!	chi chi	shame on you!
khao	eat!	æto	so
oshOb	all that	peTuk	gluttonous
eimattro	just now		

Grammar point: saying that something exists

One of the things people often talk about is that something is or is not there. They may say, for example, that 'there is a lot of rice' or that 'there is food in the kitchen'. In Bengali, such sentences are not difficult to make: you mention the thing in question and then add the verb **ache** 'is/are'. If you want to mention the place where the thing is, you put that at the beginning of the sentence. Such place expressions usually end in **-e**. The result is sentences such as:

> **duiTa kOla ache.** There are two bananas.
> **Tebile bhat ache.** There is rice on the table.

To make these sentences negative, you need the negative form of the verb **ache**. This, quite exceptionally, is not formed by adding the word **na**. Instead, the form is: **nei** or **nai** (Eastern). Both mean: 'is not/are not'.

> **kono kOla nei.** There isn't any banana/ There is no banana.
> **Tebile kono bhat nai** (E). There isn't any rice/There is no rice on the table.

Note the use of the word **kono** 'any' in both examples. This word is just like English 'any': it is often used in negative sentences and in questions (e.g. **kono khabar ache?** 'Is there any food?').

Exercise 6

Make sentences saying that:

1 There is a new (**notun**) Bengali restaurant.
2 There is food in the kitchen (**rannaghOre**).
3 There isn't any room (**jaega**).
4 There is no money (**Taka**) in your pocket (**pOkeTe**).
5 There is mango and there is pineapple (**anarOsh**).
6 There is no apple and there is no banana.

Unit 2: *Are these your cousins?*

Exercise 7

The following sentences have two contrasting halves. Complete them. The first sentence would become: **ekhane kono jaega nei kintu okhane jaega ache.**

1 ekhane kono jaega nei kintu . . . (okhane)
2 amar bā hate ækTa Taka ache kintu . . . (Dan hate)
3 rannaghOre am ache kintu . . . (anarOsh)
4 kham ache kintu . . . (DakTikiT = stamp)
5 kOlom ache kintu . . . (kagOj = paper)
6 tomar pleTe bhat ache kintu . . . (amar pleTe)

Dialogue 3 (Audio 1:47)

There is going to be a big party today at Ishita's place. She talks about the preparations with her friend Shumi. Read their conversation and answer: why does Ishita feel confident about the party?

shumi: tomader baRite aj ke ke ashben?
ishita: amar kaka-kaki o mama-mamira ashben. amar cacato o mamato bhai-bonra o ashbe. aro Oneke ashben.
shumi: tomar bhagne o bhagni to Ostreliate thake, tai na? tara ki ashbe?
ishita: hæ̃, tader o ami dawat korechi ebong tara eshe gæche. tara ækhon amar boner baRite ache.
shumi: tomar bandhobi mita kothae? take to dekhchi na.
ishita: she ashbe. she amaderke shahajjo korbe.
shumi: ta hole, ar kono shOmossha nei? shOb kichu Thik ache?
ishita: hæ̃, shOb kichu Thik ache.

SHUMI: *Who is coming to your place today?*
ISHITA: *My paternal and maternal uncles and aunts are coming. My maternal and paternal cousins are also coming. And many other people are coming.*
SHUMI: *Your nephew and niece live in Australia, don't they? Are they coming?*
ISHITA: *Yes, I have invited them too and they have arrived. They are now at my sister's place.*
SHUMI: *Where is your friend Mita? I don't see her.*
ISHITA: *She's coming. She will help us.*
SHUMI: *Then there isn't any further problem? Everything is OK?*
ISHITA: *Yes, everything is OK.*

Vocabulary

aj	today	ebong	and
ke ke	who (plural)	eshe gæche	(they) have arrived
ashbe	will come	bandhobi	friend (female)
ashben	will come (polite form)	shahajjo korbe	(she) will help
aro Oneke	many more people	ta hole	then
dawat korechi	(I) have invited	shOmossha	problem
		shOb kichu	everything

Bengali script: seven more consonants and one special sign

Learn the following consonant letters:

g	গ	গাল **gal** cheek	রাগ **rag** anger
gh	ঘ	ঘর **ghOr** room	আঘাত **aghat** blow
j	জ	জীবন **jibon** life	মেজো **mejo** second eldest
jh	ঝ	ঝাল **jhal** hot, spicy	মাঝি **majhi** boatman
th	থ	থুতনী **thutni** chin	মাথা **matha** head
dh	ধ	ধান **dhan** rice, paddy	দধি **dodhi** yoghurt
f	ফ	ফল **fOl** fruit	ফুপু **fupu** aunt (which one?)

Do you remember that vowels can be nasalised? In writing, this is shown by a little sign above the vowel. If the vowel follows a consonant, the sign is often written over that consonant.

আঁকা **āka** to draw, sketch   চাঁদ **cād** moon

Exercise 8

Next to each of the following Bengali letters, write its transcription. The first few have been done for you. If necessary, also look at pages 26 and 37.

ক	k	খ	kh	গ	g	ঘ	gh
চ		ছ		জ		ঝ	
ত		থ		দ		ধ		ন
প		ফ		ব		ভ		ম
ট		র		ল			

Unit 2: *Are these your cousins?*

Exercise 9 (Audio 1:48)

Here's a short conversation between Bulbul and his uncle. Read it, using the table you have just made and the clues given (though there is one symbol that you have to guess – the last word of the text should help you in this). After reading, say for each of the persons mentioned: what is their family relationship to Bulbul's uncle?

বুলবুল: আদাব খালু। কেমন আছেন?
খালু: আদাব। আমি ভালো আছি। তুমি কেমন আছো?
বুলবুল: ভালো আছি। খালা কোথায় (kothae)?
খালু: তোমার খালা বাড়ীতে (baRite)। তোমার ভাই বোনরা কোথায়?
বুলবুল: ওরা বাইরে (= outside)। আম্মা-আব্বা ও বাইরে গেছেন (= have gone)।
খালু: আচ্ছা। তাহলে আমি এখন যাই (jai)। খোদা হাফেজ।
বুলবুল: খোদা হাফেজ।

Exercise 10 (Audio 1:49)

Here is a very short conversation between Shontu and his teacher, about pronouns (**shOrbonam** সর্বনাম). What two pronouns does Shontu know?

– এই ছেলে, দুইটা সর্বনামের উদাহরণ (= examples) দাও (= give)।
– কে? আমি?
– বাঃ বাঃ খুব ভালো তো!

3 ওনার কয়টা বাড়ী আছে?
onar kOeTa baRi ache?

How many houses does he have?

In this unit you will learn how to:
- refer to people respectfully
- talk about people's jobs, characteristics and possessions
- ask and answer questions about numbers
- recognise some further Bengali letters

Dialogue 1 (Audio 1:51)

At his school, Dipu has met Nazma, a young lady who – it turns out – is from the same town as his family.

nazma: ta hole apni nishcOe-i amar kakike cenen?
dipu: onar nam ki?
nazma: tãr nam razia sultana. tini shonargão hai skuler prodhan shikkhika.
dipu: hæ̃, ami onake cini. apnar kaka o to æki skuler shikkhOk, tai na?
nazma: hæ̃, Thik bolechen.
dipu: amar didi oi skuler chattri chilen. mone hOe tini apnar mamato boner shOnge æki klashe poRten. tar nam rini na?

Unit 3: *How many houses does he have?*

nazma: bah! apni dekhchi amader poribarer shObaike cenen! æk din amader baRite ashben tahole. amra ækshathe khabo.
dipu: dhonnobad. Obossho-i ashbo.
NAZMA: *Then you must know my aunt.*
DIPU: *What is her name?*
NAZMA: *Her name is Razia Sultana. She is the headmistress of Sonargaon High School.*
DIPU: *Yes, I know her. Your uncle too is a teacher at the same school, isn't he?*
NAZMA: *Yes, you're right.*
DIPU: *My elder sister was a student at that school. I think she used to study in the same class as your maternal cousin. Isn't her name Rini?*
NAZMA: *My my! I see you know everyone in our family! Come to our house one day then. We will have dinner together.*
DIPU: *Thank you. I will certainly come.*

Vocabulary

cenen	(you) know (polite form)	poRten	used to study (polite form)
prodhan	main, head		
shikkhika	teacher (female)	poribar	family
cini	(I) know	din	day
æki	the same	ashben	(you) will/must come (polite form)
shikkhOk	teacher (male)		
bolechen	(you) have said (polite form)	ækshathe	together (E)
		dhonnobad	thanks, thank you
chattri	student (female)	Obossho-i	certainly
apnar boner shOnge	with your sister	ashbo	(I) will come

Grammar point: more pronouns

In addressing someone respectfully, you would use not **tumi** (or its plural: **tomra**) but **apni** (plural: **apnara**). In the same way, if you want to refer to someone respectfully, you would use a third person polite form (i.e. a polite form of 'he'/'she'/'they'). We give them here in Bengali script, because you should be able to read them by now (certainly if we tell you that none of them has an inherent vowel). You can check the transliteration on page 221.

	Subject	Possessive	Object
polite sing.			
'he/she' (close by)	ইনি	এনার/এঁর	এনাকে/এঁকে
'he/she' (far off)	উনি	ওনার/ওঁর	ওনাকে/ওঁকে
'he/she' (other)	তিনি	তাঁর	তাঁকে
polite plur.			
'they' (close by)	এনারা/এঁরা	এনাদের/এঁদের	এনাদের/এঁদের
'they' (far off)	ওনারা/ওঁরা	ওনাদের/ওঁদের	ওনাদের/ওঁদের
'they' (other)	তাঁরা	তাঁদের	তাঁদের

Just as with the ordinary forms, there are different polite forms to refer to a person close by or far off. In spoken Bengali you are likely to hear the forms এনার, এনাকে etc. ('this one') and ওনার, ওনাকে etc. ('that one'), while in written Bengali the forms এঁর, এঁকে etc. and ওঁর, ওঁকে etc. are more usual. To refer politely to someone who has already been identified, the forms তিনি, তাঁর etc. (sometimes also উনি, ওনার etc.) are used. All the plural object forms can have an extra **-ke** at the end.

Exercise 1

Go back to the list of your relatives that you made for Exercise 2 in Unit 2. For each, make a sentence of the following type:

| about Susan: | **o amar choTo bon.** | She is my younger sister. |
| about uncle Ben: | **uni amar bORo mama.** | He is my mother's elder brother. |

Also describe the relationship by saying 'I am . . .', as follows:

| about Susan: | **ami or dada** (or: **didi**) | I'm her elder brother (or: sister) |
| about uncle Ben: | **ami onar bhagne** (or **bhagni**) | I'm his sister's son (or: sister's daughter) |

You may need the following words:

bhaipo nephew, i.e. brother's son   **bhaijhi** niece, i.e. brother's daughter

Exercise 2

You are at Ishita's party. You don't know most of the people there, so you discreetly ask Shumi. Of course, you do so in Bengali.

Unit 3: *How many houses does he have?*

1 Who is he? What is his name? [said about a gentleman sitting at the far end of the room]
2 Is that (**uni**) his wife? [about the same gentleman]
3 Who (**kara**) are they? What are their names (**nam**)? [about two gentlemen sitting next to you].
4 Are these their children? Do you know them (**tumi ki . . . ceno**)?
5 Where are your father and mother? Has Ishita invited them (**dawat koreche**)?

Vocabulary point: jobs

Below are several Bengali job names. Some of them have distinct masculine (M) and feminine (F) forms. As you can see, some words have been taken over from English (and there are many more like that, such as **akaunTenT, kompiuTar programar, injiniar** (engineer), etc.).

shikkhOk (M)/ **shikkhika** (F)	teacher	**draibhar**	driver
		pulish	policeman
chattro (M)/ **chattri** (F)	student	**cashi**	farmer
		jele	fisherman
dhopa (M)/**dhopi** (F)	washerman/ washerwoman	**kaTh-mistri**	carpenter (lit.: wood mechanic)
ukil	lawyer	**dokandar**	shopkeeper
shangbadik	journalist	**cakor**	servant

Talk about jobs can start with questions such as:

apni ki kaj/ki cakri kOren? What work/what job do you do?
apni ki kOren? What do you do?

The answer can take the following form:

ami ækjOn dokandar. I'm a shopkeeper.

Note the use of the word **ækjOn**: it means 'a(n)' and is used when the following word refers to a person (for objects, the form would be **ækTa**). In the sentence given here, **ækjOn** could also be left out.

Exercise 3

Khaled is a journalist. His wife is a lawyer, his brother an engineer, his uncle a teacher and his father was a driver. What would Khaled reply to the following questions?

1 apni ki kaj kOren?
2 apnar stri ki kaj kOren?
3 apnar bORo bhai ki kOren?
4 apnar kaka ki dokandar?
5 apnar baba ki korten (= used to do)? [use chilen (= was) in the reply]

Exercise 4 (Audio 1:52)

You see someone holding a fishing net (jal). You draw the obvious conclusion:

> amar mone hOe she ækjOn jele – tar hate ækTa jal ache.
> I think (lit.: in my mind is) he is a fisherman – there's a net in his hand.

Draw the appropriate conclusion (in Bengali) for people holding:

ækTa shaban (= bar of soap)
ækTa kodal (= spade)
ækTa hatuRi (= hammer)
kichu (= some) khucra Taka (= loose change)
ækTa laThi (= stick, baton)
ækTa jhaRu (= broom)

Dialogue 2 (Audio 1:53)

Jenny has gone to pick up her visa for Bangladesh. At the High Commission, she meets a Bengali lady. Does the lady work there?

jeni: maf korben, apni ki bangali?
mohila: ji, ami bangali ebong bangladeshi duiTai. apni dekhchi bangla janen?
jeni: ami ækhono shikhchi. amar Onek bangali bondhu-bandhobi ache.
mohila: khub bhalo. apni ki kaj kOren?
jeni: ami ækjOn shebika. apni ki kOren?
mohila: ækhon ami grihini. age cakri kortam.
jeni: apnar ki chele-me-e ache?
mohila: ji, amar chele ache, tar bOyosh tirish bOchor, ar duiTi me-e ache. bORo me-er bOyosh aThash o choTo me-er unish.
jeni: tara ki kaj kOre?
mohila: cheleTa shangbadik, bORo me-e shikkhika, o choTo me-eTi ækTa ofishe cakri kOre.

Unit 3: *How many houses does he have?*

jeni: bah! ora to besh bhalo kaj korche.
mohila: ji, amar bhaggo bhalo. abar dækha hObe. ækhon jai. adab.
jeni: adab.

JENNY: *Excuse me; are you Bengali?*
LADY: *Yes, I'm both Bengali and Bangladeshi. You know Bengali, I see?*
JENNY: *I am still learning. I have many Bengali friends.*
LADY: *Very good. What work do you do?*
JENNY: *I'm a nurse. What do you do?*
LADY: *I'm a housewife now. Before, I used to work.*
JENNY: *Do you have children?*
LADY: *Yes, I have a son; he is 30. And I have two daughters. My eldest daughter is 28 and my youngest daughter is 19.*
JENNY: *What work do they do?*
LADY: *My son is a journalist, my eldest daughter is a teacher, and my youngest daughter works in an office.*
JENNY: *Well! They have quite good jobs, really.*
LADY: *Yes, I am lucky. I'll see you again later. Now I'm going. Goodbye.*
JENNY: *Goodbye.*

Vocabulary

maf korben	excuse me	bOyosh	age
duiTai	both	tirish	thirty
ækhono	still	bOchor	year
bondhu-bandhobi	male friends and female friends	aThash	twenty-eight
		o	and
grihini	housewife	unish	nineteen
age	before, in the past	bhaggo	luck, fate
kortam	(I) used to do		

Grammar point: expressing possession 🎧 (Audio 1:54)

To make a sentence expressing possession or ownership, you need the name of the owner (in the possessive form), the word for the thing that he/she owns, and the verb **ache** 'is/are' (or its negative: **nei/nai** E). Put them one after the other and you have a simple but extremely useful sentence type.

amar ækTa saikel ache	I have a bike (lit.: of me – a bike – is)
babuler ækTa gaRi ache	Babul has a car (of Babul – a car – is)
tomar ki bhai-bon nei?	Don't you have brothers or sisters? (of you – KI – brother-sister – are not?)

In the word **babuler** in the second example, you can see the regular possessive marker: **-er**. But if a noun ends in a vowel (e.g. the name **babu**), the possessive marker is simply **-r**:

babur ækhon kono Taka nai. (E)	Babu doesn't have any money now.

Exercise 5

Take the objects from Unit 1, Exercise 2 once again. Put the কলম, বই, খাতা, খাম and কাপ close to you on the table (they are yours), and the other objects further off (they are not yours). Then say what you have and don't have:

amar ækTa kOlom ache, boi ache, khata ache, kham ache, kap ache.
amar kono piric nei, pensil nei, kãci nei, khOborer kagoj nei, cabi nei.

Move the objects around several times. Each time, say what you have and don't have.

Dialogue 3 (Audio 1:56)

Ishita tells Shumi about her wealthy aunt and uncle. Is Ishita's aunt happy?

shumi:	oi mohila ke?
ishita:	uni amar khala.
shumi:	uni khub shundori. ar oi lOmba bhOddrolok ke?
ishita:	uni amar khalu.
shumi:	tomar khalu ki kaj kOren?
ishita:	uni ækjOn khub dhoni bæbshayi. onar baroTa dokan ache.
shumi:	o ma, tai na ki? tomar khalu æto dhoni? onar kOeTa baRi ache?
ishita:	gulshane onar poneroTa baRi ache!
shumi:	bap-re bap! tomar khalar tahole shukher Obhab nei!

Unit 3: *How many houses does he have?*

ishita: na, na. khala motei shukhi nOn. khalur Onek dokan-baRigaRi ache, kintu tãr kono helikopTar nei. sheTa-i khalar dukkho.
SHUMI: *Who is that lady?*
ISHITA: *She is my mother's sister.*
SHUMI: *She is very beautiful. And who is that tall gentleman?*
ISHITA: *He is my uncle.*
SHUMI: *What work does your uncle do?*
ISHITA: *He is a very rich businessman. He has twelve shops.*
SHUMI: *Oh my, is that so? Is your uncle so rich? How many houses does he have?*
ISHITA: *He has fifteen houses in Gulshan.*
SHUMI: *My goodness! Then your aunt must be very happy.*
ISHITA: *No, no. My aunt is not happy at all. Because uncle has many shops, houses and cars, but he doesn't have a helicopter. That is a source of sadness to my aunt.*

Vocabulary

shundori	beautiful	bap-re bap!	my goodness! (lit.: dear father, father)
lOmba	tall		
dhoni	rich	shukh	happiness
bæbshayi	businessman	shukher Obhab	lack of happiness
dokan	shop		
o ma!	oh my! (lit.: oh mother)	shukhi	happy
		motei nOn	is not at all
æto	so	sheTa-i	that (thing)
gulshan	Gulshan (expensive area in Dhaka)	dukkho	sadness

Vocabulary point: personal characteristics

The following sentences contain adjectives describing people's characteristics. The construction is simple: you only need to mention the person and the characteristic – no 'is' or 'are' is needed. A word meaning 'very' or 'so' can be put before the adjective.

uni khub shundori.   tomar khalu æto dhoni?
She is very beautiful.   Is your uncle so rich?

Some useful adjectives are:

dhoni	rich	buddhiman	clever
gorib	poor	boka	stupid
lOmba	tall	kutshit	ugly
khaTo	short	shundor	beautiful
moTa	fat	shundori	beautiful (of woman)
patla	thin		

Exercise 6

Describe the following pairs of people, using the adjectives given above. For the first pair, you could say:

    ishitar choTo bon khaTo kintu tar choTo bhai lOmba.

1 ishitar choTo bon o choTo bhai
2 khaled o tãr baba
3 apnar bhagne o bhagni
4 ei bæbshayi o tãr stri
5 tomar cakor o amar cakor

Counting point: some further numerals (Audio 1:58)

You can already count from 1 to 10 (and back). Now learn the Bengali numerals 11–20, 30, 40, 50 and also the words for 100 and 1000.

11	১১	ægaro
12	১২	baro
13	১৩	tæro
14	১৪	couddo
15	১৫	ponero/ponoro
16	১৬	sholo
17	১৭	shOtero/shOtoro
18	১৮	aTharo
19	১৯	unish
20	২০	bish or kuRi
30	৩০	tirish/trish
40	৪০	collish
50	৫০	pOncash

Unit 3: *How many houses does he have?* 59

100 ১০০ æk shOto or æksho
1000 ১০০০ æk hajar

Count from 1 to 20. Check how many seconds it takes and try to improve your speed (a native speaker can do this in 6 or 7 seconds, without the words becoming unintelligible).

Grammar point: numerals in sentences

When numerals are part of a sentence, they usually get the ending -Ta or -Ti (with -Ti expressing a certain intimacy or affection). If the numeral refers to people, the ending -jOn (lit.: person) is often used.

tãr baroTa dokan ache.   amar duiTi me-e ache.
He has twelve shops.   I have two daughters.
dOshTa kolkatae, duiTa Dhakae. ækshojOn mehman esheche.
Ten are in Kolkata, two   One hundred guests have
  in Dhaka.   come.

As you can see, the noun itself (**dokan, me-e, mehman**) does not get a plural form: the numeral suffices to express plural.

Putting the numeral after the noun is equivalent to inserting 'the' in English:

dokan baroTa the twelve shops (compare: **baroTa dokan**
                                     twelve shops)
cashi duijOn the two farmers   (compare: **duijOn cashi** two
                                     farmers)

To ask 'how many', different forms are used for things and people:

Tebile kOTa (E: kOeTa) boi ache?   kOejOn mehman esheche?
How many books are there on   How many guests have
  the table?   come?

Exercise 7

Ishita's aunt and uncle are describing their wealth, saying things like:

khala: amar bishTa hirar angTi (= diamond ring) ache.
khalu: amader pãcTa Tibhi-seT ache.

How would they describe their other possessions:

fourteen cars, two jeeps (**jip**), one hundred saris, eighteen servants?

Bengali script: five more consonants

ঠ	Th	ঠিক **Thik** right, correct	কাঠ **kaTh** wood
ড	D	ডাকা **Daka** to call	ডাব **Dab** green coconut
ঢ	Dh	ঢাকা **Dhaka** Dhaka	ঢাল **Dhal** shield
য	j	যাই **jai** I go	যোগী **jogi** yogi
য়	e	কোথায় **kothae** where	ছয় **chOe** six

The letter য stands for **j** (in Bangladesh sometimes **z** or **dz**) – just like the letter জ. The similar-looking য় is more complicated. First, it represents **e** when this is the second element of a diphthong. Second, it also represents the sound **y** (as in English *yes*, but pronounced very lightly) occurring between two vowel sounds: বয়স **bOyosh** 'age'. Because য় is considered a consonant, it can be followed by the inherent vowel **O** or **o**; the word বয়স is in fact an example. In some words with a sequence of two vowels, য় is written but usually left unpronounced: মেয়ে **me-e** 'girl', ভারতীয় **bharotio** 'Indian'. Third, য় is used with the vowel letter ও to form ওয় – this represents the sound **w**. It occurs in words like যাওয়া **jawa** 'to go' and in several loanwords, e.g. ওয়ার্ড **warD** 'ward'.

Exercise 8

Match each question with the appropriate answer.

1 তুমি কোথায় থাকো?
2 ঠিক আছে?
3 তোমার বাবা কি এখানে?
4 আমি এখন যাই?
5 উনি কি খাবেন?
6 তোমার কয়টা দোকান আছে?
7 কয়জন কর্মচারী (= employees) তোমার দোকানে কাজ করে?

a হ্যাঁ, তুমি এখন যাও।
b আমার নয়টা দোকান আছে।
c উনি এক গেলাস পানি (=ওয়াটার) খাবেন।
d পনের জন কর্মচারী কাজ করে।
e আমি ঢাকায় থাকি।
f না। উনি বাইরে।
g হ্যাঁ, ঠিক আছে।

4 কালীমন্দিরটা কোন দিকে?
kalimondirTa kon dike?

In what direction is the temple of Kali?

In this unit you will learn how to:

- talk about features of a city
- ask for and understand directions
- talk about some present situations
- recognise more Bengali letters

Dialogue 1 (Audio 1:60)

Jenny is going to work in Bangladesh for six months. She has travelled to Kolkata first and will travel on to Dhaka later. She is now walking around in Kolkata and asks someone for directions. Which road is she directed to?

jeni:	nOmoshkar. apnake ki ækTa prosno korte pari?
bhOddrolok:	Obossho-i.
jeni:	kalimondirTa kon dike, apni janen?
bhOddrolok:	hæ̃. sheTa khub ækTa dure nOe. ekhan theke bæ̃e hā̃Tun. pāc miniT pOre Dane ghurun. tahole-i kalighaT roD paben. oi roDe-i kalimondir.
jeni:	ei rastae dækhar mOton ar kichu ache?

bhOddrolok:	na, nei. eTa ækTa abashik elaka. kOe-ækTa dokan ache.
jeni:	accha. tahole ami kalimondire jacchi. dhonnobad.
bhOddrolok:	apnake-o dhonnobad.
JENNY:	*Hello. Can I ask you a question?*
GENTLEMAN:	*Certainly.*
JENNY:	*In what direction is the temple of Kali, do you know?*
GENTLEMAN:	*Yes. It's not very far. Walk to the left from here. After five minutes, turn right. Then you'll see Kalighat Road. The temple of Kali is on that road.*
JENNY:	*Is there anything else worth seeing in this street?*
GENTLEMAN:	*No, there isn't. This is a residential area. There are a couple of shops.*
JENNY:	*OK. Then I'll go to the temple of Kali. Thank you.*
GENTLEMAN:	*My pleasure.*

kalimondir

Unit 4: *In what direction is the temple of Kali?*

Vocabulary

kali	Hindu goddess	ghurun	turn!
mondir	temple	paben	you will get/see
dik	direction	rasta	street
dur	far	dækhar mOton	worth seeing
nOe	is not	ar kichu	anything else
khub ækTa dure nOe	it is not very far	abashik elaka	residential area
ekhan theke	from here	kOe-ækTa	a couple
hãTun	walk!	jacchi	I'm going
pOre	later, after		

Vocabulary point: right, left, close by, far off

To make clear the location of places, the following expressions are commonly used:

mondirTa apnar bãe/apnar bã hate   the temple is at your left (hand)
apnar Dane/apnar Dan hate   at your right (hand) is a
   ækTa jadughOr ache   museum.

bajarTa ki Onek dure?   Is the market very far?
na, sheTa kache-i.   No, it's close by.
ei dike shoja hãTun.   Walk straight in this direction.

ækTa cOoRa rasta dekhte   You'll see a broad street.
   paben.
okhane bãe ghurun.   There, turn left.
bajarTa rastar shesh mathae.   The market is at the end of the street.

Exercise 1 (Audio 1:62)

Complete this mini-dialogue. Then say: which is closer by, the Nakhoda Mosque or the Jain Temple?

jeni: nakhoda mosjidTa kothae, apni ki janen? ekhan theke ki Onek _____?
dokandar: na, dure nOe, besh _____. ei dike dOsh miniT _____ hãTun. tarpOre (= after that) bãe _____. okhane rastar shesh _____ apnar bã _____ moshjidTa dekhte paben.

jeni:	accha. ar join mondirTa _____?
dokandar:	Onek dure. kintu sheTa Obossho-i _____ mOton ækTa mondir.
jeni:	accha. dhonnobad.

Grammar point: demonstratives

The words **e**, **o**, and **she** are used as personal pronouns but also as demonstratives:

e	this
o	that
she	that/the (used to refer back to something already mentioned)

They can be given some emphasis by adding **i**:

e/ei rastaTa khub cOoRa.	This street is very wide.
o/oi dike hāTun.	Walk in that direction.
she/shei rastae kono dokan nei.	There are no shops in that/the street.

If **e(i)**, **o(i)** and **she(i)** don't combine with a following noun but are used on their own, they get the ending **-Ta**:

e(i)Ta shOrkari bhObon.	This is a government building.
o(i)Ta ækTa purano durgo.	That is an old fortress.
she(i)Ta khub ækTa dure nOe.	That/it is not very far.

In the plural, **-Ta** is changed into **-gulo** or **-guli**. The form **-guli** can suggest a more sympathetic attitude to the things being referred to. It is also more common in E. Bengali, which also has **-gula**.

e(i)gulo adhunik sheTu.	These are modern bridges.
o(i)guli jadughOr bhObon.	Those are museum buildings.
she(i)gulo Onek dure.	Those/they are very far off.

Exercise 2 (Audio 1:63)

You are guiding two Bengali visitors around your home town. How do you point out the following features to them? Your first sentence would be: **eTa park roD**.

1 this: Park Road
2 that: River Street
3 those: shops

Unit 4: *In what direction is the temple of Kali?*

4 this building: a museum.
5 mosque: not very far – at the end of that street.
6 the market: not very close by – walk in that direction for 20 minutes, you'll see a bridge, turn right there.

Grammar point: expressing 'a' and 'the'

The rules for expressing 'a' and 'the' with nouns are as follows:
- To express 'a(n)', use **ækTa** for things, **ækjOn** for persons, e.g. **ækTa dokan** 'a shop', **ækjOn dokandar** 'a shopkeeper'. These words can be preceded by an adjective: **bhalo ækTa dokan** 'a good shop' (lit.: good a shop), **moTa ækjOn mohila** 'a fat lady'.
- To express 'the' (singular), add **-Ta** or **-Ti** to the noun. The form **-Ti** often conveys an affectionate attitude to the thing referred to. Examples: **rastaTa** 'the street', **baRiTi** 'the (nice little) house'.
- To express 'the' (plural), add **-gulo** or **-guli**. The form **-guli** can express affection or sympathy (but in E. Bengali, it often lacks special overtones; the form **-gula** is also used there). Examples: **rastagulo** 'the streets', **baRiguli** 'the (nice) houses'.
- Use of **-Ta/-Ti/-gulo/-guli** is quite acceptable with words for children (e.g. **me-eTi** 'the girl', **chelegula** (E) 'the boys') but with other human nouns, it can convey a lack of respect (e.g. **lokTa** 'that fellow').
- Before a word with **-Ta/-Ti/-gulo/-guli**, there can be a demonstrative: **oi rastagulo** 'those streets', **ei me-eTi** 'this girl'.
- A noun on its own can also have plural meaning:

   okhane dokan ache.   There are (some) shops there.
   oi elakar rasta khub   The streets of that neighbourhood
      shoru.   are very narrow.

Mini-exercise

Now you say:

The museum is open.
But the shop is closed.
The temples are close by.
There's also a fortress there.
It's very big.

Grammar point: possessives and locatives

Remember: the possessive ending of nouns is **-er** (but **-r** if the noun ends in a vowel). Its meaning is like "*'s*' or 'of' in English.

shOhor town	**shOhorer rastagulo** the streets of the town
desh country	**desher rajdhani** the country's capital
amar bon my sister	**amar boner ofish** my sister's office

Nouns also have a locative ending: **-e**. If the noun ends in a vowel, it is **-te** (but if the noun ends in **a**, it can also be **-e**). The locative can express a stative location or movement. It corresponds to English words like 'in', 'on' or 'to'.

oi shOhore kono park nei.	There aren't any parks in that town.
ei deshe Onek nodi ache.	There are many rivers in this country.
amra kolkatae jacchi.	We're going to Kolkata.

The possessive and locative markers can also be attached to words ending in **-Ta/-Ti** or **-gulo/-guli**:

shOhorTar rastagulo shoru.	The streets of the town are narrow.
shOhorTae kono park nei.	There are no parks in the town.
oi deshgulote Onek nodi ache.	There are many rivers in those countries.

Exercise 3 (Audio 1:64)

Read the following description of a street. Is it a shopping street or a residential street? What other feature does it have?

ei rastar nam shonargão roD. rastaTa besh cOoRa. æk pashe (= on one side) **dokan ache. dokangulote kapoR** (= clothes) **bikkri hOe** (= are sold). **onno pashe baRi ache. baRigulo khub ækTa bORo nOe. oi baRite dokandarra o dorjira** (= tailors) **thake. rastaTar shesh mathae ækTa choTo mondir ache.**

Exercise 4

Mita and her husband Upol have visited several European cities. What do they say about them? Their comments about London could be:

Unit 4: *In what direction is the temple of Kali?* 67

mita: lOnDone Onek jadughOr ache.
upol: kintu oi jadughOrgulote kono bhalo bangali resTurenT nei.

1 Mita: London – many museums
 Upol: in those museums – no good Bengali restaurant
2 Mita: Paris – a beautiful river
 Upol: streets of Paris – no good rickshaws (**riksha**)
3 Mita: Amsterdam – many bridges
 Upol: streets of that city – very narrow.
4 Mita: Florence – beautiful buildings
 Upol: not the capital of Italy
5 Mita: Berlin – many wide streets
 Upol: no good wall (**dewal**).

Dialogue 2 (Audio 1:65)

Mita and Upol, who are from Bangladesh, are in Kolkata. They ask a lady the way to Howrah railway station.

upol: haoRa steshonTa kothae, apni janen?
mohila: hæ̃, jani. ami steshoner kache kaj kori. oidike pãc miniT shoja hãTun.
mita: Onek dhonnobad. amra ei shOhorer rastaguli cini na.
mohila: apnara ki TurisT? na ei desher nagorik?
upol: na, amra ei desher lok na, amra bangladeshi. amra Dhakae thaki.
mohila: tai na ki? amar baba majhe majhe Dhakate jan. karon amar choTo bhaiTi Dhaka bissho-biddalOe-e pORe.
mita: shune khushi holam. accha, amra ækhon ashi.

UPOL: *Do you know where Howrah Station is?*
LADY: *Yes, I do. I work near the station. Walk in that direction for five minutes.*
MITA: *Thank you very much. We don't know the streets of this city.*
LADY: *Are you tourists? Or citizens of this country?*
UPOL: *No, we are not people of this country. We are Bangladeshi. We live in Dhaka.*
LADY: *Is that so? My father goes to Dhaka regularly, because my little brother is a student at Dhaka University.*
MITA: *I'm happy to hear that. OK, we are going now.*

Vocabulary

steshoner kache	near the station	shune	hearing, having heard
majhe majhe	regularly	khushi	glad
jan	goes	holam	I am/we are
karon	because	ashi	I/we are going now
bissho-biddaloe	university		(lit.: I/we come)
pORe	s/he studies		

Grammar point: the present tense – part 1 (Audio 1:66)

Here is the present tense of the verb **thaka** 'to live/stay':

ami/amra	thaki	I/we live
tumi/tomra	thako	you live
tui/tora	thakish	you live
e/o/she/era/ora/tara	thake	(s)he/they live
apni/ini/uni/tini/apnara/ēra/ enara/ōra/onara/tāra	thaken	you etc. live

There are five separate verb forms: for the first person, second person familiar, second person intimate, third person, and a polite form. Singular and plural verb forms are the same.

These general rules apply to all verbs in all tenses. When you memorise them, it is best to do so with the pronouns **ami**, **tumi**, **tui**, **she** and **apni** (but remember that the verb forms can also occur with the other pronouns given above). The endings (-i, -o, etc.) in the present tense of **thaka** are found in the present tense of all verbs.

The form **thaka**, which we use to identify the verb, is not a present tense. We shall call it the verbal noun.

Here are some common verbs whose present tense is made just like **thaka**:

rakha	to put/place		hasha	to laugh
asha	to come		kāda	to cry
hāTa	to walk		jana	to know
bhaba	to think/worry		mara	to hit/beat

The verb 'to be' is another one: its forms are **ami achi, tumi acho, tui achish, she ache, apni achen**.

As in English, Bengali sentences with a present tense usually refer to a situation that has some permanence or general validity:

Unit 4: *In what direction is the temple of Kali?*

amra majhe majhe ekhane ashi   We come here regularly.
she shObshOmOe khub hashe   He/she always laughs a lot.

Exercise 5

Write each pronoun on a slip of paper. Also make a slip for each verb given above (write the verbal noun on it: **rakha**, etc.). Then take one slip from each pile and make the correct present tense verb form. For example, if you have a slip saying **apnara** and one saying **mara**, make: **apnara maren**. Repeat until your performance is satisfactory.

Exercise 6

Fill in the correct present tense forms. Choose from the words in the box:

kãde	bhaben	mare	hãTe	thaki	thake (twice)
mari	hashe	janen	jani	jano	

1 **amra ei rastae** _____.
2 **amar dada tar bæbsha nie** (about his business) **khub** _____.
3 A: **o shObshOmOe tomake** _____ **kæno?**
   B: **karon ami take** _____.
4 **rajnitibidra** (the politicians) _____, **jOnogOn** (the people) _____.
5 **protidin** (every day) **ora parke æk ghOnTa** (hour) _____.
6 A: **jadughOrTa kothae, apni ki** _____?
   B: **na, ami** _____ **na.**
7 A: **ora kothae** _____, **tumi** _____?
   B: **ora dillite** _____.

Exercise 7

You already know how to say 'How are you?' and 'I am fine', using forms like **achi/acho**. For negative replies, **nei** or **nai** (E) are used: **ami khub ækTa bhalo nei** 'I am not very well'. Note that **khub** 'very' changes to **khub ækTa** in negative sentences.

Now ask Dipu how various people are doing. Also give his answers. The first exchange would be: **apnar ma kæmon achen? uni bhalo achen.**

1 dipur ma – bhalo
2 dipur bOro mama – bhalo
3 dipur choTo bhai – khub ækTa bhalo na
4 dipu – khubi bhalo
5 dipu o dipur stri – bhalo

Dialogue 3 (Audio 1:67)

A journalist is interviewing a politician. The journalist is hoping they can have a serious conversation. But do they?

shangbadik: apni ki apnar desh nie kOkhono bhaben?
rajnitibid: ji, ami deshTa nie shObshOmOe khub bhabi. bhabi ar kãdi.
shangbadik: kæno? apni kãden kæno?
rajnitibid: karon jOnogOn amar kache ashe na. amar shOnge hãTe na. shangbadikra amar Obostha bojhe na.
shangbadik: apnar dharona Thik nOe. amra apnake nie bhabi. majhe majhe bhabi: 'onar Taka-pOesha uni kothae rakhen?'
rajnitibid: amar kono Taka-pOesha nei. ami khub gorib. tai amar stri amake nie hashe. ami jani apnara-o amake nie hashen. amar cokher pani kothae rakhi?
sangbadik: ami dukkhito. ami ki apnake ækTa rumal debo?

JOURNALIST: *Do you ever worry about your country?*
POLITICIAN: *Yes, I always worry a lot about the country. I worry and I cry.*
JOURNALIST: *Why? Why do you cry?*
POLITICIAN: *Because the people don't come to me. They don't walk with me. The journalists don't understand my situation.*
JOURNALIST: *You are not correct. We think about you. We often think: 'Where does he put his money?'*
POLITICIAN: *I don't have any money. I'm very poor. Therefore my wife laughs about me. I know you too laugh about me. It makes me cry.*
JOURNALIST: *I'm sorry. Shall I give you a handkerchief?*

Vocabulary

| . . . nie | about . . . | **rajnitibid** | politician |
| **kOkhono** | ever | **shObshOmOe** | always |

Unit 4: *In what direction is the temple of Kali?*

jOnogOn	the people	pani (E)/jOl (W)	water
Obostha	situation	cokher pani	tears (lit.: water
bojhe	(s)he/they understand		of eyes)
dharona	idea, impression	dukkhito	sad, sorry
Taka-pOesha	money	rumal	handkerchief
tai	therefore	debo	I will give

Bengali script: the remaining simple consonants

These are the remaining simple consonants of Bengali:

sh	শ	শিব **shib** Shiva		দেশ **desh** land
sh	স	সাত **shat** seven		আসা **asha** to come
sh	ষ	ষোল **sholo** sixteen		শেষ **shesh** end
n	ণ	দীণ **din** religion		লবণ **lObon** salt (E)
ng	ঙ	ব্যাঙ **bæng** frog		ঠ্যাঙ **Thæng** thigh
ng	ং	বাংলা **bangla**		অংক **Ongko** arithmetic
h	হ	হাত **hat** hand		শহর **shOhor** town
R	ড়	বড় **bORo** big		বাড়ী **baRi** house
~	ঞ	মিঞা **miã** Mr (E)		মিঞ **miõ** miaow

The letters শ, স and ষ originally represented different **sh**-sounds. Some speakers indeed still distinguish শ (a slightly sharper **sh**) from স (less sharp). But most speakers have only one **sh** sound – how this is spelt depends on the individual word. The same is true of ণ and ন, which both represent **n**. And ঙ and ং too spell the same sound: **ng**. Finally, ঞ merely signals that the following vowel is nasalised; it is not frequent.

Exercise 8

Read the following mini-dialogue. Why does the journalist say 'thank you'?

সাংবাদিক: আপনি কি আপনার দেশকে (= দেশটা) ভালোবাসেন?
রাজনীতিবিদ: হ্যাঁ। অবশ্যই ভালোবাসি।
সাংবাদিক: তাহলে আপনার টাকা-পয়সা সব বিদেশী (= foreign) ব্যাংকে রাখেন কেন?
রাজনীতিবিদ: না! না! আপনার ধারণা ঠিক নয়। দেশী (= local) ব্যাংকে রাখি।

সাংবাদিক: বাহ্। আপনার কয়টা একাউন্ট আছে?
রাজনীতিবিদ: ছয়টা একাউন্ট আছে। প্রতি একাউন্টে অনেক টাকা আছে।
সাংবাদিক: ধন্যবাদ। দেশের জনগণ পড়ে (= reading it) খুশি হবে (= will be)।

Exercise 9

Go to <htpp://www.prothom-alo.com>, the website of the Bengali-language newspaper **prothom alo** 'First Light'. Find an article which contains at least ten words that you already know. Repeat this exercise every day for one week.

5 আপনি কি কি দেখেছেন?
apni ki ki dekhechen?

What have you seen?

In this unit you will learn how to:

- talk about visiting places
- describe events in the past
- talk about transport
- recognise some combination letters

Dialogue 1 (Audio 1:68)

Jenny is visiting Santiniketan, a centre of education in West Bengal established by Rabindranath Tagore and his father. Jenny is talking with Proshun, a student there. Is Proshun a hard-working student? What is Jenny going to listen to?

jeni:	apni ekhane ki shekhen?
proshun:	ami tObla bajano shikhi.
jeni:	apni ki Onek prakTis kOren?
proshun:	hæ̃, protidin dui ghOnTa ponDit mOshae-er kache prakTis kori. tachaRa-o shOngskrito bhasha shikhi.
jeni:	konTa beshi shoja: tObla? naki shOngskrito?
proshun:	tObla. apnake ekTu bajie shonai?
jeni:	besh to, shonan. khushi hObo.
proshun:	apni ki tOblar bol janen?

Unit 5: **apni ki ki dekhechen?**

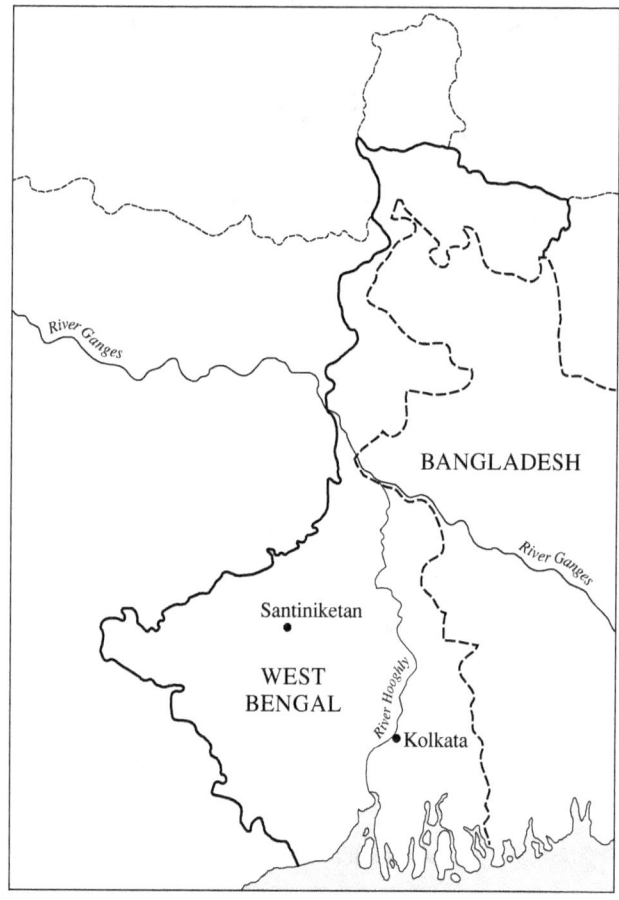

Santiniketan in West Bengal

jeni: na, jani na. bol abar ki?
proshun: bol holo tOblar Do-re-mi. prothome aste aste shuru kori, tarpOr taRa-taRi bajai. apni shonen.
jeni: accha, apni bajan. ami shuni.

Vocabulary

shekha	to learn	**ghOnTa**	hour
tObla	small drum	**ponDit**	pundit, teacher
bajano	to play	**mOshae**	sir, Mr
prakTis kOra	to practise	**... kache**	near, with ...

Unit 5: *What have you seen?* 75

shOngskrito	Sanskrit	bol	sound, scale
konTa	which one	abar	then, now (in questions)
beshi	more	prothom(e)	(at) first
shoja	simple	aste aste	slowly
bajie	playing	shuru kOra	to begin
shonai	I'll let (you) hear	tarpOr(e)	after that
besh to	yes, sure	shona	to hear, listen
hObo	I will be		

Grammar point: present tense with vowel change

We'll now tackle the present tense of verbs that don't have **a** but some other vowel in their first syllable, or stem. In some forms, this stem vowel changes. Specifically, if the ending contains the sound **i**:

> stem vowel **O** becomes **o**
> **o** becomes **u**
> **æ** becomes **e**
> **e** becomes **i**.

Here is one example for each group.

Stem vowel O: kOra to do

> ami kori (here is the change: **o** instead of **O**, due to the **i**)
> tumi kOro
> tui korish (here too: not **O** but **o** – because of the following **i**)
> she kOre
> apni kOren

(in the same way: **bOla** 'to say', **bOsha** 'to sit down', **dhOra** 'to catch, get hold of', **pORa** 'to read, study')

Stem vowel o: shona to hear, listen

> ami shuni (here it is: **u** instead of **o**)
> tumi shono
> tui shunish (and here too)
> she shone
> apni shonen

(similarly: **bojha** 'to understand', **khola** 'to open', **oTha** 'to go up, get up')

Stem vowel æ: dækha to see

ami	dekhi	(note the e)
tumi	dækho	
tui	dekhish	(here too)
she	dækhe	
apni	dækhen	

(also: **khæla** 'to play')

Stem vowel e: kena to buy

ami	kini	(so not **keni**, but **kini**)
tumi	keno	
tui	kinish	(once you know the pattern, it's simple)
she	kene	
apni	kenen	

(also: **lekha** 'to write', **fera** 'to return').

Note that all the verb endings are regular: **-i, -o, -ish, -e** and **-en**. Because these endings are usually enough to guess what the subject is, the subject itself is sometimes left out:

(ami) aste aste shuru kori	I begin slowly.
proshun ki shetar bajae?	'Does Proshun play the sitar?'
na, (she) tObla bajae.	'No, he plays the tabla.'

Exercise 1

Return to Unit 4, Exercise 5. Make further slips for the verbs given above and then repeat the exercise.

Exercise 2 (Audio 1:70)

Upol has a high opinion of himself. Here he is explaining why. Finish his sentences. The first one would be: **Oneke protidin æk ghOnTa pORe, kintu ami chOe ghOnTa poRi.**

1 **Oneke protidin æk ghOnTa pORe, kintu ami**_____ [study 6 hours]
2 **Oneke shone na, kintu ami**_____ [listen]
3 **Oneke baje kOtha** (nonsense) **bOle, kintu ami**_____ [don't talk nonsense]

4 **Oneke aje-baje khabar** (worthless food) **kene, kintu ami**_____
 [don't buy worthless food]
5 **Oneke ingreji sheke, kintu ami**_____ [learn French]
6 **Oneke boi pORe, kintu ami**_____ [write books].

Exercise 3 (Audio 1:71)

Proshun is telling Jenny about his daily activities. Add a question to each sentence, asking Jenny about her activities. Begin each question with **apni-o** 'you too'. The first one would be: **apni-o ki protidin shOkale othen?**

1 **ami protidin shOkale** (early) **uThi.**
2 **protidin car ghOnTa tObla prakTis kori.**
3 **bikale** (in the afternoon) **daba** (chess) **kheli.**
4 **protidin amar i-mel poRi o uttor** (answer) **likhi.**
5 **protidin dOshTa shOngskrito shObdo** (word) **shikhi.**
6 **shondha-bælae** (in the evening) **amar make** (mother) **fon kori.**

Grammar point: present tense of verbs ending in vowel

If a verb stem ends in a vowel, there are some special effects when the present tense endings are added. Again, several groups need to be distinguished.

Stem ending in -a: pawa **to get, receive**

ami	pai
tumi	pao
tui	pash
she	pae
apni	pan

(also: **jawa** 'to go', **khawa** 'to eat')

Some verbs have a verbal noun ending in **-ano** or **-ono** (W) (e.g. **ghumano/ghumono** 'to sleep'). They belong to this group. Their stem ends in **-a** (**ghuma-**) and their present tense is just as above (**ami ghumai, tumi ghumao**, etc.). Similarly: **shekhano** 'to teach', **paThano** 'to send'.

Stem ending in -O: hOwa 'to be(come); to happen; to grow'

ami	hoi
tumi	hOo
tui	hosh
she	hOe
apni	hOn

(also **bOwa** 'to carry' and **kOwa** 'to say' (colloquial))

The following forms require special attention: **ami noi, tumi nOo, tui nosh, she nOe, apni nOn**. They originated as the negative forms of **hOwa**. But they are now used only for the following purpose: to make the negative of a sentence in which 'to be' is omitted. In such sentences, E. Bengali often inserts the word **na** instead:

arif besh moTa	Arif is quite fat
sultana moTa nOe	Sultana is not fat.
sultana moTa na (E.)	Sultana is not fat.

To make a sentence with **hOwa** negative, **na** is simply added at the end:

inglænDe ki dhan hOe?	Does rice grow in England?
na, inglænDe dhan hOe na.	No, rice doesn't grow in England.

Stem ending in -o: showa 'to lie down'

ami	shui
tumi	sho-o
tui	shush
she	shoe
apni	shon

(also **dhowa** 'to wash')

Stem ending in -e: newa 'to take' and dewa 'to give'

These two verbs are really irregular:

ami	ni-i, nei (E)
tumi	nao
tui	nish

Unit 5: *What have you seen?*

she	næe
apni	næn

And that's it. For each verb given above, make a new slip of paper, adding it to the set you used for Exercise 1. Then repeat Exercise 1.

Exercise 4 (Audio 1:73)

Proshun has written down his morning routine. Complete his sentences, using the verbs given.

1 prothome amar hat-mukh _____ [dhowa].
2 tarpOr jOl-khabar (breakfast) _____ [khawa].
3 tarpOr dui ghOnTa tObla _____ [bajano].
4 nOeTae (at 9) ami o amar bondhura (friends) skule _____ [jawa].
5 baroTa porjonto (until 12) amader shikkhOk amaderke ingreji o shOngskrito bhasha _____ [pORano teach].
6 amra æk ghOnTa lanc-brek _____ [pawa].

Exercise 5

Proshun has given Jenny his parents' address. When back in Kolkata, she goes to visit them. Proshun's mother asks Jenny what he does all day. Use the sentences from Exercises 3 and 4 to answer her. First, say: **she protidin shOkale oThe.**

Dialogue 2 (Audio 1:74)

Jenny is now in Dhaka, where she is visiting Dipu's family. She is talking with Dipu's younger brother Tipu. He asks about her trip to Sonargaon, the centre of government during the Moghul period. Did Jenny travel to Sonargaon in historical style?

Tipu: gOto kalke apni kothae kothae giechen, apa?
jeni: kalke sonargãoe giechi. cOmotkar ækTa jaega.
Tipu: hæ̃, ta Thik. ami-o ækbar gechi. apni okhane ki ki dekhechen?
jeni: Onek kichu dekhechi. purano dalan-koTha dekhechi. jadughOr dekhechi. mogolder toiri kOra prashad dekhechi. Onek chobi tulechi.
Tipu: shekhane ki bhabe gæchen?
jeni: shOkale amra Dhaka theke base coRe gechi. shonargãoe rikshae coRe ekhane-shekhane ghurechi. shondha-bælae Dhakae firechi bebi-Tæksite. karon kono bas chilo na.

Tipu: tahole to adhunik TransporTe coRe oitihashik jaegae gæchen! hatir piThe cORen ni? mogolder prio TransporT chilo hati.
jeni: na. hatir piThe coRi ni. karon ami to mogol shahajadi na. ki dukkher bishOe!

Vocabulary

(gOto) kalke	yesterday	... theke	from ...
kothae kothae	where, what places	... coRe	by/in ...
cOmotkar	wonderful	ekhane-shekhane	here and there
ækbar	once	ghora	to turn, move
ki ki	what things	shondha-bæla	evening
Onek (kichu)	much, a lot	bebi-Tæksi	tuk-tuk
dalan	brick building	chilo	(there) was
koTha	big house	adhunik	modern
mogolder toiri kOra	built by the Moghuls	oitihashik	historical
		hati	elephant
mogol	Moghul	piTh	back
prashad	palace	cORa	to ride, drive
chobi tola	to take pictures	prio	favourite
ki bhabe	how, what way	shahajadi	princess
shOkal	morning	bishOe	matter, thing

Grammar point: the present perfect

Dialogue 2 has several examples of the present perfect tense:

    sonargãoe giechi.   I went to Sonargaon.
    ki ki dekhechen?   What things did you see/have you seen?

These verb forms describe a completed action in the past, often having a result that is still valid at the present moment (i.e. the person has experienced something or acquired a certain knowledge). The translation in English can vary, depending on the context.

To make the present perfect:

- take the stem (the verbal noun without the final **-a** or **-wa**);
- change the stem vowel as follows: **a** becomes **e**
                                  O becomes **o**
                                  o becomes **u**
                                  æ becomes **e**
                                  e becomes **i**

Unit 5: *What have you seen?* 81

- add the perfect marker **-ech-**
- add the appropriate present tense ending: **-i**, **-o**, **-ish**, **-e** or **-en**

For example, to make the form meaning 'they have come':

- take the verbal noun **asha** 'to come', but remove the final **-a** so you get the stem **ash-**;
- change **a** to **e** to get **esh-**;
- add **-ech-** to get **eshech-**;
- finally, because the subject is **tara**, add **-e**, to get **tara esheche** 'they have come'.

Some other examples:

Verb	Present perfect forms
bOla	ami bolechi, tumi bolecho, tui bolechish, she boleche, apni bolechen ('I have said' etc.)
shona	shunechi, shunecho, shunechish, shuneche, shunechen ('I have heard' etc.)
khawa	khe-echi, khe-echo, khe-echish, etc. ('I have eaten' etc.)
hOwa	hoechi, hoecho, etc. ('I have become' etc.)
dewa	diechi, etc. ('I have given' etc.)

Now repeat Exercise 1, but with the present perfect.

Exercise 6

Go online and listen to some Bengali-language news on <http://www.bbc.co.uk/bengali/radio/aod/bengali_promo.shtml>. Keep listening (and replaying) until you have identified five present perfect verbs. Concentrate on the characteristic marker **-ech-**. Also remember that the verb usually comes at the end of the sentence.

Exercise 7

Proshun's friend asks him some questions. How would Proshun reply? His first answer would be: **hæ̃, amar make fon korechi**.

1 **tumi ki tomar make fon korecho?**
2 **tumi ki tãke ciThi likhecho?**
3 **tumi ki ei shOngskrito boiTa poRecho?**
4 **tumi shOb bujhecho?**

5 tumi aj daba khelecho?
6 gOtokalke tomar choTo bon esheche?

Grammar point: irregular present perfects

A The verb **jawa** 'to go' becomes **gi-** in the present perfect:

ami giechi, tumi giecho, tui giechish, she gieche, apni giechen.

In colloquial speech, the following are often used:

ami gechi, tumi gæcho, she gæche, tui gechish, apni gæchen.

B For verbs ending in **-ano**, the perfect is made as follows: remove the final **-no** (e.g. **ghumano → ghuma-**); change the stem-final **-a** to **-i** (**ghuma- → ghumi-**); add the regular endings **-echi, -echo** etc. (**ami ghumiechi, tumi ghumiecho,** etc.). Verbs with **-e-** in the first syllable change this to **-i-** in the perfect: **ami shikhiechi** etc. from **shekhano** 'teach'. Similarly, **O** changes to **o: ami poRiechi** etc. from **pORano** 'teach'.

C Surprisingly, a perfect form (of any verb) cannot be made negative by adding **na**. Instead, the simple PRESENT tense followed by **ni** or **nai** (E, colloquial) is used.

ami boiTa poRi ni
I haven't read the book.
uni tader farshi shikhiechen kintu arbi shekhan ni.
He has taught them Persian but he has not taught (them) Arabic.

Exercise 8

Proshun's mother is talking with Proshun on the phone, and asks him: **tumi gOto-kalke ki ki korecho?** Give Proshun's answer – it consists of the sentences in Exercise 4, but with present perfect verbs: **prothome amar hat-mukh dhuechi,** etc.

After this, Proshun's younger sister Puja asks him what he has done today. Make Puja's questions, using the sentences of Exercise 3 but inserting a present perfect. Also give Proshun's answers, which – because he is getting tired of all the questions – are all negative. Their first exchange would be: **'aj apni shOkale uThechen?' 'na, aj ami shOkale uThi ni.'**

Unit 5: *What have you seen?* 83

Dialogue 3 (Audio 1:75)

Babu is telling his friend Rafiq about his upsetting day. What made it upsetting? Why didn't Babu return home by bus?

rofik: tumi kæmon acho, babu?
babu: khub ækTa bhalo nai.
rofik: kæno? ki hoeche?
babu: ami shOkale pãcTae ghum theke uThechi. nasta khai nai. saikele coRe shoja shOdorghaTe gechi. okhane Opekkha korechi car ghOnTa.
rofik: kisher jonno Opekkha korecho?
babu: amar bORo bhai gram theke cal pathiechen. lOnce ashbe. kintu lOncTa ashe nai. er-i moddhe amar mobail o Taka curi hoe gæche. thanae gechi kintu pulish amar kOthae kono kan dæe nai.
rofik: tarpOre ki korecho?
babu: tarpOre? er-i moddhe corera amar saikel-o curi koreche. tai hẽTe hẽTe bashae firechi.
rofik: tomar bhaggo bhalo je tumi nije curi hoe jao nai!

Vocabulary

pãcTae	at 5 o'clock	thana	police station
ghum	sleep	amar kOtha	my words, what
nasta	breakfast (E)		I said
shOdorghaT	Sadarghat (riverside port of Dhaka)	kan dewa	to pay attention
		tarpOre	after that
Opekkha kOra	to wait	corera	thieves
kisher jonno	for what?	curi kOra	to steal
gram	village	basha (E)/	house
cal	rice	ghOr (W)	
lOnc	launch, riverboat	je	that
er-i moddhe	in the meantime	nije	(your)self
curi hoe jawa	to get stolen		

Vocabulary point: transport

To describe what means of transport is used, the transport term (e.g. **bas**, **riksha**) is put in the locative form (**base** 'by bus', **rikshae** 'by rickshaw'). It can be followed by the word **coRe** (lit. 'riding/driving', from the verb **cOra**).

base coRe gechi. We went by bus.
bebi-Tæksite firechi. We returned by tuk-tuk.

'On foot' is **hẽTe** or **hẽTe hẽTe** (from **hãTa** 'walk'):

amar baba ofis theke hẽTe eshechen.
my father came back from his office on foot

Exercise 9

Jenny is at the wedding of one of Dipu's cousins. She asks several guests how they have travelled there. Give her questions and their replies. The first exchange would be:

– apni ki bhabe ekhane eshechen? bebi-Tæksite coRe?
– ami bebi-Tæksite coRe ashi ni, base coRe eshechi.

1 **dipur mami: bebi-Tæksi na, bas.**
2 **dipur abba-amma: gaRi.**
3 **dipur apa: lOnc**
4 **dipur dulabhai (=husband of apa): lOnc na, saikel.**
5 **rofik o babu: hẽTe**
6 **mogol shahajadi: hẽTe na, hati**

Reading text

Read the text and say:
- Where is Rangamati?
- What lake is found there?

Where necessary, consult the list on page 212.

গত পরশু আমরা ঢাকা থেকে চট্টগ্রাম এসেছি। আমরা বাসে চড়ে এসেছি। এখানে দুই দিন বেড়িয়েছি। গতকালকে আমরা গাড়িতে চড়ে রাঙ্গামাটি গিয়েছি। রাঙ্গামাটি পাহাড়ী এলাকা এবং দেখতে খুবই সুন্দর। সেখানে অনেক উপজাতীয় লোকজন বাস করে। এলাকাটা বাংলাদেশের একেবারে পূর্ব দিকে। আমরা রাঙ্গামাটিতে এসে হাতির পিঠে চড়েছি। আমরা কাপ্তাই লেক দেখেছি। সেখানে আমরা অনেক ছবি তুলেছি এবং অনেক মজা করেছি। তারপরে আমরা সন্ধ্যাবেলায় চট্টগ্রামে ফিরে এসেছি।

Unit 5: *What have you seen?* 85

Rangamati and Lake Kaptai in Bangladesh

Vocabulary

gOto porshu	day before yesterday	bash kOra	to live
cOttogram	Chittagong (city in E. Bangladesh)	ækebare	totally
		purbo	east
bæRano	to go for a trip	eshe	having come
pahaRi	hilly	mOja kOra	have fun
dekhte	to see	fire asha	to come back
upojatio	indigenous		

Bengali script: a new type of letter

You will have noticed some letters in the Reading Text that you have not seen before:

উ্ট	in	চট্টগ্রাম	– TT (cOTTogram)
ঙ্গ		রাঙ্গামাটি	– ng (rangamaTi)
ন্দ		সুন্দর	– nd (shundor)
প্ত		কাপ্তাই	– pt (kaptai)
ন্ধ		সন্ধ্যাবেলায়	– ndh (shondha-bælae)

These are conjunct or combination letters. They represent a sequence of two consonants (just like English 'x', which represents 'k' followed by 's'). Bengali has many conjunct letters. We will present them – in small batches – in the course of the following few units.

6 আপনি কি খাবেন?
apni ki khaben?
What would you like to eat?

In this unit you will learn how to:
- talk about food
- talk about events due to happen in the future
- order, instruct and urge people
- recognise double letters

Dialogue 1 (Audio 2:1)

Sumita is at her colleague Deepti's home. Who is older, Sumita or Deepti? What are they going to eat?

dipti: apni ki khaben, didi? ami ki ilish mach rãdhbo? ar begun bhãjbo?

shumita: ami kichu khabo na, dipti. ekTu age mach die bhat khe-echi.

dipti: na, na, ta hObe na, didi. aj shOkale bajar theke bhalo ilish mach enechi. ranna korte beshi shOmOe lagbe na.

shumita: kono kOsTo koro na, dipti. amra shudhu ekTu boshbo ar gOlpo korbo.

dipti: Thik ache. tahole ækhon apni am khan. pOre ilish mach die bhat khaben. gOto kalke haT theke khub misTi am kinechi.

shumita: accha, dao. ami am khub pOchondo kori.

dipti: tahole ami ranna-ghOre jai. jabo ar ashbo.

shumita: ami tomar shathe ashbo?
dipti: kæno? apni ekhane bOshen.
shumita: na, tomar shathe ashbo. jOkhon tumi am kaTbe, tOkhon ami ca banabo.

Vocabulary

ilish	hilsha	gOlpo kOra	to have a chat
mach	fish	Thik ache	that's OK
rãdha	to cook	haT	open-air market
begun	aubergine	misTi	sweet
bhãja	to fry	pOchondo kOra	to like
kichu . . . na	not . . . anything	ranna-ghOr	kitchen
. . . die	with . . .	. . . shathe	with . . . (E)
ana	to fetch, bring	jOkhon	when, while
ranna kOra	to cook	kaTa	to cut
beshi	much	tOkhon	then
lagbe	it will take	ca	tea
kOsTo kOra	to take trouble	banano	to make

Vocabulary point: food

The staple of Bengali food (**khabar**) is rice: **bhat** (which, before cooking, is called **cal**; while in the field, it is called **dhan**). It is usually served with one of several types of lentils (**Dal**) and some fried vegetable, such as:

shak	leafy greens (spinach, etc.)	kopi	cabbage
kumRa	pumpkin	shim	broad beans

Several vegetables can be cooked together (e.g. **alu, begun, mula, gajor** 'carrot'), making **niramish**.

Most Bengalis are also fond of fish (**mach**), for example:

rui	carp	koi	fish resembling telapia
ilish	hilsha	cingRi	shrimp

The well-known Bengali curries usually contain meat:

gorur mangsho (or simply goru)	beef (lit.: cow's meat)
bhæRar mangsho (bhæRa)	mutton (lit.: sheep's meat)
khashir mangsho (khashi)	goat meat
murgir mangsho (murgi)	chicken

Unit 6: *What would you like to eat?*

All these dishes contain **pẽaj** ('onion') as well as **ada-roshun** ('ginger and garlic') and different spices (**mOshla**), such as **holdi** ('turmeric'), **dhonia** (E)/**dhone** (W) ('coriander') and **tej-pata** ('bay leaf'). If a lot of **moric** (E)/**lOnka** (W) ('chilli') has been put in, the dish will be be **jhal** ('hot').

Fruits (**fOl**) abound in Bengal:

kãThal	jackfruit	**pepe**	papaya
kOmla	orange	**peara**	guava
licu	lychee		

Exercise 1

Deepti is asking Sumita about various kinds of food. Construct their dialogue. The first exchange would be:

    dipti: apni ki rui mach pOchondo kOren?
    shumita: hẽ, rui mach khub pOchondo kori.

1 Do you like carp?
2 Do you like jackfruit?
3 Does your husband (**shami**) like hot food?
4 Do your children (**chele-me-e**) like leafy greens?
5 Do you eat rice every day?
6 Does your daughter like fish?

Next, make Sumita ask Deepti.

Grammar point: the future tense

The following sentences have future tense forms:

    amra ekTu boshbo.   **tumi am kaTbe.**
    We'll sit for a while.   You will cut the mango.

They describe events due to take place in the future. The corresponding sentences in English usually contain 'will' or 'shall' (or sometimes 'going to'). In addition, the Bengali future tense can also be used to state or ask somebody's preferences, for which English might use 'would like':

    apni ki khaben?   **apnar me-e ki Tibhi dekhbe?**
    What would you like to eat?   Would your daughter like to watch TV?

To form the future tense:

- take the stem (the verbal noun without final **-a** or **-wa**)
- change the stem vowel: **O** becomes **o**
  - **o** becomes **u**
  - **æ** becomes **e**
  - **e** becomes **i**
- but if the stem ends in a vowel, or contains the vowel **a**, don't change it
- add **-b-**
- add the appropriate future tense ending for person:

-o	e.g. **ami ashbo** I'll come
-e	**tumi ashbe**, etc.
-i	**tui ashbi**
-e	**she ashbe**
-en	**apni ashben**

Some more examples:

Verb	Future tense forms
bOla	ami bolbo, tumi bolbe, tui bolbi, she bolbe, apni bolben ('I will say' etc.)
hOwa	ami hObo, tumi hObe, tui hObi etc. ('I will become' etc.) – no vowel change, because the stem (hO-) ends in a vowel
shona	shunbo, shunbe, shunbi, etc. ('I will listen' etc.)
showa	shobo, shobe, etc. ('I will lie down etc.) – no vowel change, because the stem is sho-
dækha	dekhbo, dekhbe, etc. ('I will look' etc.)
kena	kinbo, kinbe, etc. ('I will buy' etc.)
dewa	debo, debe, etc. ('I will give' etc.) – no vowel change
ghumano	ghumabo, ghumabe, etc. ('I will sleep' etc.) – the stem is ghuma-; the future is made by adding -bo, -be etc. to it

There are a few special cases:

1 Some verbs with a stem ending in **a** insert **-i-** before the ending, e.g. **ami gaibo** etc. (**gawa** 'to sing') and **ami caibo** etc. (**cawa** 'to want').
2 The form **debo** 'I/we will give' (but not **debe**, etc.) can also be **dobo** (W) or **dibo** (E).

Unit 6: *What would you like to eat?*

Exercise 2

Listen to the Bengali news on <http://www.voa.gov/stream/bangla.html> and identify five verbs in the future tense. They can all be recognised by the sound **-b-**. Are there any verbs among them that you already know?

Exercise 3

In the following dialogue, give the verbs their appropriate future tense form.

proshun: ami ki tObla [bajano]?
jeni: accha, apni bajan, ami [shona].
proshun: tarpOre apni-o ki ekTu tObla [bajano]?
jeni: na, na, ami kichu bajabo na. tObe (*but*) ækTa ingreji gan (*song*) [gawa].
proshun: kon ganTa apni [gawa]?
jeni: ami '*Wonderful world*' [gawa]. apni pOchondo [kOra].
proshun: khubi bhalo! amar bondhuder (*friends*) [Daka]. ora-o apnar gan [shona].
jeni: besh to. apni tObla [bajano], ami gan [gawa] o apnar bondhura [shona].

Dialogue 2 (Audio 2:2)

Jenny is having dinner with Dipu's parents and their son Tipu.

dipur ma: ar ekTu khao, jeni. ekTu mangsho dei?
jeni: Olpo ekTu din.
dipur baba: shono, dipur ma. tumi jenike ilish-mach dopẽaja dao ni. she koi mach-o khae ni. shOb pOd Olpo Olpo kore dao.
jeni: na, na. ami ilish o koi khe-echi. ækhon Olpo ekTu mangsho ar ekTu Dal din.
Tipu: didi, æk Tukra lebu nin. Daler shathe lebur rOsh makhie khan. khub mOja lagbe.
jeni: dhonnobad, Tipu. ami lebu makhiechi.
dipur ma: Tipu, ranna-ghOr theke ar æk baTi polao ano.
Tipu: ma, bua kothae? take Daken.
dipur ma: bua ækhon ranna ghOre nai. she baire gæche.
dipur baba: dipur ma, ami anbo?

jeni: apnara shObai bOshen – ami ani.
dipur ma: na, jeni. tumi bOsho. Tipu anuk.

Vocabulary

ar	more	rOsh	juice
din	give!	makhano	to mix
dopĕaja	onion-based dish	makhie	having mixed
pOd	item	mOja lage	it is nice
Olpo Olpo kore	a bit from everything	baTi	bowl
Tukra	piece	polao	pilau
lebu	lemon	bua	maid

Grammar point: the present imperative

The imperative of verbs is used to order, instruct or urge the listener. It is used frequently in Bengali. For example:

ar ekTu khao!   apnara shObai bOshen!
Eat a bit more!   Sit down all of you!

The imperative has a familiar form (as in the first example), an intimate one and a polite one (as in the second example). In addition, there is a 3rd person imperative, with the meaning 'Let him/her/them. . . .', e.g. **Tipu anuk!** 'Let Tipu get (it)!'.

Here are the present imperative forms of the verb **kOra**:

Present imperative

(tumi/tomra)	kOro!	('Do it!' – familiar)
(tui/tora)	kOr!	('Do it!' – intimate)
(apni/apnara)	korun! (E also: kOren!)	('Do it!' – polite)
(she/tara)	koruk!	('Let him/her/them do it!')

The imperative **tumi**-form is identical to the simple present **tumi**-form: **bOlo!** 'Say (it)!', **dækho!** 'Look!', **fero!** 'Return!' etc. The verb **asha** is irregular: **esho!** 'Come!' (but in E also **asho!**).

The imperative **tui**-form has no ending: it is the same as the stem of the verb: **bOl!**, **dækh!**, **fer!** etc. The verb **asha** is irregular: **ae!**

The imperative **apni**-form and **she**-form have the endings **-un** and **-uk**. These trigger the familiar changes in the stem vowel: O>o, æ>e,

Unit 6: *What would you like to eat?*

e>i, o>u; but **a** remains. The polite ending **-en** (E) causes no vowel change.

bolun!/E: **bOlen!**   **boluk!** Let him/her say (it)!
dekhun!/E: **dækhen!**   **dekhuk!** Let him/her look!
firun!/E: **feren!**   **firuk!** Let him/her return!

Verbs with a stem ending in a vowel also follow the above rules, but **-un** and **-uk** are reduced to **-n** and **-k**, e.g. **jan!** 'Go!' (polite) and **jak!** 'Let him/her/them go'. The **-n** causes no vowel change (e.g. **cal dhon!** 'Wash the rice!'), except in the verbs **dewa** (**din!** 'Give (it)!') and **newa** (**nin!** 'Take (it)!'). The **-k** does cause vowel change (**cal dhuk!** 'Let him/her wash the rice!').

Exercise 4

When you turn on the TV, you see there is a programme on about a Bengali restaurant that you know. Call your friend Bimola to come, sit down, look and listen.

Also tell your older brother Shujon the same. And then also your younger sister Moyna (to whom – because you are pretending to be a native speaker now – you can use the intimate form). Moyna suggests her noisy friend Diya should also come and watch – you say, 'OK, let her come, sit down, look and listen – but no noise! (**kono shObdo na!**)'.

Dialogue 3 (Audio 2:3)

Protima is about to leave for work. Her husband Shantonu has a day off. She tells him what to do. What plans did he himself have?

protima: ami jacchi. tumi jOl-khabar kheo. tarpOre bajare jeo. taja shak-shobji kino.
shantonu: Thik ache. kintu ki ki shak-shobji kinbo?
protima: ami bolchi, tumi lekho. lau, begun ar palong shak eno. lal shak eno na. pãc keji polaoer cal eno.
shantonu: ar kichu anbo?
protima: na, ar kichu na. deri koro na. taRa-taRi bajar theke esho. tarpOre amar babar baRite jeo.
shantonu: aj amar chuTir din. asha chilo je ghOre boshe aram korbo. Di-bhi-Dite ækTa hindi sinema dekhbo.

protima: bah! besh besh. ami kaje jacchi. ar tumi aram kore hindi sinema dekhbe? ta hObe na. aj tomar chuTir din, kaje-i ma-babar shOnge dækha koro. onara khushi hOben.
shantonu: Thik ache. ja bolcho, ta hObe.

Vocabulary

taja	fresh	ghOre	at home
shobji	vegetable	aram kOra	to take it easy
bolchi	I'm saying (it)	sinema	cinema; film
palong shak	spinach	kaje-i	therefore
deri kOra	to be late	dækha kOra	to meet
chuTi	holiday, day off	ja	what
asha chilo	I was hoping (lit.: there was hope)	bolcho	you are saying

Grammar point: the future imperative

Bengali has imperatives for orders meant to be carried out straight-away (the present imperative) but also imperatives for orders meant to be carried out at a later point: the future imperative.

Here is the future imperative of **kOra**:

Future imperative

(tumi/tomra)	koro	('Do it'! – familiar)
(tui/tora)	korish	('Do it' – intimate)
(apni/apnara)	korben	('Do it!' – polite)

The familiar future form is the same as the familiar present form but it always changes the stem vowel (so **a>e, O>o, o>u, æ>e** and **e>i**): **bolo!** 'Say (it)!' **dekho!** 'Look!', **firo!** 'Return!', **jeo!** 'Go!', **hesho na!** 'Don't laugh!'. If the verbal noun ends in **-ano**, the familiar future imperative ends in **-io**: **ghumio na!** 'Don't sleep!'.

The intimate form ends in **-ish** (or **-sh**, if the verb stem ends in a vowel), which triggers the changes **O>o, o>u, æ>e** and **e>i** (but stem vowel **a** remains): **bolish! dekhish! firish! jash! hashish na! ghumash na!**

The polite future imperative is identical to the polite form of the ordinary future tense: **bolben! dekhben! firben! jaben! hashben na! ghumaben na!**

Unit 6: *What would you like to eat?*

Altogether, making imperatives in Bengali is clearly not simple. Initially it may be best just to learn by heart some of the individual forms given above. But always keep in mind the difference between present and future imperative. Say things like **okhane jao!** 'Go there!' only if you want this to be done straightaway – if you are talking about a time later in the day or further into the future, you must say: **okhane jeo!**

A final little thing: the present imperative cannot be made negative. A form such as, for example, **okhane jao na!** does not at all mean what you might expect. It means 'Do go there!/Please, go there!' (a useful enough phrase, but not a negative one!). To say 'Do not go there!', you must add **na** to the future imperative: **okhane jeo na!** This form must be used also if the command is really about the here and now.

Exercise 5 (Audio 2:4)

Rina teaches in a primary school. She always tells the children what to do and also what not to do. Someone has scrambled her sentences. Pair up each of her affirmative commands with a negative one.

1 **tomra cup kOro** (= be quiet)!
2 **bOsho!**
3 **tomar kaj kOro, shumi!**
4 **bulbul, tomar khataTa amake dao!**
5 **kOlom die lekho!**
6 **ækhon shObai baire jao!**
7 **baire æk shathe khælo!**

a **khataTa bæger moddhe** (= in) **rekho na!**
b **bhitore** (= inside) **theko na!**
c **ce-ar theke uTho na!**
d **golmal koro** (= make a racket) **na!**
e **jhOgRa koro** (= fight) **na!**
f **ishitar shOnge kOtha bolo na!**
g **pensil die likho na!**

Rina's naughtiest pupil is Kajol. Whenever she says, 'Don't make a noise!' or 'Sit down!', he whispers, 'Make a noise!' or 'Don't sit down!'. What would Kajol whisper after each of Rina's commands given above?

Exercise 6

It's early in the morning. Tell your two children:

'Get up! Brush your teeth (brush = **maja**; teeth = **dãt**)! Wash your faces (**mukh**)! Eat breakfast! Don't make a racket! Now go to school! At school, don't fight! Study well (= **mon die**)! Write with a pen! Don't giggle (giggle = **hasha-hashi kOra**)! Come home at 4 (= **carTae**)!'

Bengali script: double consonants

Some conjunct letters represent a sequence of two identical consonants. Remember that such consonants are pronounced long (see section on Sounds). In spelling, they as it were get pushed together, sometimes acquiring a different shape in the process.

Here are the main ones. Most are fairly easy to recognise.

ক + ক = ক্ক	kk	ধাক্কা **dhakka** push
চ + চ = চ্চ	cc	বাচ্চা **bacca** 'child'
জ + জ = জ্জ	jj	লজ্জা **lOjja** 'shame'
ট + ট = ট্ট	TT	চট্টগ্রাম **cOTTogram** Chittagong
ড + ড = ড্ড	DD	বড্ড **bODDo** very
ত + ত = ত্ত	tt	বিত্ত **bitto** wealth; note the difference between ত্ত **tt** and ও **o** (as in ওঠা **oTha**)
দ + দ = দ্দ	DD	হদ্দ **hOddo** limit
ন + ন = ন্ন	nn	রান্না **ranna** cooking
প + প = প্প	pp	গপ্প **gOppo** gossip
ব + ব = ব্ব	bb	আব্বা **abba** (E) father
ম + ম = ম্ম	mm	আম্মা **amma** (E) mother
ল + ল = ল্ল	ll	দিল্লী **dilli** Delhi

There is also a letter for double **kh**. Historically, it stands for **kh** followed by **sh** – but it is now pronounced as a long **kh**. When it comes at the beginning of a word, it represents single **kh**.

খ + ষ = ক্ষ	kkh	অপেক্ষা **Opekkha** waiting
		ক্ষমতা **khOmota** power

Exercise 7

Answer the following questions about yourself.

1 আপনার আম্মা কি ভালো রান্না করেন? আর আপনার আব্বা?
2 আপনার কি বাচ্চা আছে?
3 আপনি কি কখনো দিল্লী বা (= or) চট্টগ্রামে গিয়েছেন?
4 আপনি কি বাংলা নিজে নিজে (= by yourself) শেখেন? নাকি কোন শিক্ষকের কাছে শেখেন?
5 আপনি এখন 'ঢাকা' বলুন। এবারে (= now) 'ধাক্কা' বলুন। পাঁচ মিনিট পরে আবার বলবেন।

7 আপনি কি রান্না করছেন?
apni ki ranna korchen?

What are you cooking?

In this unit you will learn how to:

- talk about cooking
- describe ongoing activities
- describe feelings
- make compound words
- recognise more conjunct letters

Dialogue 1 (Audio 2:5)

Jenny goes to see Sofia and gets a cooking lesson. What are the ingredients for her cooking?

jeni: sofia apa, apni ki ranna korchen?
sofia: kichu ranna korchi na. karon aj tumi-i ranna korbe. ami tomake shekhabo.
jeni: Thik ache, apa. ami ki ranna korbo?
sofia: mushurer Dal. rannar ayojon ami shOb korechi.
jeni: accha. ami ki prothome kãca moric kaTbo?
sofia: hẽ, dui bhag kore kaTo. ami tomar jonno dhonia pataguli kuci-kuci kore kaTchi. pẽaj roshun nie ki korcho?
jeni: khosha felchi. tarpOr choTo Tukra kore kaTbo.

sofia: accha, Thik ache. ækhon haRite kichu tel gOrom kOro. cular ãc ekTu baRao. pẽaj roshun badami kore bhãjo. æk ca-camoc lObon dao. moric cheRe dao. ekTu pOre Dal haRite Dhalo o adha ca-camoc holdi dao. dui kap pani haRite Dhalo. bhalo bhabe naRo.
jeni: Thik ache, naRchi. kæmon hocche, apa? ami shundor kore ranna korchi to?
sofia: hæ̃, khub-i bhalo kore korcho. tomar Dal cOmotkar hObe.

Vocabulary

mushurer Dal	red lentils	ãc	heat
ayojon	preparation	baRano	to increase
kãca	unripe, green	badami	brown
bhag	part	camoc	spoon
kuci-kuci kore	in small pieces	cheRe dewa	to let go
... nie	with ...	Dhala	to pour
khosha	skin	adha	half
fæla	to throw (away)	naRa	to stir
haRi	pan	hocche	it is going
cula	fire (of cooker)		

Grammar point: adverbs

To say how actions are carried out, English uses adverbs, as in:

I am cooking this nicely.   Stir well!

Bengali adverbs are usually formed by putting **kore** or **bhabe** after an adjective, such as **shundor** or **bhalo**:

ami shundor kore ranna korchi.   **bhalo bhabe naRo!**

To ask 'how', you can use **ki kore** or **ki bhabe**:

pẽaj ki kore kaTbo?   **ki bhabe ca banabo?**
How shall I cut the onion?   How shall I make the tea?

Another word for 'how' is **kæmne**:

pẽaj kæmne kaTbo?
ca kæmne banabo?

Some adverbs are made by adding **-e** (after a consonant) or **-te** (after a vowel) to the adjective:

Unit 7: *What are you cooking?*

shabdhan	careful, cautious	shabdhane	carefully, cautiously
nirOb	silent	nirObe	silently
deri	late (adj.)	derite	late (adv.)

Exercise 1 (Audio 2:6)

It is early in the morning. Sumita is telling her son Pial to get up, go to school, and so on. Below are some of his responses. What were her commands? The first one must have been: **oTho!**

1 hæ̃, uThbo.
2 accha, bhalo bhabe khabo.
3 accha, tarpOre taRataRi kore skule jabo.
4 hæ̃, shabdhane rasta par hObo (= I'll cross).
5 skul theke derite bashae ashbo na.
6 accha, tarpOre nirObe amar dadar shOnge daba khelbo.

Grammar point: the present progressive

In addition to the simple present tense, Bengali verbs also have a progressive present tense:

dhonia kaTchi.   apni ki ranna korchen?
I am cutting the coriander.   What are you cooking?

This form is used very much like the progressive in English ('am cutting', 'are cooking' etc.): it describes an ongoing action that is limited in duration.

The recipe for making the present tense progressive is:

- take the stem of the verb
- change the stem vowel (yes, again!): **O** becomes **o**
  - o becomes u
  - æ becomes e
  - e becomes i
- if the stem vowel is **a**, don't change it
- add **-ch-**
- add the appropriate present tense ending for person:
  - -i   e.g. ami moric kaTchi
  - -o   tumi pẽaj kaTcho
  - -ish   tui dhonia-pata kaTchish
  - -e   she roshun kaTche
  - -en   apni alu kaTchen

These rules also apply to verbs with a stem ending in a vowel, except that they don't get -ch- but -cch-. E.g. **dhowa** has the forms **ami dhucchi, tumi dhuccho,** etc.; **dewa** has **ami dicchi, tumi diccho,** etc.; **ghumano** has **ami ghumacchi, tumi ghumaccho,** etc.

Exercise 2

Find your slips of paper again, one set with pronouns and one with verbs. Use them to practise making the present progressive.

Exercise 3

You are working in a Bengali restaurant, where it is your duty to coordinate the work in the kitchen. The place is full tonight. The owner pops in to ask if everybody is pulling their weight. Answer his questions, using the clues provided.

1 **babul ki korche?** [cutting onions]
2 **saiful okhane ki dhucche?** [washing coriander]
3 **onup kothae?** [gone home]
4 **o Onadi kothae? oke dekchi na** [there; frying fish]
5 **polTu ki korche?** [stirring the lentils]
6 **shunan ki aj esheche?** [no; is studying at home]
7 **amar chele ki ekhane?** [yes; is eating rice]
8 **o tumi ki korcho?** [I am giving him rice]

Dialogue 2 (Audio 2:7)

Dipu's mother has taken Jenny to a restaurant. Why does Jenny have to be careful when eating out?

dipur ma: jeni, tomar mukh shukna kæno? tomar ki Oshustho lagche?
jeni: na, na. amar khub khide pe-eche.
dipur ma: tahole taRa-taRi khabar ODar dei. tumi ki khabe? jhal khicuRi khabe?
jeni: na, jhal khabar amar bhalo lage na. korma polao khabo.
dipur ma: ei weTar, eidike esho. amar jonno ghie bhăja poroTa o niramish ano. ar ei mohilar jonno korma polao dao.
weTar: ar ki ki debo?
dipur ma: ækhon amader dui gelash taja fOler rOsh dao ar khabar pOre amaderke TOk doi dio.

Unit 7: *What are you cooking?*

jeni:	weTar, apni ki janen korma polao ki ki die ranna kOre? karon badam khawa amar nishedh. amar ælerji ache.
weTar:	bhOe paben na. baburcike shabdhan korbo. she apnar khabare kono badam debe na.
jeni:	apnake Onek dhonnobad.

Vocabulary

shukna (E)/ shukno (W)	dry	ghi	ghee
tomar mukh shukna/shukno	you look dried out/hungry	bhāja	fried
		poroTa	paratha
		TOk	sour
Oshustho	ill	doi	yoghurt
khide/khuda	hunger	badam	nut
ODar dewa	to order	nishedh	forbidden
khicuRi	rice with lentils and vegetables	... khawa amar nishedh	I'm not allowed to eat ...
korma	rice with yoghurt, coconut milk, nuts, meat	bhOe	fear
		baburci	cook
		shabdhan kOra	to warn
eidike	here		

Grammar point: describing feelings and emotions

To describe feelings, emotions or other sensations, Bengali often uses a special type of construction. An example is:

jhal khabar amar bhalo lage na.
I don't like spicy food.

Many of such sentences feature the verb **laga**. The verb is always in the 3rd person (i.e. **lage, lagche, lagbe**, etc.). The person who has the sensation is in the possessive form (in the example above: **amar**). The cause or source of the sensation gets the object form. If the cause is a thing, that means it has no ending. But if it is a person, it will have the ending **-ke** (for the singular) or **-der(ke)** (for the plural).

The construction as a whole is called the 'impersonal' construction. It does involve a person but – unlike in other sentences – that person is not the subject of the sentence.

Here are some further examples:

oiguli amader bhalo lage na.	We don't like those.
take tomar bhalo lagbe.	You will like him/her.
jenike dipur mar bhalo legeche.	Dipu's mother liked Jenny.
amTa tomar kæmon lagche?	How do you like the mango?
(amTa) (amar) bhalo lagche.	I like the mango.

As the last sentence shows, the cause and/or the person are sometimes left out if they are clear from the preceding context.

Another verb meaning 'to like' is **pOchondo kOra** – as you saw in Unit 6, it has straightforward grammar. However, this verb usually expresses permanent likes and dislikes (e.g. **ami mach pOchondo kori**), while **bhalo laga** can also be used to express what someone likes or dislikes on a specific occasion (e.g. **ei machTa amar bhalo lagche na**).

Exercise 4

With your little son, you are visiting Deepti. She asks if you are enjoying the food she has prepared. Make her questions and give your answers. The first exchange would be: '**machTa apnar kæmon lagche?**' '**machTa amar bhalo lagche**' (or: '**bhalo lagche**')

1 **machTa?**
2 **palong shakTa?**
3 **DalTa?**
4 **shimTa?**
5 **alu-bhOrtaTa?** (**alu-bhOrta** = spicy potato-mash)
6 **doiTa?**

Then Deepti asks if your son is also liking the food. Make her questions and answer for your son: '**machTa apnar cheler kæmon lagche?**', '**tar bhalo lagche**' etc.

When you go home, Deepti gives you some food to take for your mother. When you meet again the following week, Deepti asks how your mother liked the food. Again make her questions and give your answers: '**machTa apnar maer kæmon legeche?**', '**onar bhalo legeche**' etc.

Grammar point: describing more feelings and emotions

Now that you know how impersonal constructions work, you are able to deal with a host of other impersonal expressions. Here are some more with **laga**.

amar **Oshustho** lagche	I feel/am	ill	(**Oshustho**	= unwell)
amar **klanto** lagche	"	tired	(**klanto**	= tired)
amar **khide** lagche	"	hungry	(**khide**	= hunger)
amar **pipasha** lagche	"	thirsty	(**pipasha**	= thirst)
amar **ThanDa** lagche	"	cold	(**ThanDa**	= cold)

Since these examples all describe a temporary state of affairs, they are in the present progressive (**lagche**). For a more permanent situation, the simple present (**lage**) is used:

arifer shObshOmOe khide lage.   Arif is always hungry.

Some of the above can also have the verb **pawa** (in the perfect tense):

amar **khide** pe-eche	I feel/am hungry
amar **pipasha** pe-eche	" thirsty
amar **ghum** pe-eche (also: **lagche**)	" sleepy
amar **bhOe** pe-eche (also: **lagche**)	" scared

There are also impersonal expressions with **hOwa**, some of them in the perfect tense.

take amar pOchondo hOe na.	I don't like him/her.
tomar ki hoeche?	What's happened to you/ what's the matter with you?
amar jOr hoeche.	I've got a fever. (**jOr** = fever)

There are three impersonal constructions that express the meaning 'to need':

amar æk hajar Taka lagbe	I need 1000 taka
amar æk hajar Taka cai	I need/want 1000 taka
amar æk hajar Takar dOrkar ache	I need 1000 taka (lit.: of-me of-1000-taka need is)

Exercise 5

Your sister is describing her special diet to you. Say how it will make her feel. Your first sentence is: **tahole apnar khub khide lagbe, didi.**

1 ami dui din kono khabar khabo na. hungry!
2 tarpOre æk din kono pani khabo na. thirsty!
3 tarpOre dui din ghumabo na. sleepy!
4 tarpOre æk din shudhu bOrof (ice) khabo. cold!
5 tarpOre marathon dourabo (I'll run). tired!
6 oi bhabe (that way) bish keji ojon (weight) ill!
   kOmabo (I'll lose/reduce).

Dialogue 3 (Audio 2:10)

Ishita wants to go shopping with Shumi. Why doesn't Shumi want to go? What solutions does Ishita suggest?

ishita: shumi, ami bajare jacchi. jabe amar shathe?
shumi: na, ækhon baire jabo-Tabo na. karon amar khub matha dhoreche.
ishita: shudhu ki matha-i dhoreche? naki jOr-TOr-o uTheche?
shumi: hæ̃, shei shathe peT-o bætha korche. amar ækebare-i bhalo lagche na.
ishita: tahole ækTa pærasitamol khao. kOmla apel-Tapel khao.
shumi: shOb-i khe-echi. tarpOre-o aram lagche na.
ishita: tahole ækhon resT nao. ghumao. ami jacchi. tomar jonno kichu anbo? cokleT-bishkuT anbo? cĩRa-muRi anbo?
shumi: na, kichu-i eno na. amar kono kichu-i mOja lagche na.
ishita: tahole tomar jonno ki notun kono Di-bhi-Di anbo? Ti-bhi dekhbe?
shumi: na, Ti-bhi-o dekhbo na.
ishita: tahole ki Daktar Dakbo?
shumi: na, Daktar-Taktar lagbe na. ami resT nebo. ghumabo. tate-i shustho hObo.

Vocabulary

amar matha dhoreche	I have a headache	amar aram lagche	I'm feeling comfortable
amar jOr uTheche	I've got a fever	cĩRa (E)/ cĩRe (W)	flattened rice
peT	stomach	muRi	puffed rice
bætha kOra	to be painful, to cause pain	tate shustho	through that well, healthy

Unit 7: *What are you cooking?*

Grammar point: emphasis

You already know that the sound **o** can be added to a word to express the meaning 'also, too' (as in **jOr-o uTheche** 'A fever has also come on'). The sound **i** can also be attached to a word – the effect is to emphasise it.

shOb-i khe-echi.	I've eaten all (really all).
tate-i shustho hObo.	Through that (precisely that) I'll get better.
ami-i take fon korbo.	I myself will call him.
ThanDa-i lagche.	It feels very cold.

This emphatic **-i** corresponds to various devices in English: 'very', 'really', 'myself', etc. or heavy stress in pronunciation.

Exercise 6

Complete the dialogue.
- tumi _____ jaccho?
- bashae jacchi.
- kæno?
- bhat khabo. amar khub-i _____ pe-eche.
- ki die bhat khabe?
- khashir mangsho ache, shim-Tim ache. shOb-i ranna korbo.
- tumi-i ranna korbe?
- hæ̃, _____ ranna korbo.
- khashir mangsho _____ kOro?
- hæ̃, khashir mangsho amar _____ lage.
- ar ki ki pOchondo _____?
- Onek kichu-i pOchondo kori. tumi jano na? _____ ækjOn peTuk.

Vocabulary point: compound words

The word for 'and' (which is **o** or **ar**) is often left out in phrases like 'father and mother', 'table and chair', 'rice and lentils', producing compound words such as:

ma-baba, cear-Tebil, Dal-bhat.

The Bengali fondness for compounds is also in evidence in so-called 'echo' words, where a word is doubled but the second occurrence starts with the sound **T**. This can be done with nearly all words:

cear-Tear	jabo-Tabo
chairs and things like that	I will go or something
am-Tam	ThanDa-TanDa
mango and such things	cold and so on

If the word itself already starts with **T**, the 'echo'-part gets **Th**:

Taka-Thaka (also: Taka-Tuka)	money and things like that
TOk-ThOk (also: TOk-Tuk)	sour and so on

The 'echo'-part means 'and the like/and so', but it is often difficult to translate these forms into English. Because of the jingling sound effect, they often express a playful attitude.

Exercise 7

The restaurant owner of Exercise 3 is asking questions again. Give his kitchen staff's answers, using an echo-word for the word in the question that has been underlined. Saiful would say: **na, ami ækhon kichu khabo-Tabo na.**

1 saiful, tumi ækhon kichu <u>khabe</u>? – na, ...
2 polTu, tomar ki <u>ghum</u> lagche? – na, ...
3 shunan, tumi ki <u>mangsho</u> keTecho? – ji, ...
4 Onadi, weTar ki <u>bhat</u> khe-eche? – na, ...
5 babul, tumi ki <u>shak</u> dhuecho? – na, ...
6 onup, kababe <u>lObon</u> diecho? – hæ̃, ...

Bengali script: more conjunct letters

The following conjunct letters have a consonant followed by the sound **u** – easy enough to pronounce but look carefully at the shape of the letters.

গ + ু = গু	gu	গুড় **guR** molasses
শ + ু = শু	shu	শুকনা **shukna** (E) dry
হ + ু = হু	hu	হুকুম **hukum** command
র + ু = রু	ru	রুটি **ruTi** roti
র + ূ = রূ	ru	রূপা **rupa** silver

Bengali also has a letter for the sound **ri** at the beginning of a word: ঋ. It occurs in a few words only, such as ঋণ **rin** 'debt, loan' and ঋষি **rishi** 'saint'. In other words that start with the sound **ri**, the spelling রি or রী is used: রিপু **ripu** 'passion' and রীতি **riti** 'custom'.

Unit 7: *What are you cooking?*

For the sound **ri** coming after a consonant, the symbol ৃ is sometimes used, written below the consonant, e.g: গৃহিনী **grihini** 'housewife'. Another possible spelling uses ্য ('squiggly' **r**) and ি **i**, e.g. প্রিয় **prio** 'dear, favourite'.

The sound **ri** can also occur after **h** – the combination looks as follows:

হ + ৃ = হৃ   **hri**   হৃদয়   **hridOe** heart (pronounced with a light **h**, though sometimes simply **ridOe** in E)

Exercise 8

Read the following items on a restaurant menu:

Bengali Eatery

শুকনো বড়া (= vegetable cake)	১ রুপি
ডাল রুটি	৩ রুপি
নিরামিষ পরোটা	৪ রুপি
খিচুড়ি	২.৫০ রুপি
ভাঁজা মাছ	৩ রুপি
টক দই	১.৫০ রুপি
গুড় চা	৫০ পয়সা (i.e. half a rupee)

1 Which is more expensive, the fish or the rice with lentils and vegetables?
2 Go to <http://www.calcuttaweb.com/recipes/> and try to find out for some of the items how many calories they are.

8 দেখাবো?
dækhabo?

Shall I show it to you?

In this unit you will learn how to:

- talk about quantities and prices
- ask more questions
- describe relations between things
- read some further Bengali-script texts

Dialogue 1 🎧 (Audio 2:12)

Rifat and his aunt are in the market. What do they buy?

দোকানদার:	আপনাদের কি চাই?
কাকিমা:	আধা কেজি হলদি, একশ গেরাম জিরা, আর এক পোয়া গুঁড়া ধনিয়া দিন। ভালো শুকনা মরিচ আছে?
দোকানদার:	হ্যাঁ, আছে — দেখেন।
কাকিমা:	আচ্ছা। সোয়া কেজি দিন।
দোকানদার:	আর কিছু লাগবে?
কাকিমা:	হ্যাঁ, এখন মনে পড়ছে। সরিষার তেল লাগবে। এক লিটার দিন।
দোকানদার:	আর কিছু চাচ্ছেন আপনারা?
কাকিমা:	নারিকেলের দরকার ছিলো। কিন্তু — না। থাক। আমার ভাই গ্রাম থেকে পাঠাবে।
রিফাত:	বাসায় কলা নেই কাকিমা। আমাদেরকে এক ডজন কলা দিন।
দোকানদার:	এক হালি সাগর কলার দাম তিরিশ টাকা। সব মিলিয়ে আটশ চল্লিশ টাকা আর আশি পয়সা দিন। ধন্যবাদ। আবার আসবেন।

Unit 8: *Shall I show it to you?*

Vocabulary

jira (E)/jire (W)	cumin	narikel	coconut
gũRa (E)/gũRo (W)	powder	thak	leave it!
		DOjon	dozen
mone poRche	I remember (lit.: it falls in mind)	hali	four (in counting fruits)
shorisha (E)/shorshe (W)	mustard	shagor kOla	large-size banana
		dam	price
cawa	to want	shOb milie	all together

Notes about Bengali script

The word আচ্ছা **accha** 'OK' has **cch**, written চ্ছ. It is pronounced like **ch** but the initial **t**-like part is prolonged.

The word কিন্তু **kintu** 'but' has the conjunct for **n + t + u**: ন্তু. You can see ন (the top part), ত (the middle part – the ত looks as if it has been rotated 90° counterclockwise) and ু (as in **shu** or **gu**, e.g. in গুঁড়া **guRa** – it's the little flourish at the bottom).

Vocabulary point: quantities (Audio 2:13)

You can already count to 20 in Bengali. Counting further is not easy, since many numerals up to 100 have irregular forms. It is worth the effort now to learn the sequence 21–30, because they are used relatively often.

21	২১	একুশ	ekush	26	২৬	ছাব্বিশ	chabbish
22	২২	বাইশ	baish	27	২৭	সাতাশ	shatash
23	২৩	তেইশ	teish	28	২৮	আটাশ	aTash
24	২৪	চব্বিশ	cobbish	29	২৯	উনত্রিশ	untrish
25	২৫	পঁচিশ	põcish	30	৩০	তিরিশ/ত্রিশ	tirish/trish

Also learn: 60, 70, 80, 90. For these, look at pages 216–218, where all these numerals are given.

Now count from 1 to 30, and then onwards: 40, 50, 60, 70, 80, 90, 100. Also do this backwards.

And then say:

- ২, ৪, ৬, ৮, ১০, ১২, ১৪, ১৬, ১৮, ২০, ২২, ২৪, ২৬, ২৮, ৩০
- ৫, ১০, ১৫, ২০, ২৫, ৩০

To express halves, Bengali has the following words:

adha/Ordhek	½
deR	1½
aRai	2½
shaRe tin	3½
shaRe car	4½
ittadi	etc.

¼ is **shiki**, 1¼ is **shoa æk**, 2¼ is **shoa dui**, etc. ¾ is **poune æk**, 1¾ is **poune dui**, etc.

Weights are usually expressed in grams (**geram**) and kilos (**keji**), but there are still some older measures in use:

æk sher	$c.$ 0.9 kg
æk mOn	$c.$ 37.5 kg (40 **sher**)
æk poa	$c.$ 230 grams (quarter of a **sher**)

Some less precise words are:

kichu kichu	several	**kichu kichu lok/kichu kichu boi**
Olpo ekTu	a little bit of	**Olpo ekTu jOl**
æto Tuku	so little, such a small bit of	**æto Tuku nun**
æk gada	a heap/lot of	**æk gada bhat**

Exercise 1

Turn the following shopping list into Bengali.

```
1½ kilo red potatoes
3½ litre oil
30 gram cumin
225 gram coriander powder
19 kilo pilau rice
```

Vocabulary point: prices

Stating prices is done as follows:

eTar dam collish Taka — this costs (the price of this is) 40 taka
egulir dam protiTa pOncash pOesha — these cost 50 cents a piece

Unit 8: *Shall I show it to you?* 111

eTar dam keji proti (or proti keji) this costs 40 taka per kilo
  collish Taka
collish Taka keji   40 taka per kilo

To ask for this information, say:

eTar dam koto?   What is the price of this?
koto lagbe?   How much should I pay?
koto debo?   How much should I give/pay?

Exercise 2 (Audio 2:15)

Deepti is buying food. How many kilos will she have to carry home? Also complete the last turn.

dipti: misTi alur dam koto?
dokandar: proti keji pOncash Taka.
dipti: accha, dui keji din. bhalo shim ache?
dokandar: ache, dækhen. adha keji tirish Taka.
dipti: tahole, deR keji din. bashmoti caler dam koto?
dokandar: æk mon tin hajar shatsho Taka, apa.
dipti: bapre bap – æto dam! dui keji din. kichu shukna moricero dOrkar chilo.
dokandar: poa proti shaT Taka. kOe poa can?
dipti: adha poa din.
dokandar: ei nin. tahole shOb milie _____ sho _____ Taka din.

Grammar point: more question words

You already know many question words (such as **ki? kothae? kæmne? kæno?** etc.). Here are some more.
  There are two words for 'when': **kOkhon** (to ask about the time of an event) and **kObe** (to ask on which day).

  aj kOkhon bajare jaben, kaki-ma?
  kObe bilate firben, jeni-di?

To say 'how long', **kotokkhon** is used for durations shorter than a day and **kotodin** (lit.: how many days?) if the answer is likely to be a number of days.

  kotokkhon ghumiecho?   aT ghOnTa.
  apni ekhane kotodin thakben?   pāc din.

> **Mini-exercise**
>
> Ask Jenny:
>
> When (what day) did you come here?
> Why did you come here?
> How long will you stay?
> Where will you go next (= **pOre**)?

The word for 'who' has several different forms:

ke tomake mereche?	Who has hit you?	(**ke** = subject form)
tumi kake merecho?	Whom have you hit?	(**kake** = object form)
eigulo kader saikel?	Whose bicycles are these?	(**kader** = plural possessive form)

The complete list resembles that of **she** 'he/she' (see Unit 2):

	Subject	*Possessive*	*Object*
singular	**ke**	**kar**	**kake**
plural	**kara**	**kader**	**kader**

There is also a form **ke ke**: a plural subject form meaning 'which various people?'. E.g. **ke ke ashben?** 'Which people are coming?' (note the polite form **ashben** – this means the answer is expected to include older or higher-status people). The object form is **kake kake**, as in: **apni kake kake dawat diechen?** 'Which people have you invited?'. The form **ki ki** is similar in meaning: **ki ki khe-echo, arif?** 'What things have you eaten, Arif?'.

Grammar point: more question types

Bengali does not have tag questions such as 'You will come, won't you?'. But **to** or **tai na** added to a statement creates a similar effect.

tumi ashbe to?	You will come, won't you? (I would like it)
tumi ashbe, tai na?	You will come, won't you? (that's true, isn't it?)

Unit 8: *Shall I show it to you?*

Attaching **naki** (sometimes **na ki**) also turns a statement into a question – its effect is like saying 'Please, enlighten me'. As a result, it cannot be used, for example, to make invitations – for those, ordinary **ki** is used.

tumi ashbe na ki?	Will you be coming? (what is your plan?)
tumi-o ki ashbe?	Will you also be coming? (that would be nice)

The form **naki** (sometimes shortened to **na**) is also used when asking about two alternatives. It then simply means 'or':

tumi ashbe na(ki) bashae thakbe?	Will you come or will you stay at home?
TakaTa ækhon na(ki) pOre debo?	Shall I give the money now or later?

To make indirect questions, **ki na** 'whether' is used. In such sentences, the 'whether' part often comes first, with **ki na** at the end of it:

she ashbe ki na ami jani na.	I don't know whether he'll come. (lit.: he'll come – whether – I don't know)
tumi bojho ki na bOlo.	Tell me whether you understand. (lit.: you understand – whether – tell)

$$a = \sqrt{b^2 + c^2}$$
$$E = mc^2$$

tumi bojho ki na bOlo

Exercise 3 (Audio 2:16)

Complete Rifat's questions. His aunt's answers are given.

1 আপনি _____ বাজারে যাবেন, কাকিমা? – একটু পরে যাবো।
2 বাজারে _____ কিনবেন? – চাল-ডাল আদা-রসুন কিনবো।
3 আমি আসব? নাকি _____? – তুমি এখানে থাকো।
4 এখানে _____ করবো? – তুমি টেবিল বানিও। ছয়টায় মেহমান আসবে।
5 তাই নাকি? _____ দাওয়াত দিয়েছেন? – তোমার মামা-মামি, খালা-খালু, বোন-দুলাভাই আসবেন।

Dialogue 2 (Audio 2:17)

Rifat's aunt is at the market again, now looking for clothes. What does she buy?

kaki-ma: amar me-er jonno æk seT salwar-kamij khũjchi. kOe-ækTa dækhaben?
dokandar: nishcOe-i. ei taker upore dækhen, kaki-ma. eigula shundor na? konTa neben – badamiTa? naki halka nilTa?
kaki-ma: nilTar nice ki? oi kOmlaTa dekhi? oiTar dam koto?
dokandar: ei salwar-kamijTa kintu silker. dam shaRe car hajar Taka.
kaki-ma: ki? æto dam cacchen kæno? Otoguli Taka debo na. apnake dui hajar Taka debo.
dokandar: ki bOlen, kaki-ma! æto kOme hObe na. ar ekTu baRan.
kaki-ma: dui hajar dui sho debo.
dokandar: Thik ache, Thik ache. ar ki khũjchen?
kaki-ma: amar cheler jonno lungi dOrkar. ache apnar kache?
dokandar: na, kaki-ma, ami purushder kapoR bikkri kori na. amar dokaner pechone amar bondhur dokan ache. tar kach theke kinte parben.

Vocabulary

salwar-kamij	salwar kameez	æto kOme	for so little
khõja	to look for	lungi	sarong (worn by men)
dækhano	to show	purush	male
tak	shelf	bikkri kOra	to sell
halka	light	kinte parben	you can buy
kintu	however		
Otoguli	so many		
kOm	little, less		

Grammar point: postpositions

Words such as 'after', 'under', 'for' are called prepositions in English, because they come before the noun. The corresponding words in Bengali are called postpositions, because they come after the noun:

after breakfast   **nastar pOre**
under water   **panir (E)/jOler(W) nice**
for Babul   **babuler jonno**

Some further postpositions are:

Unit 8: *Shall I show it to you?*

moddhe, bhitore	in	**baRir moddhe/bhitore** in the house
baire	outside	**ofisher baire** outside the office
upore	on, over	**taker upore** on the shelf
shamne	in front of	**apnar shamne** in front of you
pechone	behind	**dokaner pechone** behind the shop
dike	towards	**mondirer dike** towards the temple
kache	near, with	**bajarer kache** near the market
		amar kache with me/in my posssession
majhkhane	between	**boigulor majhkhane** between the books
shOnge/ shathe (E)	with	**amar shOnge/shathe** with me
age	before	**dOshTar age** before ten

The nouns in front of all these take the possessive form (**baRir, ofisher, apnar,** etc.).

Some postpositions combine with non-possessive forms:

die/nie	with (the use of)	**camoc die/nie**	with a spoon
theke	from, out of	**skul theke**	from/out of school
chaRa	without, except	**Taka chaRa**	without money

If **theke** combines with a noun denoting a person, it sometimes takes the form **kach theke**. The noun gets the possessive form:

babuler kach theke   from Babul (lit.: from near Babul)

Exercise 4

Carry out the following instructions and answer the final question.

একটা বই ও একটা খাতা নিন। খাতাটা বইয়ের নিচে রাখুন। বইয়ের উপরে একটা কলম রাখুন। আর একটা বই নিন। এখন খাতাটা বইগুলোর মাঝখানে রাখুন। আর একটা কলম নিন। ঐ (**oi**) কলমটা খাতার উপরে রাখুন। এখন আপনি ঘরের বাইরে যান। দশ সেকেন্ড (**sekenD**) পরে আবার ঘরের ভিতরে আসবেন।

এখন বলুন: খাতাটা ও কলমগুলি কোথায়?

Exercise 5

Onika has just come back from shopping. How would she reply to her mother's questions? Her first answer would be: **na, Taka nie bajare gechi.**

1 tumi ki Taka chaRa bajare gæcho? – na, _____ nie _____
2 tumi kOkhon fire eshecho? baroTar age? – na, _____ pOre _____
3 gaRiTa ki baRir shamne rekhecho? – na, _____ pechone _____
4 palong shak frijer bhitore rekhecho? – na, _____ baire _____
5 kOlagulo taker upore rekhecho? – na, _____ Tebiler _____
6 ei boiTa ki babar jonno kinecho? – na, _____ apnar _____

Vocabulary point: colours

Some common colour words are:

lal	red	holud	yellow	golapi	pink
shobuj	green	badami	brown	shada	white
nil	blue	kOmla	orange	kalo	black

There are various ways of specifying an object's colour:

ei shaRir rOng ki?	What is the colour of this sari?
eTa ækta lal shaRi	This is a red sari.
ei shaRir rOng lal	The colour of this sari is red.
eTa ækTa lal rOnger shaRi	This is a red-coloured sari. (lit.: a sari of red colour)

Note that **-Ta** or **-gulo/-guli** can be added to colour words (and also other adjectives) to express 'the ... one(s)':

| lalTa o nilgulo shundor. | The red one and the blue ones are beautiful. |
| amar shaRi lal, tomarTa nil. | My sari is red; your one (yours) is blue. |

Exercise 6

Fatema is buying clothes for the poor in her village. This is her shopping list. What would she say to the shopkeeper? Her first sentence could be: **amar bishTa nil lungi o dOshTa shobuj lungi chai. apnar kache ache na ki?**

1 লুঙ্গি (lungi) – নীল ২০টা, সবুজ ১০টা
2 শাড়ী – সবুজ ৮টা, বাদামী ৫টা, লাল ৩টা, গোলাপী ৪টা
3 সালোয়ার-কামিজ – সাদা ৪ সেট, নীল ৩ সেট
4 শার্ট – সাদা ১১টা, নীল ৭টা, সবুজ ৯টা

Unit 8: *Shall I show it to you?*

Dialogue 3 (Audio 2:18)

Jenny is in a book and stationery shop. She wants some postcards to send home and some things to read, for herself and Dipu's mother. What does Jenny buy for Dipu's mother?

jeni:	apnar kache ki gramer chobir bhiu-karD ache?
dokandar:	ji, ache. gram chaRa bideshi bhiu-karD-o ache.
jeni:	na. gramer karD-i nebo. baccader gOlper boi ache?
dokandar:	ji, ache. notun ækTa gOlper boi beRieche. dækhabo?
jeni:	besh to. dækhan. e-chaRa amar kOe-ækTa khata, rOng pensil ar pãchTa kham lagbe. ache?
dokandar:	ji, ache. ei nin.
jeni:	ei khOborer kagojTa ar mohilader oi pottrikaTa-o din.
dokandar:	dicchi.
jeni:	plasTiker shoping-bæg dite parben?
dokandar:	na, nai. poribesh montri nishedh kore diechen. apnake kagojer Thonga dicchi. apnar jinishguli Thongae bhore roshi die bẽdhe dicchi.
jeni:	besh. bhalo ækTa upae ber korechen! dhonnobad.

Vocabulary

bhiu-karD	picture postcard	nishedh kore dewa	to forbid
gOlpo	story	Thonga	bag
bæRano	to come out/be published	jinish	thing
		bhore	having put
pottrika	magazine	roshi	rope
dite parben	you can give	bẽdhe dewa	to tie up
poribesh	environment	upae	solution
montri	minister	ber kOra	to find

Grammar point: leaving out pronouns

Bengali sentences can be very brief. Often, all the pronouns (so not only the subject pronouns) are left out.

    dækhabo?   **dicchi.**
    Shall I show you (it)?   I'm giving it.

Of course, if there could be any unclarity, the pronouns can also be put in:

| apnake dækhabo | ami apnake dækhabo | ami apnake eTa dækhabo |
| ami dicchi | ami apnake dicchi | ami eTa apnake dicchi. |

Speakers of Eastern Bengali generally leave out pronouns more often than Western speakers.

Exercise 7

Here are some very short and economical sentences. For each, choose the question that it could answer.

	Questions:
1 na, shOmOe nei.	a tumi eTa bolcho kæno?
2 na, ani ni.	b kaka-kaki kothae gæchen?
3 bajare gæchen.	c amar jonno ca enecho?
4 tomake diechi to!	d tumi ki amar shOnge ashbe?
5 bolchi karon shotti.	e TakaTa kake diecho?

Bengali script: more conjunct letters

In the following conjuncts, the two separate letters are easily recognisable.

With ল:

ক + ল = ক্ল kl ক্লাশ klash class
প + ল = প্ল pl প্লেট pleT plate
ম + ল = ম্ল ml ম্লান mlan dejected

With ন:

গ + ন = গ্ন gn ভাগ্নি bhagni niece
ত + ন = ত্ন tn যত্ন jOtno care

With ব:

At the beginning of a word, ব in a conjunct is not pronounced. In the middle of a word, the conjunct represents a long consonant.

ধ + ব = ধ্ব dh ধ্বংস dhOngsho destruction
জ + ব = জ্ব j   জ্বর jOr fever
স + ব = স্ব sh স্বামী shami husband
            ssh ভূস্বামী bhusshami landowner
হ + ব = হ্ব bb জিহ্বা jibba tongue

Unit 8: *Shall I show it to you?*

Reading texts – একটু হাসুন!

দুধওয়ালা: আমি খরিদ্দার ঠকাই না। দুধে পানি মিশাই ঠিকই, কিন্তু মাপে কম দেই না।
চাল বিক্রেতা: আমিও না। তিন পোয়া চালে এক পোয়া কাঁকর মিশালে, এক সের হয় কিনা, তুমিই বল ভাই?

Vocabulary

dudh	milk	**Thik-i**	indeed
dudhwala	milkman	**map**	measurement
khoriddar	customer	**bikkreta**	seller
ThOkano	to cheat	**kãkor**	grit
mishano	to mix	**mishale**	if I mix

সাংবাদিক: ম্যাডাম, আপনার বয়স কত?
নায়িকা: দুঃখিত। আমি সব সময়ে আয়নার দিকে তাকাই। ক্যালেন্ডারের দিকে না।

Vocabulary

naika	actress	**takano**	to look
aena	mirror		

9 এই চেকটা কি এখানে ক্যাশ করে নিতে পারি?
ei cekTa ki ekhane kæsh kore nite pari?

Can I cash this cheque here?

In this unit you will learn how to:
- talk about post and bank matters
- make requests
- describe sequences of actions
- express nuances of verb meaning
- recognise further conjuncts

Dialogue 1 (Audio 2:20)

Jenny is in the post office. How much is the postage for her letters? What is wrong with the parcel she wants to send?

kOrmocari:	slamalaikum. apnar jonno ki korte pari?
jeni:	walaikum salam. ei ciThi duiTa inglænDe paThate cai.
kOrmocari:	accha, din. æarmele naki shadharon Dake paThate can?
jeni:	æarmele – rejisTri Dake. koto lagbe?

Unit 9: *Can I cash it here?*

kOrmocari:	protiTa ciThir ojon põcish geram – tar mane, æk ækTa paThate deRshOto Takar DakTikiT lagbe.
jeni:	accha. ar ækTa parsel ache. kolkatae paThabo.
kOrmocari:	parseler moddhe ki ache? apnake fOrmer upore likhte hObe.
jeni:	eTar bhitore æk pOT amer acar ache.
kOrmocari:	khabar-dabar paThate nished ache.
jeni:	thak, tahole dOrkar nai. shudhu ciThi duiTa regisTri Dake paThie din. TakaTa nin. dhonnobad.

Vocabulary

kOrmocari	clerk	æk ækTa	each one
shadharon	ordinary	DakTikiT	stamp
Dak	post	acar	chutney
rejisTri Dak	registered post	khabar-dabar	food and such things
tar mane	its meaning is/this means that		

Grammar point: the infinitive

Bengali verbs also have an infinitive, which ends in **-te**:

    apnar jonno ki korte pari?   What can I do for you?
                                 (lit.: you-for what do I-can)
    ciThi paThate cai   I want to send a letter
                            (lit.: letter send I-want)

As in English, there are several common Bengali verbs, e.g. **para** 'can, be able to' and **cawa** 'want', that combine with the infinitive. Note the word order: infinitive – other verb (**korte pari**, **paThate cai**).
    Now you say: What can he do for you?
                 What can I do for him?
               I want to send a parcel.
    Some other verbs that often combine with the infinitive:

dewa	let, allow	**tomake okhane jete debo na** (I will not let you go there)
shekha	learn	**she ranna korte shekhe ni** (he hasn't learnt to cook)
bhule jawa	forget	**ciThiTa posT korte bhule gechi** (I've forgotten to post the letter)

cesTa kOra	try	oke fon korte cesTa korbo
		(I'll try to phone him)
jawa	go	she bajar korte gæche
		(s/he has gone to do shopping)

To express 'must/have to', **hOwa** is used:

| hOwa | have to | apnake/apnar eTa likhte hObe |
| | | (you have to write it) |

Here, **hOwa** is always 3rd person. Be careful with the tense: whenever the action to be carried out lies in the future, the future tense **hObe** must be used. The person can have the object form (**apnake**) or possessive form (**apnar**).

Another use of the infinitive form, more akin to the present participle of English, can be seen in:

Tibhi dekhte dekhte ami ghumie poRechi.
Watching TV, I fell asleep.

Here the infinitive is usually doubled (**dekhte dekhte**). It describes an activity ('watching the telly') that is ongoing when another event takes place ('I fell asleep').

The infinitive is made as follows:
- take the stem of the verb
- change the stem vowel: **O>o, o>u, æ>e, e>i** (but **a** doesn't change)
- add the ending **-te**

Verbal noun	Infinitive
khola to open	khulte
dhowa to wash	dhute
lekha to write	likhte
asha to come	aste

Stem-final **a** usually becomes **e**: **khete** (from **khawa**).

But sometimes it becomes **ai**: **gaite** (from **gawa** 'to sing')
caite (from **cawa** 'to want').

Verbs with a verbal noun in **-ano** have **-ate** in the infinitive:

ghumate (from **ghumano**)

Exercise 1

How would schoolteacher Rina respond to her students? Match each of the students' sentences with one response.

Unit 9: *Can I cash it here?*

Students:

1 ami ki ekTu baire jete pari?
2 ami Ongko korte cai na.
3 aj amra ki ingreji poRte shikhbo?
4 ami ei æljabraTa korte pari na.
5 amader baire jete dicchen na kæno?

Rina's responses:

a karon tomader kaj ækhono shesh hOe ni (shes hOwa=to be finished).
b tobuo (= still) korte cesTa kOro.
c na, aj amra itihash (= history) poRbo.
d tobuo korte hObe.
e jao. kintu pãc miniTer moddhe fire esho.

Exercise 2 (Audio 2:21)

Jenny has returned to the post office with another letter. What does she say?

kOrmocari: slamalaikum. apnar jonno ki korte pari?
jeni: *(greets the clerk and says she has forgotten to give this letter to him.)*
kOrmocari: o, accha. ciThiTa din. kothae paThate hObe?
jeni: *(says she wants to send it to Kolkata.)*
kOrmocari: Thik ache. kintu apni ThikanaTa banglae likhechen. ingrejite lekhen ni kæno? antorjatik (= *international*) ciThi-pOttrer (ciThi-pOttro = *letter*) Thikana ingrejite likhte hOe.
jeni: *(says she has learnt to write in Bengali.)*
kOrmocari: banglate likhechen – Thik ache. kintu ami banglar pashe *(= next to)* ingrejite ThikanaTa abar likhchi. kichu mone korben na *(= don't mind)*.
jeni: *(tells him to write it and says thank you.)*

Dialogue 2 (Audio 2:22)

Shukla is in a travel agency in Kolkata. She wants to make a trip to Agra with some friends to see the Taj Mahal.

shOhokari: agrate apnara kotodin thakte can? dilli hoe jete hObe. dillite kichudin beRie tarpOre agrate jete parben.

shukla:	hæ̃, dillite amra æk din thakte cacchi. dillir lal kellaTa dekhte cai. tarpOr agrate gie car din thakbo.
shOhokari:	tahole prothome apnara shondhar Trene haoRa isTeshon theke dillite jete paren. okhane shOkal bælae põuche shoja hoTele gie mal-pOttro rakhte parben. tarpOr lal kella dekhte jete paren. pOrer din shOkaler Trene agrae põuchben.
shukla:	dilli theke agrate jete kotokkhon lagbe?
shOhokari:	dui-aRai ghOnTa lagte pare. car din pOre ækibhabe abar kolkatae fire ashben.
shukla:	programTa to bhalo-i mone hocche. amar bandhobider shOnge alap kore abar eshe buking debo. ækhon jacchi tahole. nOmoshkar.
shOhokari:	ashun. nOmoshkar.

Vocabulary

shOhokari	assistant	mal-pOttro	luggage
... hoe	via ...	pOrer din	the next day
kichudin	a couple of days	ækibhabe	the same way
kella	fort	alap kOra	to consult
shondha	evening	buking dewa	to make a booking
põuchano	to arrive	ashun	goodbye (lit.: come!)

Grammar point: the past participle – meaning

Another important verbal form is the past participle. It always ends in -e. Its basic meaning is that of an action completed in the past.

> *Examples:*   **eshe** (from **asha** come)   having come
>   **dekhe** (from **dækha** see)   having seen
>   **fire** (from **fera** return)   having returned

This form can be used to describe a sequence of actions carried out by one and the same person. It is then used for all actions except the last:

> **shOkal bælae põuche hoTele gie mal-pOttro rakhte parben**
> After arriving in the morning and going to the hotel, you can put away your luggage.
> (lit.: Having arrived in the morning, having gone to the hotel, you can put away your luggage)

Thikana likhe ciThiTa posT koro
Write the address and post the letter.
(lit.: having written the address, post the letter)

To say that an action was not carried out, use **na** plus past participle. English might use the word 'without':

she jOl-khabar na khe-e skule gieche.
He went to school without eating breakfast.
(lit.: he, not having eaten breakfast, went to school)

Exercise 3 (Audio 2:23)

Read Puja's description of her daily routine and say: what are Puja's hobbies?

ami protidin shOkale uThe hat-mukh dhue æk ghOnTa homwark kore jOl-khabar khe-e nOeTae skule jai. bikal (afternoon) **carTae abar fire eshe æk kap ca khe-e proshun-dadake ækTa i-mel paThie amar bandhobir shOnge æk hat daba** (game of chess) **kheli. tarpOr ingreji poRi. pORa sheshe** (= after studying) **bhat khe-e æk ghOnTa Tibhi dekhe ghumate jai.**

Grammar point: the past participle – form

To make the past participle of a verb, take the present perfect form (see Unit 5) and remove everything after the **-e-**.

Present perfect	*Past participle*
korechi I have done	**kore** having done
diechi I have given	**die** having given
giechi I have gone	**gie** having gone
baniechi I have prepared	**banie** having prepared

Exercise 4

Sofia is telling Jenny what to do, using pairs of sentences. Combine each pair into one sentence with a past participle. The first sentence would be: **ranna-ghOre eshe amar kOtha shono.**

1 **ranna-ghOre esho. amar kOtha shono.**
2 **haRiTa bhalo bhabe dho-o. tarpOr cular upore rakho.**

3 pẽ-ajTa kaTo. tarpOr amake dao.
4 Dal ranna kOro. tarpOre bhat ranna koro.
5 bhat khao. tarpOre bashae jeo. [convert this into, 'Do not go home without eating'; use **na** twice]
6 agami kalke (= tomorrow) abar esho. mach ranna korbe.

Exercise 5

The following exchanges describe several sequences of actions. Change them so that each action is described in a sentence of its own. The first exchange would become:

A: tumi ei kajTa shesh korbe. tarpOre ki korbe?
B: ami bhat khabo. tarpOre ghumabo.

1 A: tumi ei kajTa shesh kore ki korbe? (shes kOra = finish)
   B: ami bhat khe-e ghumabo.
2 A: kaj shesh kore ekhane esho.
   B: na, kaj shesh kore ami bashae jabo.
3 A: tomaderke dekhe she ki bolbe?
   B: ki bolbe? amaderke dekhe she khushi hObe.
4 A: arif fon kore boleche, 'bashae khabar nei'.
   B: ami bashae gie take dhOmok debo (dhOmok dewa = give a scolding)

Dialogue 3 (Audio 2:24)

Opu is at the bank to cash a cheque. He also enquires about a transfer and about opening a savings account. Is Opu's visit successful?

opu: amar bhai amar cOloman hishabe æk lakh Taka paThieche. TakaTa ki eshe gæche? dOya kore ekTu khõj kore dekhben?
kerani: dekhchi – apnar akaunT nOmborTa koto?
opu: nOmborTa holo 1546398. amar nam opu ganguli.
kerani: ji, gOtokalke apnar akaunTe TakaTa jOma hoe gæche.
opu: shune khushi holam. ækhon ami ki ækTa shOncoyi hishab khule ei TakaTa shei akaunTe jOma rakhte parbo?
kerani: nishcOe-i parben. ei fOrmTa puron kore din.
opu: Thik ache. ar ækTa kaj ache. ækTa cek pe-echi. cekTa ki ekhane kæsh kore nite pari?

Unit 9: *Can I cash it here?*

kerani: hæ̃, paren. kintu tar jonno pasher kaunTare jete hObe.
opu: accha. apnake Onek dhonnobad.

Vocabulary

cOloman	current	jOma hOwa	to be credited
hishab	account	shOncoyi hishab	savings account
lakh/lokkho	100,000	jOma rakha	to deposit
dOya kore	please	puron kOra	to complete
khõj kOra	to seek out, to enquire	kæsh kOra	to cash
kerani	official	pasher	next, adjoining

Grammar point: combinations with the past participle

A second use of the past participle is in combination with another verb, which conveys a nuance of meaning like suddenness, completion or benefit. An example is **fæla** – literally 'to throw', but when combined with a past participle (e.g. **khe-e**, from **khawa**), it expresses suddenness or completeness:

    arif shOb khabar khe-e feleche.   Arif has eaten up all the food.

It is best to think of **khe-e fæla** as a fixed unit, like 'eat up' in English. Other examples are **heshe fæla** 'burst into laughter' and **poRe fæla** 'read to the end/read all of it'.

A past participle combined with **newa** means that the subject of the sentence benefits from the action, while **dewa** conveys that somebody else does. These verbs can even combine with their own past participles.

TakaTa bæger moddhe rekhe nin.	Put the money in the bag. (suggesting: for yourself)
TakaTa bæger moddhe rekhe din.	Put the money in the bag. (suggesting: for somebody else)
she TakaTa nie nieche.	She took the money (for herself).
she TakaTa die dieche.	She gave the money (to somebody).

A past participle combined with **jawa** conveys that the subject of the sentence is completely affected by the action.

shune jao!	Listen (attentively)! (**shona** = listen)
kapTa bhenge gæche.	The cup has broken. (**bhanga** = break)

Some verbs are seldom used in the ordinary perfect tense, because speakers prefer to use past participle plus **gechi/gæcho** etc.

    tomar nam bhule gechi.   I have forgotten your name.
          (**bhola** = forget)
    she gOtokalke cole gæche.   He left yesterday. (**cOla** = go, leave)

Other combinations feature the verbs **oTha** (lit. 'go up', but here conveying an unexpected action), **bOsha** (lit. 'sit', but here expressing that the action is undesirable) and **pORa** (lit. 'fall', but here conveying suddenness):

    me-eTi kĕde uTheche   The girl burst out crying (**kăda** = cry)
    arif shOb am khe-e   Arif has eaten all the mango (how
      bosheche   annoying!)
    amar dada eshe poReche   My brother has (suddenly) arrived

All of the above are best learned as fixed units. You will come across more of them further on, where you should be able to recognise that they consist of a past participle plus another verb.

Given a fixed unit such as **cole jawa** 'leave', how to say: 'I want to leave'? You will need **ami cai** 'I want'; since this verb combines with an infinitive, you need the infinitive **cole jete**; the result is: **ami cole jete cai** 'I want to leave'. This is just like **ami aste cai** 'I want to come', except that **aste** is a one-word unit while **cole jete** is a two-word unit – but both are infinitives.

Exercise 6 (Audio 2:25)

Protima comes home from work and asks her husband Shantonu about various things he was going to do. Complete his replies, using the clues provided. To the first question, he could answer: **hæ̃, ciThigulo paThie diechi.**

1 'tumi ki posT ofise gie ciThigulo paThiecho?'
   'hæ̃, ciThigulo _____ [paThie dewa]'
2 'amar jonno ækTa pottrika kinecho?'
   'hæ̃, _____ [kine newa]'
3 'dudh ache? naki nai?'
   'nai. dudhTa _____ [shes kore fæla]'
4 'tumi amar make fon korecho?'
   'na, _____ [bhule jawa]'
5 'tomar i-mel poRecho?'
   'hæ̃, amar shOb i-mel _____ [poRe fæla]'

Unit 9: *Can I cash it here?* 129

6 'tomar bon esheche?'
'hĩ, she baroTae _____ [eshe pORa]'

Bengali script: some further conjunct letters

With ম:

The letter ম as second element in a word-initial conjunct is not pronounced. In the middle of a word, the first consonant is pronounced long and the following vowel is nasalised. Exception: ন combined with ম is pronounced **nm**.

শ + ম = শ্ম   sh   শ্মশান **shOshan** cremation ground
দ + ম = দ্ম   dd   পদ্মা **pOddā** river Padma
ন + ম = ন্ম   nm   জন্ম **jOnmo** birth

With ত:

The ত is always pronounced. Note how **kt** is written.

ক + ত = ক্ত   kt   যুক্তরাজ্য **jukto-rajjo** United Kingdom
ন + ত = ন্ত   nt   ক্লান্ত **klanto** tired
স + ত = স্ত   st   পাকিস্তান **pakistan** Pakistan

With থ and দ:

The pronunciation is straightforward but look carefully at the shape of the conjuncts with থ.

ত + থ = ত্থ   tth   উত্থান **utthan** emergence
ন + থ = ন্থ   nth   পান্থ **pantho** passer-by
স + থ = স্থ   sth   অসুস্থ **Oshustho** ill
ন + দ = ন্দ   nd   সুন্দর **shundor** beautiful
ব + দ = ব্দ   bd   শব্দ **shObdo** sound

With ধ:

The pronunciation is straightforward but ধ gets a distinctive shape.

দ + ধ = দ্ধ   ddh   বুদ্ধি **buddhi** intelligence
ন + ধ = ন্ধ   ndh   বন্ধ **bOndho** closed
ব + ধ = ব্ধ   bdh   ক্ষুব্ধ **khubdho** enraged

With র:

Note the following two conjuncts with 'squiggly' **r**:

ত + ্র = ত্র   tr   ত্রিশ **trish** thirty (= তিরিশ **tirish**)
ক + ্র = ক্র   kr   ক্রিকেট **krikeT** cricket

Finally, here are two letters used (in a few words) for the diphthongs **oi** and **ou**.

ৈ (following a consonant) oi   কৈ **koi** type of fish
ঐ (elsewhere) oi   ঐতিহাসিক **oitihashik** historical
ৌ (following a consonant) ou   বৌ **bou** bride (also: বউ)
ঔ (elsewhere) ou   ঔদার্য **oudarjo** generosity

Exercise 7

Go to <http://www.anandabazar.com/>. Choose one article and try to transcribe its first 25 words. How many can you transcribe confidently? How many do you already know?

Reading text – আবার একটু হাসুন!

প্রযোজক: আমরা শুধু নামকরা লেখক চাই। নতুন লেখক নেই না।
লেখক: ঠিক আছে। তাহলে আমার ছদ্মনামটা ব্যবহার করুন।
প্রযোজক: আপনার ছদ্মনামটা কি?
লেখক: রবীন্দ্রনাথ ঠাকুর।

Vocabulary

projojok	director	**chOddonam**	pseudonym
namkOra	famous	**bæbohar kOra**	to use
lekhok	writer		

10 এখানে কেউ থাকে না?
ekhane keu thake na?

Doesn't anyone live here?

In this unit you will learn how to:

- tell the time
- describe homes
- refer to people
- read more conjunct letters

Dialogue 1 (Audio 2:26)

Sumita is talking with her young son Pial. Why is Pial less than keen to do his homework?

pial: mamoni, ami ækhon Tibhi dekhbo. karTun dækhabe.
shumita: karTun shuru hObe kOkhon?
pial: shoa pãcTae.
shumita: ækhon ki shoa pãcTa baje?
pial: na, shoa pãcTa bajte ækhono tirish miniT baki.
shumita: tahole tumi ei adha ghOnTa Ongko kOro.
pial: mamoni, Onko khub koThin. æka æka parbo na. baba kOkhon ashben?
shumita: tomar baba shaRe shatTae ashben. tahole ækhon ingreji pORo.
pial: mamoni, ingreji poRte pÕca lage.

shumita: tahole bhugol poRte jao. agamikal tomar bhugol porikkha, tai na?
pial: ji. tahole tirish miniT bhugol poRbo. tarpOre ami kintu karTun dekhbo.
shumita: Thik ache. poRte jao. karTun shuru hole tomake Deke debo.

Vocabulary

mamoni	mother (affectionate form)	põca	rotten
		põca lage	it is unpleasant
shuru hOwa	to begin	agamikal	tomorrow
baja	to strike	bhugol	geography
baki	left over	porikkha	examination
koThin	difficult	shuru hole	when it begins
æka æka	alone	Deke dewa	to call

Vocabulary point: telling the time

To tell the time, you need numbers. You already know the numerals up to 30. But you also want to understand times like 3.36 or 4.55 – so now learn by heart the sequence 30–60 (see page 217).

Mini-exercise 1

Say: 45 minutes;
      55 minutes;
      59 minutes;
      33 minutes;
      25 minutes.

To say what time it is, the verb **baje** (lit.: 'it strikes') is used:

ækTa baje, duiTa baje, etc.
It's one o'clock, it's two o'clock, etc.

Half-hours are expressed with the words for 1½, 2½, 3½ etc.

deRTa baje, aRaiTa baje, shaRe tinTa baje, etc.
It's half past one/two/three, etc.

Unit 10: *Doesn't anyone live here?*

Quarters are expressed as follows:
>**poune ækTa baje, poune duiTa baje**, etc.
>It's a quarter to one/two etc.
>
>**shoa ækTa baje, shoa duiTa baje**, etc.
>It's a quarter past one/two etc.

Mini-exercise 2

Say: 'Is it half past ten?'
'No, it is half past eleven.'

'Is it a quarter to five?'
'No, it's a quarter past five.'

Other times are expressed as follows:
>**ækTa bajte baro miniT baki ache.**
>It is twelve to one (lit.: to strike one, there are 12 minutes left)
>
>**ækTa beje baro miniT.**
>It is twelve past one (lit.: having struck one, 12 minutes)

All these sentences can answer the question:
>**kOTa baje?/kOeTa baje?** (E)   What time is it?

Now you say: 'It's one minute to twelve.'
'No. It's one minute past twelve.'

To say at what time things happen, the time expression is put in the locative form:

ækTae, duiTae	At one, at two
deRTae, aRaiTae, shaRe tinTae	At 1.30, 2.30, 3.30
poune ækTae, poune duiTae	At 12.45, 1.45
shoa ækTae, shoa duiTae	At 1.15, 2.15
ækTa dOshe, ækTa bishe	At 1.10, 1.20

To specify the part of the day, use the following words:

bhore	in the early morning (till *c.* 6 a.m.)
shOkale	in the morning
dupure	in the early afternoon
bikale	in the late afternoon (3 to 6)
shondhae	in the evening (6 to 8)
rattre	in the night (locative of **rat**)

These words are given here in the locative form (with **-e**). They have their simple form if they are followed by an expression of the precise time:

kOTae/kOeTae (E) how late? **shOkal aTTae** at 8 a.m.
                                  bikal tinTae   at 3 p.m.
                                  rat aTTae   at 8 p.m.
                                  rat tinTae   at 3 a.m.

This is a general principle in Bengali grammar: if several nouns form a unit, only the last word of the unit gets an ending. Other examples are:

mita-upoler fon-nOmbor (not **mitar-upoler**)
Mita and Upol's phone number

tomar boi-pottrikagulo bhule jeo na (not **boigulo-pottrikagulo**)
Don't forget your books and magazines.

Further useful time phrases are the following:

kOTar/kOeTar (E) **shOmOe?**   At what time?
põetrish miniT age/pOre   35 minutes earlier/later
ækTa theke duiTa porjonto   from 1 until 2
æk ghOnTa dhore   for one hour
proti ghOnTae/proti dui ghOnTae every hour/every 2 hours
pãcTae shuru hObe o chOeTae shesh hObe. It will start at 5 and end at 6.
okhane jete æk ghOnTa lagbe.   It will take one hour to get there.

Exercise 1

Study the following TV timetable and say:

1 'mOnco kOtha' shuru hOe kOeTae?
2 'shOngbad' kotokkhon colbe?

Unit 10: *Doesn't anyone live here?*

3 'uDi uDpekar' shes hOe kOeTae?
4 kon onusthan shaRe tinTae shuru hObe?
5 kon onusthan duiTa collishe shes hObe?

onusthan shuci (= programme timetable)

dupur 2Ta shOngbad. 2Ta 15 miniT muktir pOthe. 2Ta 40 miniT mOnco kOtha. 3Ta 05 miniT uDi uDpekar. 3Ta 30 miniT shukhi poribar. 4Ta khObor. 4Ta 05 miniT shObar jonno. 4Ta 30 miniT kon gramer me-e? 5Ta khObor.

shOngbad	news	mOnco	stage, theatre
mukti	freedom	shObar	possessive of shObai

Exercise 2

Read the following description of Pial's evening and answer the questions.

pial shoa pācTa theke poune chOeTa porjonto Tibhi dekheche. ækhon chOeTa pōcish baje. pial tar ghOre gie bhugol poRche. ponero miniT pOre she nice (= down) gie tar choTo bhai o boner shOnge bhat khabe. bhat khe-e shaRe shatTae she tar babar kache Ongko shikhbe. rat nOeTae she ghumate jabe.

1 pial kotokkhon Tibhi dekheche?
2 kOeTae she bhat khabe?
3 kader shathe she bhat khabe?
4 kar kache Ongko shikhbe?
5 pial kOeTae ghumate jabe?

Exercise 3

Answer the following questions.

1 ækhon kOeTa baje?
2 apni koto miniT dhore bangla poRchen?
3 apni protidin kOeTa theke kOeTa porjonto bangla pORen?
4 apni aj kOeTae ghum theke uThechen?
5 apni gOto kalke ghumate gæchen kOeTae?

Dialogue 2 (Audio 2:29)

Jenny is back in England for two weeks. Sofia has come with her. They have arrived at Jenny's family home, where they will be staying.

jeni: dækho, sofia. eTa amader paribarik baRi. ami dOrjaTa khulchi.
sofia: kæno? khali baRi naki? ekhane keu thake na?
jeni: shudhumattro amar ma thaken. tini bodh hOe kothao gæchen. bhitore esho. ei shĩRi die dotOlae jao. dotOlae Dandiker ghOre tumi thakbe.
sofia: tomader baRiTa ki shundor! paTatonguli ki cOmotkar karukaj kOra! tomar shobar ghOr konTa?
jeni: tomar pasher ghOrTa-i amar. oi konae gosholkhana. tachaRa nictOlae-o ækTa TOeleT ache. almarite toale pabe. jodi ar kichu lage, bolo. cOlo amra ækhon nice gie ca banie khai.
sofia: hæ̃, cOlo. amar khub ca khete iccha korche.
jeni: ca nie baire bagane gie boshi.
sofia: accha. boshe boshe ca khai ar tomar maer jonno Opekkha kori.

Vocabulary

paribarik baRi	family home	**kona**	corner
dOrja	door	**gosholkhana** (E)/	bathroom
khali	empty	**snan-ghOr** (W)	
shudhumattro	only	**nictOla**	ground floor
bodh hOe	it seems	**almari**	wardrobe
shĩRi	staircase	**toale**	towel
dotOla	first floor (lit.: second storey)	**jodi**	if
		cOlo	let's (lit.: go!)
ghOr	room	**nice**	down
ki shundor!	how beautiful!	**iccha (icche** W)	to want
paTaton	ceiling	**kOra**	(impersonal)
karukaj kOra	decorated	**bagan**	garden
shobar ghOr	bedroom		

Exercise 4

Match each of the objects with the place in the house where it is normally found.

Objects	Places
আলমারি	রান্নাঘর
সোফা	শোবারঘর
চুলা	বাগান
চায়ের কাপ	গোসলখানা/স্নানঘর
গাছ (= tree)	খাবারঘর
সাবান	বসারঘর (= sitting-room)

Grammar point: indefinite pronouns

Indefinite pronouns express the meanings 'anyone', 'anything', etc. Most derive from a question word:

Question word	Indefinite pronoun
ke who	**keu** anyone (poss. **karo/karur**, obj. **kauke/kakeo**)
ki what	**kichu** anything
kon which	**kono** any
kothae where	**kothao** anywhere
kOkhon when	**kOkhono** ever, at any time
kObe when	**konodin** ever, any day

The indefinites are used in yes–no questions and in sentences with **jodi** 'if'. They are also frequent in negative sentences.

keu esheche?	Has anyone come?
tumi okhane kauke dekhecho?	Did you see anyone there?
jodi kichu korte pari	If I can do anything
kothao jeo na!	Don't go anywhere!
amar kono shOmOe nei.	I don't have any time/I have no time.

Elsewhere, indefinites are less usual. But with something added to them, **keu** and **kichu** can mean 'somebody' and 'something':

keu ækjOn fon koreche.	Someone (lit.: anyone-a-person) has phoned.
tomake kichu ækTa bolbo.	I will tell you something. (lit.: anything-one)

Forms with **onno** 'other' plus indefinite pronoun have the meaning 'someone else'/'another person', etc.

onno keu kajTa shes korbe.	Someone else will finish the work.
onno kauke dekhi ni.	I have not seen anyone else.
tahole onno kothao jabo.	Then I'll go somewhere else.
onno kono khabar nei?	Isn't there any other food?

Exercise 5

Sumita has to get some shopping and is leaving her son Pial alone at home. She tells him what to do in case different things happen. Complete her sentences. The first one would be: **jodi keu ashe**

1 **keu ashbe na, kintu jodi _____, tahole dOrjaTa khulo na.**
2 **kichu ghoTbe na (ghOta** = happen), **kintu jodi _____, tahole amar mobaile fon koro.**
3 **ami karo shOnge tader bashae jabo na, kintu jodi _____, tahole taRa-taRi fire ashbo.**
4 **tomar baba fon korbe na, kintu jodi _____, tahole bolo je ami dOsh miniTer moddhe firbo.**
5 **onno keu fon korbe na, kintu jodi _____, tahole bolo je ami rannaghOre bæsto** (= busy) **achi.**
6 **kono brisTi** (= rain) **poRbe na, kintu jodi _____, tahole baganer dOrjaTa bOndho koro.**

Exercise 6

Today is Ishita's birthday. Her friend Shumi has come and wants to talk, but all she gets is grumpy negative replies. What does Ishita say? Her first sentence would be: **keu ashbe na.**

1 **aj ke ke ashbe?**
2 **tara kOkhon ashbe?**
3 **tara tomar jonno ki ki upohar** (= present) **nie ashbe?**
4 **tumi taderke ki khawabe?** (**khawano** = give to eat)
5 **tumi ki kono sinema dekhte cao?**
6 **tomar ki mon kharap hoeche?** (= have a bad mood)

Reading text 1 (Audio 2:30)

- What did the writer's friend do?
- What are his prospects?

amar bondhuke gOtokal pulishe dhore nie gæche. she ækjOn chattroneta ebong pulisher onumoti chaRa-i michile gie netritto dieche. aj shOkale ami amar bondhur babake nie ækjOn ukiler kache gechi. ukil shahebke shOb ghOtona amra khule bolechi. kintu ukil shaheb bolechen, je amar bondhu shOhosha-i chaRa pabe na. pulish tar biruddhe boma mamla daer koreche. amra korT-kacarite gie besh kOejOn kOrmocariderke ghush diechi. kintu Taka khe-e-o amader keu kono shahajjo kOre ni. amar bondhu ækhono jel-khanae aTka ache.

Unit 10: *Doesn't anyone live here?*

Vocabulary

neta	leader	... biruddhe	against (with possessive)
onumoti	permission		
michil	demonstration	boma	bomb
netritto dewa	to lead	mamla	case
shaheb	mister, sir (Muslim term of respect)	mamla daer kOra	to bring a case
		korT-kacari	court
ghOtona	event, incident	besh kOejOn	quite a few
khule bOla	to explain	ghush	bribe
shOhosha-i	quickly	ghush khawa	to take bribes
chaRa	release	jelkhana	prison
		aTka	detained

Grammar point: human nouns

Nouns referring to humans have several distinctive forms. Here, as an example, are the forms of **bon** 'sister'.

	Singular	*Plural*
subject form	**bon**	**bonra**
possessive form	**boner**	**bonder**
object form	**bonke**	**bonder(ke)**

> ### Mini-exercise 3
>
> Say: What is your sister's phone number?
> Give this to your sister.
> My sisters live in Delhi.
> I will phone my sisters tonight.

If a noun ends in a vowel (e.g. **bondhu**), the singular possessive has **-r**: **amar bondhur saikel** (my friend's bike). If the vowel is **-o** (e.g. **chattro**), **-o** can also be dropped and possessive **-er** added: **ei chattrer/ chattror boigulo** (this student's books). For short nouns ending in **-a**, both **-r** and **-er** are possible: **amar mar/maer bandhobira** 'my mother's friends'.

The plural subject ending **-ra** sometimes has the form **-era**:

bonra/bonera sisters
shikkhOkra/shikkhOkera teachers

Plural **-ra** and **-der** can be added to a first name to express: 'X and his/her family or friends'.

shunanra kothae?	Where are Shunan and his friends/family?

Like inanimate nouns, human nouns are often unmarked for plural if plural meaning is signalled through another word:

duijOn ukil eshechen.	Two lawyers have come.
kOe-ækTa bacca kãdche.	Several children are crying.

Remember that **ækjOn** is put before a human noun to say 'a(n)':

ækjOn ukilke fon kOro!	Phone a lawyer!

The endings **-er**, **-ke**, **-ra** and **-der** themselves can convey the meaning 'the':

ukilke fon kOro!	Phone the lawyer!
baccara kothae?	Where are the children?

Nouns for humans (and animals) sometimes get the ending **-e** (**-te** after a vowel) when they function as a plural indefinite subject:

pulishe oke dhore nie gæche.	Policemen have arrested him.
gorute ghash khae.	Cows eat grass.

Exercise 7

Do you know the story of Snow White (**tushar kOna**, lit.: snow's flake)? Below are several sentences about her, the seven dwarfs (**shat bhai bamon**, lit.: seven-brother dwarf), the wicked queen (**dusTo rani**) and the prince (**rajkumar**). But the whole story is wrong! Correct it.

Example:

bamonra tusarkOnar kap-pleT shorieche (= have moved) →
na, na: tusarkOna bamonder kap-pleT shorieche

1 **tusharkOnar baba mara gæchen.**
2 **bamonra tusharkOnar baRite esheche.**
3 **tusharkOna bamonder tar baRite thakte dieche.**

Unit 10: *Doesn't anyone live here?* 141

4 ækdin dusTo rani kOmla nie esheche.
5 tusharkOna dusTo ranike apel dieche.
6 apel khe-e dusTo rani ghumie poReche.
7 Onek bOchor pOre ækjOn rajnitibid põuche gæche.
8 tusharkOna rajkumarke cuma (= kiss) dieche.

Bengali script: more conjunct letters

In a conjunct, স gets a rather different shape and sometimes also causes the other letter to change form. You have already seen স্ত st and স্থ sth. Two other ones are:

স + প = স্প   shp   স্পর্শ shpOrsho touch
ক + স = ক্স   ksh   বাক্স baksho box

Conjuncts with ষ are:

ষ + ক = ষ্ক   shk   পরিষ্কার porishkar clean
ষ + ট = ষ্ট   sT   স্টেশন sTeshon station
ষ + ণ = ষ্ণ   shn   কৃষ্ণ krishno Krishna

In the following conjuncts (except the last) the individual letters are still easily recognisable:

ল + প = ল্প   lp   গল্প gOlpo story
ল + ট = ল্ট   lT   পল্টু polTu Poltu
ম + প = ম্প   mp   কম্পিউটার kompiuTar computer
ম + ভ = ম্ভ   mbh   সম্ভব shOmbhOb possible
ন + ত = ন্ত   nt   ক্লান্ত klanto tired
ণ + ট = ণ্ট   nT   ঘণ্টা ghOnTa hour
ণ + ঠ = ণ্ঠ   nTh   কণ্ঠ kOnTho voice
ণ + ড = ণ্ড   nD   পণ্ডিত ponDit pundit, teacher

The following are really irregular spellings, used in a few words only.

ক্ষ + ম = ক্ষ্ম   mm   ব্রাহ্মণ brammon/brammhon Brahmin
              kkh   লক্ষ্মী lokkhi Hindu goddess Lakhsmi
ক্ষ + ন = ক্ষ্ন   khn   লক্ষ্নৌ lOkhnou Lucknow

The next four represent combinations with the rare letters ঙ and ঞ. It is simplest to remember that the conjuncts represent the sounds **ng**, **gg** (but **g** word-initially and **gæ** in the combination জ্ঞা), **nc** and **nj**:

ঙ + গ = ঙ্গ   ng   গঙ্গা gOnga Ganges
জ + ঞ = জ্ঞ   gg   জিজ্ঞেস jiggesh question

	জ্ঞা	gæ̃	জ্ঞান gæ̃n knowledge
ঞ + চ = ঞ্চ		nc	পঞ্চাশ pOncash fifty
ঞ + জ = ঞ্জ		nj	গঞ্জ gOnj riverside marketplace

Exercise 9

Find the correct transliteration for each of the following words.

1	আফগানিস্তান	a	jOngol jungle
2	ট্যাক্সি	b	biggæ̃n science
3	স্ট্যাম্প	c	lauDspikar
4	স্পঞ্জ	d	Tæksi
5	নান্টু-সন্টু	e	sTæmp
6	পণ্ডিত	f	ponDit
7	ফ্যাক্স	g	læmp
8	অল্প	h	fæks
9	বিজ্ঞান	i	bangla (old-fashioned spelling)
10	জঙ্গল	j	Olpo
11	লাউডস্পিকার	k	inci inch
12	ল্যাম্প	l	afganistan
13	বাঙ্গলা	m	sponj sponge
14	ইঞ্চি	n	nanTu-shonTu Nantu and Shontu

Reading text 2

Read the text and say:

- What has happened?
- Has the government provided any help yet?

গতকাল সন্ধ্যা সাড়ে সাতটায় নারায়ণগঞ্জে একটা ভয়াবহ ভূমিকম্প হয়েছে। ভয়ে বহু মহিলা ও শিশুরা অজ্ঞান হয়ে গেছে। তারপরই শুরু হল প্রচণ্ড ঝড়বৃষ্টি। ঠাণ্ডায় বহুলোক অসুস্থ হয়ে পড়েছে। কিছু কিছু রাস্তাঘাট ভেঙ্গে গেছে। আজ দুপুরে ট্যাক্সিতে চড়ে ডিসি সাহেবের স্ত্রী ঘটনাস্থলে এসেছিলেন। তিনি অল্প কিছু সাহায্য দিয়েছেন। বহু মূল্যবান স্থাপত্য নষ্ট হয়ে গিয়েছে। এমন ভূমিকম্প লোকে আগে কখনো দেখে নি।

Unit 10: *Doesn't anyone live here?*

Narayangonj in Bangladesh

Vocabulary

narayongOnj	Narayangonj (district close to Dhaka)	rasta-ghaT	roads and streets
bhOeabOho	horrific	Disi	district commissioner
bhumikOmpo	earthquake	sthOl	place
bohu	many	eshechilen	came
shishu	baby, infant	mulloban	valuable
Oggæn hOwa	to faint	sthapotto	monument
procOnDo	severe, violent	nOsTo	ruined, destroyed
jhOR	storm	æmon	such a

11 তারপরে কি হল?
tarpOre ki holo?
What happened next?

> **In this unit you will learn how to:**
> - describe events and ongoing actions in the past
> - specify days of the week
> - describe reflexive actions
> - understand words relating to politics and crime

Dialogue 1 (Audio 2:32)

An election has been announced. A journalist is interviewing an opposition leader about this. What has the opposition party already done? What else are they going to do?

shangbadik: mongolbare nirbaconer khObor shune apni ki korlen?
rajnitibid: khOborTa shune-i shoja amader dolio karjalOe-e gelam. amra shOrashori desher onnanno jela-karjalOe-e jogajog korlam. tarpOr shOngbad shOmmelon korlam.
shangbadik: budhbar bORo ækTa michil holo. kintu shOrkar to age-i nirbacon ghoshona die dieche. michil-Tichiler ki dOrkar chilo?
rajnitibid: protibader dOrkar Obossho-i chilo. karon jOnogOn jane je ei shOrkar nirbacon nie protarona korbe. tai gOto budhbarer michile lokkho lokkho lokjon hajir hoechilo o michiler pOre amader netar boktrita shunlo.

Unit 11: *What happened next?*   **145**

shangbadik: apnara ki onnanno birodhi dOlgulor shOnge jot-gOThon korben?

rajnitibid: amra agami shombare shOngshOde prodhan-montrike onurod korbo jate tini tOttabodhayok shOrkarer kache khOmota die dæn. amader dabi na manle amra cobbish ghOnTar jonno hOrtal Dakbo. jOnogOner bijOe Obossho-i hObe!

Vocabulary

nirbacon	election	boktrita	speech
dolio karjalOe	party office	birodhi dOl	opposition party
shOrashori	straightaway	joT-gOThon	coalition
onnanno	other, different	shOngshOd	parliament
jela	district	prodhan-montri	prime minister
jogajog kOra	to contact	onurod kOra jate	to request that...
shOngbad shOmmelon	press conference	tOttabodhayok khOmota	caretaker, interim power
shOrkar	government	dabi	demand
ghoshona dewa	to announce	na manle	if they don't comply with
protibad	protest		
protarona kOra	to cheat	hOrtal	general strike
hajir hoechilo	appeared	bijOe	victory

Exercise 1

Arrange the following words into two groups, on the basis of shared meaning.

    hOrtal   dabi
    prodhan-montri   shOrkari dOl
    michil   protibad
    khOmota   protarona kOra
    shOrkar   birodhi dOl

Exercise 2

Complete the following radio news item, in which there were several words that you did not catch.

aj shOrkar _____ ghoshona koreche. montrira shObai _____ bhObone eshechen. _____ ækTa spic diechen. bolechen je nirbacon epril mashe (= month) hObe. tarpOre _____ dolio neta spic diechen. uni _____ korechen. bolechen je tOttabodhayok shOrkarer kache khOmota die dite hObe. birodhi dOlgulo agami kalke _____ korbe o agami budhbare _____ Dakbe.

Grammar point: the simple past tense

The dialogue above contains several examples of verbs in the simple past tense:

    amader dolio karjalOe-e gelam.   I went to our party office.
    ækTa michil holo.   A demonstration took place.

These forms are used to describe an event that was entirely completed in the past. They are often used in narratives.

    tushar-kOna apel nilo. bhalo bhabe dekhlo. tarpOre khelo.
    Snow White took the apple. She looked at it carefully. Then she ate it.

As these examples illustrate, the simple past tense consists of the verbal stem followed by the sound **l** and the appropriate person ending. The verb **Daka** 'to call', for example, has the following simple past forms:

Personal pronoun	*Simple past*
ami	**Daklam** (also **Daklum** W)
tumi	**Dakle** (sometimes **Dakla** in colloquial E)
tui	**Dakli**
she	**Daklo**
apni	**Daklen**

As you can see, the vowel **a** in the stem does not change in the simple past. But all other vowels do, in the expected way:

Verbal noun	*Simple past*
kOra to do	korlam, korle, korli, korlo, korlen
khola to open	khullam, khulle, khulli, khullo, khullen
dhowa to wash	dhulam, dhule, dhuli, dhulo, dhulen
dækha to see	dekhlam, dekhle, dekhli, dekhlo, dekhlen
lekha to write	likhlam, likhle, likhli, likhlo, likhlen
dewa to give	dilam, dile, dili, dilo, dilen

Unit 11: *What happened next?*

A stem-final **a** also changes (into **e**). But verbs with a verbal noun ending in **-ano** have **-alam** in the simple past:

Verbal noun	Simple past
khawa to eat	**khelam** etc. (but **gawa** 'sing' and **cawa** 'want' have **gailam**, etc. and **cailam**, etc.)
ghumano to sleep	**ghumalam**, etc.

The simple past tense of **jawa** is irregular: **ami gelam, tumi gele, tui geli, she gælo, apni gelen**. The verb **asha** has the irregular form **ami elam**, etc. (but also **ashlam**, etc. in E).

Corresponding to the present tense forms **ami achi, tumi acho**, etc., the simple past forms are **ami chilam, tumi chile**, etc. Unlike the present tense, the past tense of this verb cannot be omitted:

tumi ki Oshustho?	Are you ill?
tumi kalke ki Oshustho chile?	Were you ill yesterday?

Also note that this verb only has a simple present and simple past. If any other verb form is needed, a form of the verb **thaka** has to be used:

kalke she shustho thakbe.	He'll be fit tomorrow. (future **thakbe**)
ami Oshustho thakte cai na.	I don't want to be ill. (infinitive **thakte**)

There are a few cases where the simple past form does not describe an event in the past. First, it can describe an action that is about to happen. This is common especially with the forms **collam** and **gelam** 'I'm going (now)' (lit.: 'I went'). Second, the form **holo** (3rd person past tense of **hOwa**) often means 'is/are': **e holo amar skuler bondhu** ('this is my schoolfriend'). In this use, **holo** always comes in the middle of the sentence, never at the end.

Exercise 3

Write down and learn the simple past tense of **dækha, shona, newa, kOra, hOwa** and **showa**. Then find your slips of paper with pronouns and verbs and practise making the simple past tense.

Exercise 4 (Audio 2:33)

Read the following text about a protest demonstration and say:
- How many opposition parties took part in the demonstration?
- What did the demonstrators do?

গতকালকে রমনায় একটা বিক্ষোভ মিছিল ছিল। মিছিলে অন্যান্য দশ-বারোটা দল যোগ দিলো। পাঁচজন নেতা নেতৃত্ব দিলেন। তাঁদের পেছনে হাজার হাজার লোকজন ছিলো। সবাই শ্লোগান দিতে দিতে প্রেস-ক্লাবের সামনে এলো। সেখানে এসে তারা নেতাদের বক্তৃতা শুনলো। তারপরে বিভিন্ন দলের কর্মীরা প্রেসিডেন্ট-ভবনে যেতে স্থির করলো। কিন্তু পথে পুলিশ কর্মীদের বাধা দিলো। তখন পুলিশ ও মিছিলকারীদের মধ্যে সংঘর্ষ শুরু হল। এবং কয়েকজন নেতাকে গ্রেফতার করলো। সন্ধ্যার দিকে পুলিশ সব রাস্তা থেকে মিছিলকারীদের সরিয়ে দিলো।

Vocabulary

rOmna	area in central Dhaka	pOth	path, way
bikkhobh	protest	badha dewa	to stop, prevent
jog dewa	to join	michilkari	demonstrator
shekhane	there	shOngghOrsho	clashes
bibhinno	different	greftar kOra	to arrest
kormi	worker	shorie dewa	to remove
sthir kOra	to decide		

Vocabulary point: days of the week

The days of the week are:

shombar	Monday
mongolbar	Tuesday
budhbar	Wednesday
brihOshpotibar/bisshudbar	Thursday
shukrobar	Friday
shonibar	Saturday
robibar	Sunday

Unit 11: *What happened next?*

shombar	shukrobar
mongolbar	shonibar
budhbar	robibar
brihOshpotibar	

If further specification is needed, the terms **gOto** 'last' and **agami** 'coming, next' are used. These words are also used to disambiguate the words **kal** (locative: **kalke**) 'yesterday'/'tomorrow' and **porshu** 'the day before yesterday'/'the day after tomorrow'.

gOto robibar	last Sunday
agami shonibar	this coming Saturday
gOto kal	yesterday
agami porshu	the day after tomorrow

To say on what day something happens, the locative ending **-e** can be attached to the name of the day (**gOto budhbare elo** 's/he came last Wednesday') but often the bare name is used (**gOto budhbar elo**).

Mini-exercise

Say: Snow White came last Monday.
On Tuesday she cleaned the house.
On Wednesday she did the shopping.
On Thursday she cooked rice.
On Friday she ate an apple and fell asleep.
On Saturday the dwarves cried.
On Sunday, a prince came and kissed her.

Exercise 5

Mr Roy is a politician. Below are some entries from his diary of last week. The Nina that is mentioned is his youngest daughter and Minoti is his wife.

shombar	10.00	misTar coudhurike fon kOra
	10.30–15.00	dOler nirbahi (executive) shObha (meeting)

	16.00	ninar jonno shoping kOra
	20.30	ninar jOnmodiner parTi (birthday party)
mongolbar	9.00	budhbarer boktrita cek kOra
	13.00	dOler kormider shOnge alocona (discussion)
	15.00	ciThipOttro pORa
	20.00	minotir shOnge mondire jawa
budhbar	11.00	chattro-chattrider jonno boktrita dewa
	13.00	sromik (labourer) netader shOnge alocona
	14.00	shangbadikder shakkhatkar (interview) dewa
	17.00	em-pi-der shathe ca khawa

Mr Roy indeed did all these things last week. Describe what he did at the different times on the different days.

The first few sentences will be: **shombar shOkal dOshTae misTar rOe misTar chowdhurike fon korlen. shaRe dOshTae uni dOler nirbahi shObhae gelen. bikal tinTae shObha shesh holo.**

Dialogue 2 (Audio 2:35)

Onika is at the police station, reporting the theft of her handbag. Were there any witnesses?

onika: o-si shaheb, ami apnar Thanae ækTa chintaier reporT korte cai.
o-si: Obossho-i, boshun. ki ghoTeche bolun.
onika: ami rasta die hãTchilam ar amar mobaile kOtha bolchilam. amar kãdhe ækTa bæg jhulchilo. oiTa chintai hoe gæche.
o-si: bæger moddhe ki ki chilo?
onika: amar pasporT, poricOepOttro, nOgod Taka, baRir cabi o onnanno bektigOto jinishpOttro chilo.
o-si: eirOkom chintai protidin-i hocche. ghOTonaTa ki onno keu dekheche?
onika: ta ami bolte parbo na. tObe maTher moddhe ækTa lok jadu-khæla dækhacchilo. Oneke-i khæla dekhchilo. hote pare tader keu chintaikarike dekheche.
o-si: Thik ache. Dairi kore rakhlam. ækjOn pulish-ofiserke ghOTonasthOle paThacchi. she tOdOnto korbe. amra apnake janabo.

Unit 11: *What happened next?*

Vocabulary

o-si	officer in charge	jinishpOttro	things
chintai	mugging	eirOkom	such (a)
reporT kOra	to report	tObe	but
ghOTa	to happen	maTh	field
kãdh	shoulder	jadu-khæla	magic
jhola	to hang	hote pare	perhaps
chintai hOwa	to get stolen	chintaikari	mugger
poricOepOttro	identification	Dairi kore rakha	to record
nOgod Taka	cash money	tOdOnto kOra	to investigate
bektigOto	personal	janano	to let know

Grammar point: the past progressive

You have seen that Bengali verbs (e.g. hãTa 'walk') have, amongst others, the following tenses:

	Simple	*Progressive*
present	hãTi I walk	hãTchi I'm walking
past	hãTlam I walked	

You won't be surprised to learn that they also have a past progressive tense:

ami rasta die hãTchilam.   I was walking in the street.
ækTa lok jadu-khæla   A man was showing some magic.
dækhacchilo.

These forms express that an action or activity was ongoing at some moment in the past. The most natural translation in English is usually with a past progressive ('was walking/showing').
  The forms of the past progressive are not difficult to make:

- take the first person form of the present progressive (i.e. **likhchi**, **nicchi**, **dekhchi**, **khulchi**, **korchi**, **hãTchi**, etc. – see Unit 7)
- add the same endings as in the simple past (i.e. add **-lam**, **-le**, **-li**, **-lo** and **-len**).

The result is forms such as:

ami likhchilam, tumi likhchile, tui likhchili, she likhchilo, apni likhchilen (I was writing, you were writing, etc.)

Some further examples:

'fon bajchilo; 'The phone was ringing;
TibhiTa pura bholume colchilo; the TV was playing at full
volume;
baccara kãdchilo; the children were crying;
protibeshira citkar korchilo.' the neighbours were shouting.'
'o tumi ki korchile?' 'And what were you doing?'
'ami khOborer kagoj 'I was reading the newspaper.'
poRchilam'

Exercise 6

A customer in Harun's tea shop has been shot by another customer after an argument. A policeman is interrogating witnesses, asking each of them: **jOkhon gulir** (guli=bullet) **shObdo shunlen, tOkhon apni ki korchilen?** Give their answers.

1 (Harun's employee:) [making tea]
2 (Harun:) [talking with my friend]
3 (Harun's two sons:) [washing cups in kitchen]
4 (a customer:) [drinking my tea]
5 (another customer:) [talking on my mobile]

Vocabulary point: crime and criminals

You already know several words relating to unlawful behaviour. Here are some more words for criminals and their activities:

cor thief   curi kOra to steal
pokeTmar pickpocket   pokeT mara to pick pockets
Dakat robber   Dakati kOra to commit robbery
jaliat counterfeiter   jal Taka chapano to print counterfeit money
kalobajari black marketeer   jinishgulo kalo bajare bikkri kOra sell things on the black market
khuni murderer   khun kOra to murder
cãdabaj extortionist   cãdabaji kOra to take extortion money
dhõkabaj cheat   dhõkabaji kOra to cheat

Exercise 7

The police have caught several criminals red-handed. One by one, they are brought before the judge. A policeman says who they are

Unit 11: *What happened next?* 153

and what they were caught trying to do. Complete his sentences. The first one would be: **she ækTa saikel curi korte cesTa korchilo.**

1 **ei lok ækTa cor. she...** (was trying to steal a bicycle)
2 **ei lok ækTa pokeTmar. she...** (was trying to pick pockets)
3 **ei lok ækTa jaliat. she...** (was trying to print counterfeit money)
4 **ei lok ækTa kalobajari. she...** (was trying to sell things on the black market)
5 **ei lok ækTa cādabaj. she...** (was trying to take extortion money)
6 **ei lok ækTa chintaikari. she...** (was trying to mug a lady for her bag)

The defendants deny all charges. Thus the first one says: **na, na, ami cor noi. konodin saikel curi kori ni.** What would the others say?

Dialogue 3 (Audio 2:37)

Babu and Rafiq are talking together. Babu is not looking good and Rafiq asks him why.

rofik: ei je, babu, idaning aenae nijeke dekhecho?
babu: na bhai, nijer cehara dekhe ar ki hObe?
rofik: kæno? ki hoeche? tomake khub hOtash mone hocche?
babu: ar bolo na, bhai. gOto rattre baRite Dakat eshe amar strir gOenagāti shOb nie gæche.
rofik: tomra Dakatder badha dite cesTa kOro ni?
babu: na, ora baRite Dhuke-i amaderke cearer shOnge doRi die bẽdhe felechilo. ora shObkichu nie cole gælo. tarpOre amra nijera nijederke chaRalam.
rofik: tarpOre ki holo? thanae riporT korecho?
babu: hæ̃, pulisher kache gechi. kintu tara bollo je amader nijeder jinisher dike nijeder-i kheal rakhte hObe.
rofik: bOlo ki? thanar lokjon tomake shahajjo korte cailo na kæno?
babu: karon agami mashe nirbacon. pulish ækhon michil-miTing nie bæsto.

Vocabulary

ei je	hey!	doRi	rope
idaning	recently	bẽdhe fæla	to tie up
cehara	face	chaRano	to free, release
hOtash	dejected	kichur dike	to keep an eye
gOenagāti	jewelry	kheal rakha	on something
Dhoka	to enter	bæsto	busy

Grammar point: reflexive pronouns

Dialogue 3 has some sentences which describe an action directed at the subject:

aenae nijeke dekhecho?   Have you seen yourself in the mirror?
amra nijederke chaRalam.   We freed ourselves.

They contain the reflexive pronoun **nije**. Like other pronouns, it has different forms depending on its number and its function in the sentence.

	Subject	*Possessive*	*Object*
singular	**nije**	**nijer**	**nijeke**
plural	**nijera**	**nijeder**	**nijeder(ke)**

Further examples are:

tara aenae nijeder dekhe nilo.
They looked at themselves in the mirror.
(**nijeder** is object in the sentence)

me-eTa nijeke khub shundori mone kOre.
The girl considers herself very beautiful.
(**nijeke** is object)

she nijer chobi dewale jhulalo.
She hanged her own photo on the wall.
(**nijer** expresses possession)

she nijer jonno salwar-kamij o tar maer jonno ækTa shaRi kinlo.
She bought a salwar-kameez for herself and a sari for her mother.
(possessive **nijer** because **jonno** requires a possessive form)

A personal pronoun can be added as well:

tara aenae tader nijeder dekhe nilo
she tar nijer chobi dewale jhulalo

Sometimes **nije** does not express reflexive action but simply emphasis:

babu nije boleche.   Babu himself has said so.

Unit 11: *What happened next?*

Exercise 8

Upol is comparing himself again with other people. Complete his sentences, using the clues given.

1 **tumi tomar nijer saikel meramot korte paro na, kintu ami** _____ (can repair my own car).
2 **amar bondhura nijederke bhalo bhabe bojhate pare na, kintu ami** _____ (can express myself very well).
3 **Oneke-i nijeke bhalobaste pare na, kintu ami** _____ (am able to love myself).
4 **Oneke-i nijer bæpare kOtha bolte cae na, kintu ami** _____ (am always willing to talk about myself).
5 **amar stri nijeke aenae dekhe khushi hOe na kintu ami** _____ (am happy when I see myself in the mirror).

Reading text 🎧 (Audio 2:38)

Here is a Bengali lullaby. In it, the baby's mother is confronting some pirate-robbers, who are demanding 'tax'. But she tells them that the **bulbuli** *(which are tiny birds) have eaten all the paddy and asks them to wait for the newly sown garlic to grow (i.e. wait several months).*

বর্গী এলো দেশে

খোকা ঘুমালো, পাড়া জুড়ালো –
বর্গী এলো দেশে।
বুলবুলিতে ধান খেয়েছে –
খাজনা দেব? কি সে!
ধান ফুরালো – পান ফুরালো
খাজনার উপায় কি?
আর ক'টা দিন সবুর করো –
রসুন বুনেছি।

Vocabulary

borgi	pirate	**furano**	to be finished
khoka	little boy	**dhan-pan**	crops
paRa	neighbourhood	**kOTa**	a few
juRano	to be quiet	**shobur kOra**	to wait
bulbuli	Indian nightingale	**bona**	to sow
khajna	tax		

12 আপনারা স্কুলে কি কি পড়তেন?
apnara skule ki ki poRten?
What did you study at school?

In this unit you will learn how to:

- talk about the way things used to be
- describe events in the more distant past
- specify dates
- make requests and give permission

Dialogue 1 (Audio 2:39)

Jenny is back in Dhaka. She is talking with Dipu's grandfather about his schooldays. What two differences from today does Dipu's grandfather mention?

jeni:	dadabhai, apnader amole skul kæmon chilo? skule ki ki poRten?
dada-bhai:	jOkhon ami choTo chilam, tOkhon amra jetam paThshalae.
jeni:	paTh-shala abar ki, dadabhai?

Unit 12: *What did you study at school?*

dada-bhai: paTh-shala holo gach-tOlae khola skul. amaderke ækjOn ponDit-mOshae pORaTen.
jeni: gacher tOlae skul! khub mOjar bæpar to.
dada-bhai: bæparTa motei mOjar chilo na. shOb pORa amader mukhostho korte hoto. na parle ponDit-mOshae bet die piTaten. baRite eshe abar babar hate piTuni khetam.
jeni: o ma! tahole to piTunir bhOe-e Onek kichu mukhostho korte hoeche. ækhono ki kono kichu mone ache?
dada-bhai: Obossho-i – namta mukhostho korechi, jæmon: pãc ække pãc, pãc dugune dOsh, tin pãce ponero, car pãce kuRi – eibhabe namta mukhostho kortam.
jeni: shune khub mOja pelam, dadabhai. skule amrao namta mukhostho kOrte shikhechi... kintu apnader mOton na.

Vocabulary

dada(bhai)	grandfather (father's father)	bet	cane
amol	time, days	piTano	to beat
paTh-shala	village school	piTuni	beating
gach-tOla	foot of tree	khawa	to suffer, endure
mOja	fun	amar mone ache	I remember
bæpar	thing, matter	namta	multiplication table
motei na	not at all	jæmon	such as, for example
pORa	reading, studying	dugune	twice (used with numbers)
mukhostho kOra	to learn by heart	eibhabe	in this way
		mOja pawa	to enjoy oneself
na parle	if we were unable	mOton	like... (with possessive)

Grammar point: *habitual past tense*

Dialogue 1 has several sentences with a new verb form:

  skule ki ki poRten? What did you study at school?
  babar hate piTuni khetam I used to get beaten by my father.

These forms are habitual past tenses: they are used to describe actions that took place repeatedly in the past. The corresponding English sentences have 'used to', though a simple past tense is often also possible. But in Bengali, to describe a past action that was habitual, you have to use the past habitual tense.

The forms of the habitual past tense are identical to the simple past tense (see Unit 11), except that they do not have the sound **l** but the sound **t**. Examples are:

	pORa	*khawa*
ami	poRtam (also poRtum W)	khetam (or khetum)
tumi	poRte (also poRta in colloquial E)	khete (or kheta)
tui	poRti	kheti
she	poRto	kheto
apni	poRten	kheten

We saw that **jawa** and **asha** have an irregular simple past tense. But their habitual past tense is regular: **ami jetam, tumi jete** etc. and **ami astam, tumi aste** etc.

Note that **gawa** and **cawa** differ from **khawa** in changing their stem vowel to **ai (ami gaitam/caitam,** etc.), just as in the simple past tense **(ami gailam/cailam)** and the infinitive **(gaite/caite).**

Exercise 1

Dipu's grandfather is reminiscing about the past. He mentions several things that were different. Finish his sentences. The first one would be: **ami ar farshi boi poRi na, kintu age Onek poRtam.**

1 **ami ar farshi boi poRi na, kintu age . . .**
2 **ar piTuni khai na, kintu age . . .**
3 **kobita** (= poems) **mukhostho korte ami ar pOchondo kori na, kintu age . . .**
4 **baccara ar gach-tOlar paTh-shalae jae na, kintu . . .**
5 **ami ækhon bhalo bhabe fuTbOl khelte pari na, kintu age . . .**
6 **mohilader shathe gOlpo korte amar ar bhalo lage na, kintu age . . .**
7 **ami ar robindro-shongit** (= songs of Rabindranath) **gai na, kintu age . . .**

Exercise 2

Answer the following questions.

1 **apnar choTobælae** (= youth) **apni kon shOhore thakten?**
2 **kon skule poRten?**

Unit 12: *What did you study at school?*

3 ki kore skule jeten?
4 kon khæla (= game) khelte pOchondo korten?
5 chuTite apni kothae jeten?
6 apnar ma apnar jonno kon khabar ranna korten?

Dialogue 2 (Audio 2:40)

After the summer vacation (May to June in Bengal), teacher Rina asks several students how they spent their holidays and when they came back. What did the students like best about their holidays?

rina: tomra grissher chuTite ki ki korechile?
bina: amra shObai mile mama-baRite giechilam. khub mOja kore am khe-echi. me-er aTharo tarikhe amra fire eshechi.
bishu: choTo mama pukur theke bORo bORo rui-mach dhorechilen. mama-baRi theke amra Onek mach nie eshechi.
rina: bah. tomra dui bhai-bon mile to khub mOja korecho. tarpOr didar, tumi tomar chuTi ki bhabe kaTiechile?
didar: amra chuTite choTo khalar baRite lOnDone giechilam. shekhane pOhela jun theke couddoi jun porjonto chilam. amra bibhinno jadughOre giechilam.
rina: tomra Taoar jadughOre-o giechile?
didar: ji. giechilam. shekhane kohinur hiraTi dekhechi. æto shundor jinish prithibite ar ditioTa nai.
rina: tumi dekhi ækTa oitihashik chuTi kaTiecho. cOmotkar.

Vocabulary

grissho	summer	pukur	pond
mile	together	kaTano	to pass, spend
mama-baRi	mother's paternal home	hira	diamond
		prithibi	world
tarikh	date	ditio	second

Grammar point: double adjectives

Dialogue 2 has the phrase **bORo bORo ruimach** (lit.: big big carpfish). The double adjective **bORo bORo** conveys emphasis: 'really

big'. But in addition it also conveys plural meaning: the whole phrase means 'some/several really big carp-fish'.
Some further examples:

misTi misTi am	really sweet mangos
dami dami jinish	really expensive things

As with other nouns, plural can also be expressed by adding **-gulo/ guli**. An additional demonstrative (**ei**, **oi**) is also possible.

misTi misTi amgulo	really sweet mangos
ei shundor shundor hiragulo	these really beautiful diamonds

Exercise 3

Rifat's aunt is at the market again. Four different shopkeepers call out to her, saying the following. What kind of shop does each shopkeeper have?

1 kakima, bhalo bhalo am kinben?
2 apnar taja taja mach cai?
3 gOrom gOrom rOshgolla (= a round milk-based sweet) khan.
4 ashun, kakima. shundor shundor shaRi ache.
5 bOro bOro rui neben?
6 notun notun salwar-kamij khũjchen?
7 choTo choTo kOla nie jan.

Grammar point: past perfect

Dialogue 2 has several examples of the past perfect tense:

chuTite ki ki korechile?	What did you do in the holidays?
bORo bORo rui-mach dhorechilen.	He caught several big carp.

This tense is used to describe an action in the past. Sometimes that action precedes another one that is also mentioned. In such cases, English would also use the past perfect:

jadughOrTa age dekhechilam. tai tader shOnge gelam na.
I had seen the museum before. So I did not go with them.

In addition, the Bengali past perfect is used to describe events that took place long ago:

Unit 12: *What did you study at school?* 161

briTishra bharot theke kohinurTa nie giechilo
The British took the Kohinoor from India.

It can also be used for events that happened more recently, as in the examples above from the Dialogue. But if there is a direct connection to the present, as in the following example, the present perfect is more usual.

duiTa bORo bORo mach dhorechi. amra aj rattre khabo.
I've caught two big fish. We'll eat them tonight.

The past perfect is easy to make: take the past participle (e.g. **kore, dhue, gie**) and add one of the endings **-chilam** (also **-chilum** W), **-chile** (also **-chila** in colloquial E), **-chilo, -chili, -chilen** (i.e. what you add is the simple past tense of 'to be'). The result is:

kOra	*dhowa*	*jawa*
ami korechilam	dhuechilam	giechilam
tumi korechile	dhuechile	giechile
tui korechili	dhuechili	giechili
she korechilo	dhuechilo	giechilo
apni korechilen	dhuechilen	giechilen

For **giechilam**, etc., the shorter forms **gechilam**, etc. are also used.

Like the present perfect tense, the negative of the past perfect is formed by the simple PRESENT tense followed by **ni** (**nai** in colloquial E):

ami lOnDone gechilam kintu amar bhai jae ni.
I went to London but my brother didn't go.

Exercise 4

Here is the story of Dipu's grandfather's life. Choose the appropriate verb forms.

dipur dadabhaier unishshOto pōcish shale jOnmo [hoto/hoeche]. cho-Tobælae murshidabade (= town in W. Bengal) [thaklen/thakten]. unishsho shatcollish shale uni purbo-pakistane [eshechen/ashchilen]. okhane bibhinno bORo bORo kompanite kaj korten. unishsho shaT shale uni poshcim-pakistane (= West Pakistan) disTrikT-komishonar [hocchilen/hoechilen]. 1966 theke 1971 porjonto kOracite (= Karachi) bash korten. 1971-er pOre ar pakistane thakte [ce-echilen na/can ni].

1972 januari mashe shadhin (= free) bangladeshe cole [ashlen/ashten]. shekhane ponero bOchor shikkha montronalOe-e (= ministry of education) kaj korlen. 1986 shale reTair [korben/korechen].

A boxed history of Bengal

	Before 1947	1947–1971	1971–now
West Bengal	part of British India	one of the states of India	one of the states of India
Bangladesh	part of British India	part of Pakistan	independent nation

Vocabulary point: specifying dates

For the months, the English names are generally used, pronounced as: **januari, februari, marc, epril, me, jun, julai, agosT, sepTembor, OkTobor, nobhembor, Disembor**. To indicate the day of the month, these are put in the possessive form, followed by the appropriate numeral and the word **tarikh** 'date' (in the locative: **tarikhe**). It is also possible to insert the word **masher** – the name of the month is then in the basic form.

januarir æk tarikh	1 January
julaier põcish tarikhe bæRate gelam.	On 25 July we went for a trip.
agosT masher car tarikhe fire elam.	On 4 August we came back.

An alternative way to specify dates uses words meaning 'first, second, third', etc.:

pOhela (or **pOela**)	(১লা)	first
doshora	(২রা)	second
teshora	(৩রা)	third
couTha	(৪ঠা)	fourth
pãci	(৫ই)	fifth
chOei	(৬ই)	sixth
ittadi	(ইত্যাদি)	etc.
aTharoi	(১৮ই)	18th
unishe	(১৯শে)	19th
bishe	(২০শে)	20th
ittadi		etc.

Unit 12: *What did you study at school?*

These words are followed by the name of the month (which gets the locative form to express 'on such and such a day').

pOhela januari   1 January
shOtoroi eprile nirbacon hObe   The election will be on 17 April.

Mini-exercise

Now say: Today is 1 July.
We came back from London on 18 June.
School will start on 10 July.
On 20 July, our grandfather will come.
In December, we are going to London again.

The basic units of time are:

sekenD	second (but outside clock-watching contexts, **muhurto** 'moment' is used)
miniT	minute
ghOnTa	hour
din	day (the word **bar** is only used in the days of the week: **uni gOto budhbare elen; dui din thaklen; gOto shukrobare abar cole gelen**)
shOpta	week
mash	month
bOchor	year (but to specify the calendar year, the word **shal** is used: **2001 shale lOndone gelam; tin bOchor thaklam; 2004 shale abar fire elam**)
dOshok	decade
shOtabdi	century

Exercise 5

Go back to Unit 11, Exercise 5. If Mr Roy did all these things as scheduled, how would he himself say so? Make his sentences, using the past perfect and specifying the time and date on which he did the various things. The dates were: 18, 19 and 20 October.

He would start as follows:

aTharoi OkTobor shOkal dOshTae ami misTar chowdhurike fon korechilam. shaRe dOshTae ami dOler nirbahi shObhae gechilam.

Exercise 6

Go to the website of the daily newspaper **ittefak** <htpp://www.ittefaq.com>. Browse through it and find 10 sentences which mention dates. Can you work out what the events on these dates are?

Exercise 7

Test your knowledge of time and dates.

1 এক মিনিটে কয় সেকেন্ড?
2 সাড়ে তিন ঘণ্টায় কয় মিনিট?
3 এক দশকে কয় মাস?
4 এক শতাব্দীতে কয় দশক?
5 ডিসেম্বর মাসের কত তারিখে ক্রিসমাস?
6 কোন তারিখটা আগে? অক্টোবরের চব্বিশ তারিখ? না ছাব্বিশে অক্টোবর?
7 কোন তারিখটা আগে? মে মাসের চৌদ্দ তারিখ? না চৌঠা মে?

Dialogue 3 (Audio 2:42)

Arif is outside the headmaster's office. What is his problem?

arif:	sar, ami bhitore aste pari?
prodhan shikkhOk:	hæ̃, asho. ki bæpar?
arif:	sar, amake baRi jete onumoti din. amar khub matha dhoreche. jOr-jOr bodh hocche. monojog die kichu-i korte parchi na.
prodhan shikkhOk:	Thik ache. ami Daktar Deke anacchi. Daktar eshe porikkha kore dekhuk ki hoeche tomar.
arif:	sar, apnake onurod korchi dOya kore Daktar Dakben na. baRite gie bissram nebo. tahole-i ami shustho hoe uThbo.
prodhan shikkhOk:	Thik ache, kintu tomake æka jete dite parbo na. tomar obhibhabokder khObor dicchi. tader keu ækjOn eshe tomake nie jaben.
arif:	sar, onuggrohopurbok eTa korben na. ami æka-i jete parbo.
prodhan shikkhOk:	aha – bujhte parchi. tomar ækhon ar skule thakte iccha hocche na, tai na? ækhon gie tomar klashe bOsho. carTae klash shesh hObe. tarpOre baRi jeo.

Unit 12: *What did you study at school?*

Vocabulary

jOr-jOr	feverish	anano	to let someone fetch
amar bodh hocche	I'm feeling... (impersonal)	bissram	rest
		obhibhabok	guardian
monojog die	with concentration	onuggrohopurbok	please

Vocabulary point: wanting, requesting and getting permission

Here are some words to express wishes and desires. Note the ways they are used to form sentences.

upol cole jete cae	Upol wants to leave
amra cai na (je) upol cole jak	We don't want Upol to leave (**je** 'that' is optional; the verb is imperative: **cole jak**)
(amar) mon cae baRite jai	I want to go home (lit.: my mind wants that I go home)
ca khete amar iccha hOe	I want/would like to drink tea (an impersonal construction)

There are also several ways to request things. The first two sentences feature the verbs **onurodh kOra** 'ask, request' and the last one has the word **onuggrohopurbok** 'please' (another possibility would be: **dOya kore**).

arif jete onurodh kOrlo.	Arif requested to be allowed to go. (lit.: Arif requested to go)
onurodh korchi (je) apni ekTu khan.	I am asking you to eat a little. (**je** 'that' is optional; the verb is imperative)
onuggrohopurbok chuTi din.	Please/kindly give me a day off.

Finally, here are some ways of giving or refusing permission. They feature the verbs **onumoti dewa** 'to give permission', just **dewa** 'allow, let' and **para** 'can, be allowed to'. These all combine with infinitives.

tini amake jete onumoti dilen na.	He didn't give me permission to go.
tini amake jete dilen na.	He didn't allow me to go.
jete parbe na.	You can't go/may not go.

Exercise 8

Finish the sentences, using the clues provided.

1 ækjOn chattro: sar, _____ cai. _____ onumoti din.
   (I want to go home; give me permission to go).
2 shikkhOk: na, _____ parbe na. tomake _____ debo na.
3 ækTa bacca: ma, _____ iccha hOe na. _____ pari?
   (don't feel like studying; can I watch TV?)
4 misTar rOe: prodhan montri, amra cai na je _____
   (don't want there to be an election on 1 January)
5 ækjOn cashi: malik, onurodh korchi je _____
   (landlord, I'm asking you to help us please)

Exercise 9: revision of tenses

A politician is making a speech, in which he says what he has always done, always does, and will always do in the future too (or has never done, never does, and never will do). 'In the future' is **bhobisshote**; 'never' is **konodin... na**. Make his sentences for him. The first one would be:

ami apnaderke bolchi je ami shObshOmOe shotti kOtha bolechi, shObshOmOe shotti kOtha boli o bhobisshote-o shotti kOtha bolbo.

1 **shotti kOtha** (= the truth) **bOla**.
2 **apnader jonno porissrom kOra** (= work hard)
3 **mittha kOtha** (= lies) **bOla**.
4 **amar deshTake bhalobasha** (= love)
5 **ghush khawa**.
6 **nirbaconer shOmOe apnaderke Taka dewa**.

Then the politician turns to the topic of what his opponent (**protipOkkho**) always or never does. Make his sentences. The first one is: **amar protipOkkho konodin shotti kOtha bOle ni, konodin shotti kOtha bOle na o bhobisshote-o shotti kOtha bolbe na.**

Reading text – একটু হাসুন।

সোভিয়েত রাশিয়ার আমলে একজন মার্কিন শিক্ষক রাশিয়ার কোন একটি স্কুলে অংক করাতেন। একদিন ক্লাশে অংক বোঝাতে গিয়ে তিনি জিজ্ঞেস করলেন:

Unit 12: *What did you study at school?*

শিক্ষক – বল তো, পাঁচ রুব্‌লে একজোড়া মোজা কিনে যদি আমি বিশ রুব্‌লে বিক্রি করি, তবে আমি কি পাবো?
ছাত্র – সাইবেরিয়ায় সাত বছর!

Vocabulary

kono ækTa	a, some	**bojhano**	to explain
kOrano	to make (somebody) do	**moja**	sock

13 জমি হাল দেওয়ার জন্য কি ব্যবহার করেন?
jomi hal dewar jonno ki bæbohar kOren?

What do you use for ploughing the land?

> **In this unit you will learn how to:**
> - talk about village life and the countryside
> - state obligations
> - report what people have said
> - recognise the remaining conjuncts

Dialogue 1 (Audio 2:44)

Jenny and Tipu are visiting Tipu's Aunt Jamila, who lives in a village. Why is Jamila worried?

jomila-fupu: ei je, jeni-Tipu. tomra fire eshecho? sharadin kothae kothae ghurle?

jeni: noukae coRe nodite ghurechi. tarpOr hẽTe hẽTe shara gramTa ghure dekhechi. ækTa baRite Dhuke Daber pani o khejurer rOsh khe-echi.

Unit 13: *Ploughing the land*

ækTa nouka

jomila-fupu: ki shOrbonash! Tipu, tui jenike nie noukae uThechili kæno?

jeni: fupu, Tipuke bokben na. ami bhalo shātar jani. noukae coRte pere ami khub anondo pe-echi. æmon tOk-toke porishkar gram ami konodin dekhi nai.

jomila-fupu: sharadin ghure ghure tomader niscOe-i khide pe-e gæche. cOlo shObai mile chade gie ca khai. jeni, akasher dike ce-e dækho. mish-mishe kalo akashe taraguli jhOk-jhOk korche.

jeni: ish – Opurbo shundor lagche. lOnDoner akashe kOkhono æmon cãd-tara dekhi nai.

Tipu: Obak korlen, jenidi. apnader lOnDoner akashe cãd oThe na naki? bangladesher shadharon akash dekhe Obak hoe gelen?

jeni: bhai Tipu, lOnDone shararat caridike bijli bati jolte thake. tai cãd-tarar eirOkom miTi-miTi alo shekhane dækha jae na.

Vocabulary

shara	whole, all	**khejur**	date (the fruit)
ghora	to turn, go	**ki shOrbonash**	how terrible!
nouka	small boat	**oTha**	to board
Dab	green coconut	**bOka**	to scold

shătar	swimming	Obak hOwa	to be surprised
anondo	pleasure, joy	caridike	on all sides
chad	roof	bijli	electricity
cawa	to look	bati	lamp
cãd	moon	jOla	to burn
tara	star	jolte thaka	to burn continuously
Opurbo shundor	extremely beautiful	alo	light
Obak kOra	to surprise	dækha jae	it can be seen

Vocabulary point: repeating words

Bengali has many 'repeating' words, consisting of two identical or near-identical parts. The parts themselves do not mean anything – but their combination does.

taraguli jhOk-jhOk korche	the stars are shining
tOk-toke porishkar	sparkling clean

Many of these words combine with the verb **kOra** to make a verb. When they do not, they usually get an **-e** at the end. The vowel **O** in front of this **-e** then changes to **o**. Thus, there is **tOk-tOk kOra** 'to sparkle, glare' but **tOk-toke porishkar** 'sparkling clean'. Other examples are:

mish-mishe kalo	pitch black	pæn-pæn kOra	to nag
miTi-miTi alo	a twinkling light	Tuk-Tuke cehara	a lovely face
bhOn-bhOn kOra	to buzz	miT-miTe shOetan	a deceitful devil
bOkor-bOkor kOra	to chatter	khiT-khiT kOra	to fret, grumble

Exercise 1

Complete the sentences, choosing from the words in the box:

```
khiT-khiT     miT-miTe      bhOn-bhOn
jhOk-jhOk     bOkor-bOkor
```

1 she misTi kOtha bOle kintu ashole (= really) she ækjOn _____ shOetan.

Unit 13: *Ploughing the land* 171

2 amra ækTa hoTele uThechilam, kintu shararat mOshagulo (= mosquitos) _____ korchilo – ækebare-i ghumate pari ni.
3 tar stri sharadin _____ korto o she _____ korto.
4 porishkar akashe taraguli _____ korchilo.

Vocabulary point: more emotions

Here are some more phrases expressing feelings and emotions. The first three are 'impersonal' constructions. For each, note way the source of the feeling is expressed (usually with a past participle or an infinitive).

cãd dekhe amar Obak lagchilo	I was surprised to see the moon
gramTa dekhe amar anondo lagchilo	I felt happy to see the village
tara dekhte cOmotkar laglo	I found it wonderful to see the stars/I found the stars wonderful to see
shune ami Obak holam	I was surprised to hear it
gramTa dekhe anondo pe-echilam	I was happy to see the village
shune khushi holam	I was happy to hear it
dekhe ami bisshito holam	I was amazed to see it

There are also many phrases to describe less happy feelings:

shune amar hOtash lagchilo	I felt disappointed to hear it
dekhe dukkho lagchilo	I felt sad to see it
okhane jete amar kOsTo hocchilo	I felt sad/troubled to go there
oke dekhe amar maya lagchilo	I felt pity seeing him/her
shune amar birokto lagchilo	I felt irritated to hear it
amar hingsha lagchilo	I felt jealous
amar mon kharap lagchilo	I felt bad/upset

Exercise 2

In describing her trip to the village, how would Jenny say that:

1 she was amazed to see such a big river;
2 she found the sunset (**shurjasto**) wonderful to see;
3 the stars were shining;
4 Tipu was surprised to hear her words;
5 she felt sad leaving the village;
6 she will go there again next month.

Her first sentence would be:

æto bORo nodi dekhe ami bisshito holam.

Dialogue 2 (Audio 2:45)

Jenny is talking with a farmer who is working on the field. How was this farmer affected by the recent flood?

jeni:	apnar jomite ki ki fOshol fOlan?
cashi:	dhan paT Dal moric alu shorisha ittadi. Olpo Olpo kore shObkichur-i cash kori.
jeni:	jomi hal dewar jonno ki bæbohar kOren? kono TrakTor ache?
cashi:	na, amar kono meshin nai. ami goru die hal-cash kori. amar duiTa teji hali-goru ache.
jeni:	apnar ar ki ki jib-jontu ache?
cashi:	amar aro duiTa dudhel-gai ache. goTa caræk chagol-bokri ache.
jeni:	hãsh-murgi palen na?
cashi:	hãsh-murgi chilo. amar stri palto. kintu gOto masher bonnae hãsh-murgiguli panite bheshe gæche. bonnar shOmOe-e goru-chagol pala khub kOsTer bæpar chilo. karon ghash-kuTa kenar Taka chilo na.
jeni:	shune khub dukkho pelam. cash-bash kOrar kaj ashole khub koThin.
cashi:	ji, goru-bachurer jOtno korte hOe. jomite hal-cash kore fOshol folate hOe. tarpOr ajkal pouro kOr dewar kono shesh nai.
jeni:	apnar to Onek daitto ache dekhchi. prithibir shOb deshe-i cashider jibon Onek kOsTer.

Vocabulary

jomi	land	jib-jontu	animal
fOshol	crop	dudhel-gai	milk cow
fOlano	to grow	goTa caræk	about four
paT	jute	chagol	goat
cash	farming	bokri	male goat
hal dewa	to plough	hãsh	duck
hal-cash kOra	to plough	pala	to keep, tend
teji	strong	bonna	flood
hali-goru	plough-ox	bhasha	to float

Unit 13: *Ploughing the land*

bheshe jawa	to float away	jOtno kOra	to take care of
kOsTo	difficulty		(with possessive)
ghash	grass	ajkal	nowadays
kuTa	hay	pouro shObha	local council
cash-bash kOra	to farm	kOr	tax
ashol	real	daitto	duty, obligation
bachur	calf		

Grammar point: verbal noun

The verbal noun ends in **-a** (e.g. **kOra**) or, for some verbs, **-ano/-ono** (W) (e.g. **ghumano/ghumono**). When this form is used in sentences, it usually corresponds to an English verb form ending in '-ing' (or sometimes an infinitive).

> **goru-chagol pala kOsTer bæpar chilo.**
> keeping cows and goats was a difficult matter

> **jomi hal dewar jonno** **ghash-kuTa kenar Taka**
> for ploughing the land   money for buying grass and hay

The verbal noun can be the subject of the entire sentence; then it gets no special ending (hence simply **pala** in the first example). It can also combine with a postposition; it then gets the appropriate ending (hence **dewar** in the second example, because of **jonno**). And it can also combine with a noun; the verbal noun then has the possessive form (hence **kenar** in the third example, because it combines with the noun **Taka**).

Some more examples:

> **TrækTor kena shOmbhOb chilo na**
> It was not possible to buy a tractor
> (lit.: buying a tractor was not possible)

> **kajTa shes kOrar pOre bashae jabo**
> I'll go home after finishing the work.

> **bonna shuru hOwar shOmOe-e cashi baRite chilo na**
> When the flood started, the farmer was not at home
> (lit.: at the time of the flood starting)

The possessive of the verbal noun sometimes has the ending **-bar**. The stem vowel then changes in the expected way (but **a** does not change). Thus, instead of **shesh kOrar pOre** or **TrækTor kenar Taka**, you may also find **shesh korbar pOre** and **TrækTor kinbar Taka**.

Exercise 3

Now answer the following questions about Dialogue 2.
1 fOshol fOlanor jonno cashiTar ki poriman (= amount) jomi ache, apnar dharona ki?
2 she hal-cash kOrar jonno kono TrækTor bæbohar kOre na kæno?
3 bonna hObar age, cashir hãsh-murgi chilo?
4 hãsh-murgi pala kar kaj chilo? cashi nije korto naki tar stri?
5 jib-jontur jOtno kOra chaRa, cashir ar ki ki kaj thake?

Exercise 4

Turn each of the following sentence pairs into one sentence, using the clues given. The first one would become: **noukae oThar pOre Onek chobi tullam.**

1 age noukae uThlam. tarpOre Onek chobi tullam. (oThar pOre)
2 noukae uThchilam. oi muhurte brisTi shuru holo. (oThar shOmOe-e)
3 nodite ghurechi. tarpOre gramTa dekhechi. (ghorar pOre)
4 onno gramgulite jete iccha hocchilo. kintu brisTir fOle (= because of) jete pari nai. (shOmbhOb chilo na)
5 cashir ghash-kuTa kinte holo. tar jonno take kichu Taka diechi. (kenar jonno)
6 goshol korechi. tarpOre fupur shOnge chade ca khe-echi. (khabar age)

Vocabulary point: duties and obligations

You are already familiar with the following impersonal construction:

cashir ghash-kuTa kinte hObe
The farmer has to buy grass and hay.

Some other expressions describing duties and obligations feature a verbal noun:

amar bajar kOra ucit
I have to do some shopping.
(lit.: my doing shopping is necessary)

gOto kalke bajar kOra ucit chilo
I had to do some shopping yesterday.

Unit 13: *Ploughing the land*

amar baRi jawar proyojon chilo
It was necessary for me to go home.
(lit.: of my-going-home was a need – the verbal noun is possessive: **jawar**)

tar oshudh khawar dOrkar chilo
He had to take medicine.
(here too a possessive: **khawar**)

To say what should not be done, there is a special construction, with an infinitive followed by **nei** (E. **nai**). The person is usually not specified.

eishOb kOtha bolte nei.
You/One should not say these things.

Exercise 5

Various people are telling you what they want. Say what they have to do then. Use the clues provided. Your first piece of advice would be: **tahole tomake prodhan shikkhOker kache jete hObe.**

1 **ami baRite jete cai.** (go to the headmaster) **[hObe]**
2 **amar ca khete iccha korche.** (make tea) **[dOrkar]**
3 **mon cae ækTa hirar angTi kini.** (husband has to buy it) **[ucit]**
4 **iccha korche je cashike ækTa goru kine dei.** (give him money) **[proyojon]**
5 **ami cai na je tumi Oshustho hOo.** (eat a lot of oranges) **[dOrkar]**
6 **ami cai na je tomar khide laguk.** (cook some rice for me) **[hObe]**

Dialogue 3 (Audio 2:47)

A farmer and his wife are talking about taxes. Who is the more optimistic of the two?

cashi: pouro cearmæn-shaheb bollen je tini amader fOshol dekhte ashben.
cashi-bou: ashuk. bhOe pawar kono karon nai.
cashi: shObai bollo je eibar cashider Onek beshi pouro kOr dite hObe.
cashi-bou: tomra shObai mile cearmænke bOlo je, 'apnar ashar dOrkar nai. amra ei bOchore kono khajna dite parbo na. karon bonnae amader khub khoti hoeche.'

cashi: ei kOtha bole ki labh hObe? tini ashben bole ghoshona korechen.
cashi-bou: tumi ki jiggesh korecho je tini kObe ashben?
cashi: ta jene ki hObe? cintae matha ghurche.
cashi-bou: kono cinta koro na. shigghro-i notun fOshol uThbe. paT bikkri kore kichu Taka dite parbo.
cashi: paTer fOlon eibare kæmon hObe, ke jane.
cashi-bou: inshallah bhalo hObe.

Vocabulary

karon	reason	amar matha ghurche	my head is spinning
eibar(e)	this time	cinta kOra	to worry
khoti	damage	shigghro	quickly
labh	use, benefit	fOlon	harvest
cinta	worry	inshallah	God willing (Muslim)

Grammar point: reporting speech

In Bengali – as in English – people often report what somebody else has said. This usually takes the form of direct speech, in which the actual words used (or thought to have been used) are repeated. The speech verb is usually **bOla** 'to say' (or, very colloquially, **kOwa** 'to say'). Other speech verbs (e.g. 'to shout', 'to answer') are often given the form of a past participle, which then combines with **bOla**.

arif bollo, 'amar khide lagche.'
Arif said, 'I am hungry.'

sultana citkar kore bollo, 'amake birokto koro na!'
Sultana shouted (lit.: having-shouted said), 'Don't bother me!'

Indirect speech also occurs:

arif uttor die bollo (je) tar khide lagche.
Arif answered (lit.: having-answered said) that he was hungry.

Use of the word **je** 'that' is optional. It is also sometimes used in direct speech: **arif bollo je, 'amar khide lagche'**.

Tense in indirect speech is the same as in direct speech – that is why **arif bollo je tar khide lagche** 'Arif said that he was hungry' has a present tense **(lagche)**. In English, the past tense 'was hungry' is used, because 'said' is a past tense. But Bengali does not have this rule and keeps the tense of the direct speech version.

Instead of **je**, the word **bole** (past participle of **bOla**; so literally 'having-said') is sometimes used with the meaning 'that'. It follows the reported words and is itself followed by the verb of saying:

tini ashben bole ghoshona korlen.
He announced that he would come.
(lit.: he will come – that – he announced)

tar khide lagche bole arif bollo.
Arif said that he was hungry.
(lit.: he is hungry – that – Arif said)

Finally, look at this indirect question:

ami jiggesh korlam je tini kObe ashben
I asked when he would come
(lit.: I asked that he when will-come?)

Such sentences differ from English in the following respects:

- they can have the word **je** 'that' introducing the question;
- the question word (here: **kObe**) is not at the front of the question, but in the middle – this is a general feature of Bengali questions, direct and indirect.
- the question word **ki na** 'whether' is special, since it always comes at the end of the indirect question; the indirect question as a whole often comes first (see Unit 8):

she ashbe ki na, tumi jano?
(or: **tumi jano she ashbe ki na?**)
'do you know whether he is coming?'

Exercise 6

Convert the following sentences into indirect speech, using the clues provided. The first one would become: **fupu jiggesh korlen tara kothae kothae ghurlo.**

1 jeni o Tipu, tomra kothae kothae ghurle?
  (fupu jiggesh korlen tara ...)
2 amra noukae coRe nodite ghurechi.
  (tara ... bole jeni bollo)
3 jeni, gramTa dekhte tomar bhalo legeche?
  (jenir ... kæmon ... , fupu jiggesh korlen)
4 akashe taraguli jhOk-jhOk korche
  (jeni dekhlo je ...)

5 jeni, lOnDoner akashe-o cãd oThe to?
   (Tipu jenike jiggesh korlo . . . ki na)
6 Tipu, tumi baje kOtha (= nonsense) bolo na!
   (fupu bollen je tini can na je . . . boluk).

Bengali script: the remaining conjunct letters

Some conjuncts combine not two but three letters. We give the main ones here. There are some more, but their components are easily recognisable and they are used in few words only.

A first group involves combinations ending in **ru**:

ত + র + ু = ত্রু   tru   শত্রু shottru enemy
দ + র + ু = দ্রু   dru   দ্রুত druto fast
ভ + র + ু = ভ্রু   bhru   ভ্রু bhru eyebrow
শ + র + ু = শ্রু   sru   অশ্রু osru tear

Another group has final **r**:

ন + ত + র = ন্ত্র   ntr   মন্ত্রী montri minister
ষ + ট + র = ষ্ট্র   str   রাষ্ট্র rastro state, country
স + ত + র = স্ত্র   str   স্ত্রী stri wife

A third group has final ব, written but not pronounced:

জ + জ + ব = জ্জ্ব   jj   উজ্জ্বল ujjol shiny
ত + ত + ব = ত্ত্ব   tt   তত্ত্ব tOtto theory
ন + দ + ব = ন্দ্ব   nd   দ্বন্দ্ব dOndo quarrel

We end our survey of the Bengali letters with a simple letter: ৎ, as in চমৎকার **cOmotkar** 'wonderful'. This stands for **t**, so it is like ত. But ৎ is only used when there is no vowel following the sound **t**.

Exercise 7

Match these words with their transliterations.

1 শ্রুতি   a **bhumitOtto** geology
2 ভূমিতত্ত্ব   b **mistri** mechanic
3 ত্রুটি   c **drutota** swiftness
4 দ্রুততা   d **Onujjol** dull, not shiny
5 অনুজ্জ্বল   e **istri** clothes-iron
6 মিস্ত্রী   f **sruti** hearing
7 সান্ত্রী   g **shantri** guard
8 ইস্ত্রী   h **truti** flaw

Unit 13: *Ploughing the land*

Exercise 8

Go to the website of the newspaper **jOnokOnTho** ('People's Voice') at <http://www.dailyjanakantha.com/>. Find one article there for which you are able to identify the general topic. Repeat this every day for a week.

Reading text – একটু হাসুন।

নির্বাচনে জয় লাভ করার পরে প্রধানমন্ত্রীর সাক্ষাৎকার নিতে এলেন সাংবাদিকরা –

সাংবাদিক	– মন্ত্রী পরিষদ গঠন করার আগে নিশ্চয়ই কারো পরামর্শ নেবেন?
প্রধানমন্ত্রী	– অবশ্যই! কিন্তু আমার স্ত্রীকে আবার এর মধ্যে টেনে আনছেন কেন?

Vocabulary

jOe labh kOra	to win	**gOThon kOra**	to form
shakkhatkar	interview	**pOramOrsho**	advice
montri porishOd	cabinet	**Tana**	to pull, drag

14 ফ্লাইট দশটায় ছাড়লে ক'টায় রিপোর্ট করতে হবে?
flaiT dOshTae chaRle kOTae riporT korte hObe?

If the flight leaves at ten, at what time should I check in?

In this unit you will learn how to:
- talk about air travel
- describe conditions and causes
- make comparisons
- make sentences that are packed with information

Dialogue 1 (Audio 2:49)

*Opu is travelling to Kolkata tomorrow. He has called the airline and is asking an assistant (**shOhokari**) about check-in times. Why can't Opu check in via the Internet?*

অপু — হ্যালো। আমি অপু গাঙ্গুলী বলছি। আমি আপনাদের কোম্পানীর বিমানে আগামীকালের ফ্লাইটে কোলকাতা যাচ্ছি।

সহঃ — জ্বি বলুন।

অঃ — শুনেছি ইদানীং আন্তর্জাতিক ফ্লাইটে নিরাপত্তার কারণে অনেক চেক হয়। ফ্লাইট দশটায় ছাড়লে ক'টায় রিপোর্ট করতে হবে?

Unit 14: *If the flight leaves at ten*   **181**

সহঃ – ডিপার্চারের আড়াই ঘণ্টা আগে রিপোর্ট করবেন। সময় মতন যদি পৌঁছাতে পারেন, তাহলে চিন্তার কিছু নেই।
অঃ – ইন্টারনেটের মাধ্যমে চেক-ইন করার চেষ্টা করেছিলাম। কিন্তু বোর্ডিং-পাসটা প্রিন্ট করতে পারি নি।
সহঃ – সরি স্যার। এই মুহূর্তে আমাদের ওয়েবসাইটে একটু ডিস্টার্ব আছে। যদি আজ চেক-ইন করতে না পেরে থাকেন, তাহলে কালকে বিমানবন্দরে করতে পারবেন।
অঃ – আচ্ছা। ইনফর্মেশন দেবার জন্য ধন্যবাদ।
সহঃ – আপনাকেও ধন্যবাদ। বিমানবন্দরে সমস্যায় পড়লে, আমাদের অফিসে যোগাযোগ করবেন।

Vocabulary

biman	aeroplane	**maddhome**	through (with possessive)
antorjatik	international		
nirapOtta	safety, security	**prinT kOra**	to print
karone	because of (with possessive)	**disTarb**	internet problem
		bimanbOndor	airport
reporT kOra	to check in	**shOmossha**	problem
shOmOe mOton	in good time	**shOmosshae pORa**	to run into problems

Spelling point: abbreviating words

When words are abbreviated, only the first few letters are kept and ঃ is written after them.

    সহঃ for: সহকারী **shOhokari**   অঃ for: অপু **opu**

Further examples are:

    মিঃ খান for: মিস্টার খান **misTar khan** Mr Khan
    ডাঃ সরদার for: ডাক্তার সরদার **Daktar shOrdar** doctor Sarder

The same symbol ঃ is sometimes used to signal a following long consonant, e.g. দুঃখিত **dukkhito** 'sorry'.

Grammar point: conditional sentences

Conditional sentences consist of two parts. The first part contains the word **jodi** 'if' – this word can come at the front but it often occurs as the second element of the sentence or even later:

jodi apnar flaiT carTae chaRe, tahole deRTae aste hObe.
If your flight leaves at four, then you have to come at 1.30.

flaiT jodi Dile hOe, amra apnake fon kore janabo.
If the flight is delayed, we will let you know by phone.

apnar aj shOmOe jodi na thake, tahole kalke fon korben.
If you do not have time today, then phone tomorrow.

The first part of the sentence usually has a verb in the present tense (**chaRe, hOe**). To make the verb negative, **na** is put in front of it, e.g. **jodi Dile na hOe** 'if there is no delay'.

The **jodi**-part of the sentence cannot contain **ache** (or **nei**) – instead, a form of **thaka** (or **na thaka**) must be used. It can also not be a perfect (of any verb). Instead, past participle plus **thaka** is used, e.g. **jodi ora eTa bole thake** (instead of **boleche**) 'if they have said so'.

The second part of a conditional sentence often starts with **tahole** 'then'.

Bengali also has unreal conditions – these describe situations that are hypothetical. They feature the habitual past tense in both sentence parts:

proshun jodi janto, tahole niscOe-i bolto.
If Proshun knew it, he would certainly say so.
or: If Proshun had known it, he would certainly have said so.

If the **jodi**-part is omitted, the result is sentences such as the following:

bhalo hoto. That would be good.
oke tumi ki bolte? What would you have said to him?

Exercise 1

Combine each of the sentence pairs into one sentence, using **jodi**. The first example would become:

apnar flaiT jodi rat dOshTae chaRe, tahole shaRe shatTae biman-bOndore aste hObe.

1 **apnar flaiT ki rat dOshTae chaRbe? tahole shaRe shatTae biman-bOndore aste hObe.**
2 **apni shOmOe mOton aste parben? tahole kono shOmossha hObe na.**
3 **apni amar kOtha bojhen na? tahole bolben.**
4 **apnar pasporT ache to? tahole kono cintar karon nei.**

Unit 14: *If the flight leaves at ten*

apnar pasporT ache to?

5 apni dilli hoe kolkatae jete can? tahole dillite kanekTing flaiT nite hObe.
6 apnar stri ki apnar shOnge jaben? tahole amader janaben.

Grammar point: conditional participle

Instead of using **jodi**, a conditional sentence can also be made using the conditional participle. This form always ends in **-le**, no matter what its subject is. Some examples:

amar kOtha na buhjle, bolben.	If you don't understand me, say so.
flaiT Dile hole, amra apnake janabo.	If the flight is delayed, we'll let you know.
amar Taka thakle ditam.	If I had money, I would give it.

The word **na** comes before the participle. There is no conditional participle of **ache** – instead **thakle** is used. If the sentence describes a hypothetical situation, the second part of the sentence has a habitual past tense.

The conditional participle has exactly the same form as the **tumi/ tomra** form of the simple past tense (see Unit 11):

Verbal noun	Conditional participle
kena	kinle 'if I/you/(s)he/we/they, etc. buy'
bikkri kOra	bikkri korle 'if I, etc. sell'
jawa	gele 'if I, etc. go'

Mini-exercise 1

Say: If I have time, I will go.
If you go, I will also go.
If Arif wants, he can also come.
If he is hungry, we'll go to a restaurant.

If **-o** is added to the participle, it means 'even if/though' (e.g. **kinleo** 'even if/though I/you, etc. buy it'). The same meaning can be expressed by **jodio** 'even if/though'.

brisTi poRleo, flaiT Thik shOmOe-i chaRlo
Though it rained, the flight left on time.

jodio brisTi pOrchilo, tobuo flaiT Thik shOmOe-i chaRlo
Though it rained, still the flight left on time.

Exercise 2

Several people ask you questions. Give each person an answer containing a condition. To sentence 1, you could reply:

jodi brisTi na hOe (or: **brisTi na hole**), **tomader baRite ashbo.**

1 apni ki kalke amader baRite ashben? (brisTi na hOwa)
2 apni ki agami mashe kolkatae jaben? (bimaner TikeT kinte para)
3 amake æk hajar Taka deben? (amar Taka thaka)
4 Onko nie amake shahajjo korben? (tumi na bojha)
5 ami ki Tibhi dekhte pari? (homwark shesh kore thaka)
6 amra aj ilish-mach khabo? (tumi khete cawa)

Dialogue 2 (Audio 2:51)

Opu, his wife Lila and their young son are on the plane. The stewardess comes to bring food. Do they get the food they ask for? Whose blanket does their son get – Opu's or Lila's?

Unit 14: *If the flight leaves at ten*

sTuwarDesh:	dOya kore apnar TebilTa khule patun. ebong cearTa shoja korun. apni ki khaben? ciken, bif na bhejiTarian?
opu:	bheji din. amar strir jonno-o æki Dish. amader baccaTar jonno dudh hObe?
sTuwarDesh:	Obossho-i hObe. baccar fiDarTa din. kicen theke gOrom dudh bhore ene dicchi.
opu:	dhonnobad. age amra nijera-i shOnge kore dudh-Tudh nie astam. ækhon nishedh hoe jawate ani ni. bæRano ager ce-e Onek koThin hoe gæche.
sTuwarDesh:	sori. baire jhOR shuru hoeche. apnader Tebilgulo bhãj kore felun. ebong siTbelT bẽdhe nin. jhOR shesh hole khabar poribeshon korbo.
lila:	ki hoeche? plenTa kãpche kæno?
opu:	bhOe peo na. ekTu jhOR boiche.
lila:	ami janalar pashe boshbo na. amake ailsiTe bOste dao. khokamoni amader majhkhaner siTe ghumate parbe.
opu:	Thik ache. kintu or kOmbolTa tomarTar ce-e Onek patla. tomarTa khokake dao.

Vocabulary

pata	to extend, spread	poribeshon	to distribute
hObe?	can you give/ arrange?	kOra	
		kãpa	to shake
fiDar	bottle	bOwa	to blow
bhOra	to fill	janala	window
shOnge kore	with us	pashe	next to (with possessive)
bhãj kOra	to fold (up)	khoka-moni	little boy (affectionate)
bãdha	to bind, fasten	kOmbol	blanket

Grammar point: comparisons

The following sentences express comparisons:

> **ei kOmbolTa oiTar ce-e patla.**
> This blanket is thinner than that one.

> **shunan tomar theke 2 inci lOmba.**
> Sunan is two inches taller than you.

anas shObce-e lOmba. Anas is tallest.
rakin o shunan shOman lOmba.
Rakin and Shunan are equally tall/Rakin is as tall as Shunan.
ke beshi lOmba, rakin na tumi? Who is taller, Rakin or you?

The word 'than' is **ce-e** (also: **ce**) or **theke**. They combine with a possessive form (**oiTar ce-e, tomar theke**). This combination is followed by the adjective (**oiTar ce-e patla, tomar theke lOmba**). The word **shObce-e** (lit.: than all) expresses superlative degree and **shOman** (lit.: equal) expresses identical degree (also: **æki shOman** and **æki rOkom**). The adjective usually has its basic form, but sometimes the word **beshi** 'more' is put in front of it (**beshi lOmba**).

And that is all you need to know in order to make comparisons.

bangla ingrejir ce Onek shoja, tai na?

Exercise 3

Use the following data to answer the questions below.

	bOyosh (age)	*uccota* (height)
opu	42	1 m 65 cm
Tipu	38	1 m 65 cm
kamal	78	1 m 50 cm
shujon	41	1 m 80 cm

1 **bORo** (= older) **ke, Tipu na shujon?**
2 **kamal opur ce lOmba? na opu kamaler ce lOmba?**
3 **ke shObce bORo?**
4 **shujon kamaler theke koto senTimiTar beshi lOmba?**
5 **kara æki shOman lOmba?**

Exercise 4

Compare Bengal with your own country, pointing out that:

1 rivers in Bengal are bigger
   (i.e. **banglar nodiguli amader desher nodigulir ce bOro**)
2 the weather (**abohawa**) in Bengal is hotter;
3 the trees (**gach**) in Bengal are taller;
4 Bengali politicians are equally (**æki rOkom**) clever;

Unit 14: *If the flight leaves at ten*

5 the food is hotter;
6 the language is easier.

Dialogue 3 (Audio 2:53)

*Opu, Lila and their son have arrived in Kolkata. A customs officer (**shulko kOrmokOrta**) asks them some questions. Next, Opu goes outside to try and find his sister. Does the **shulko kOrmokOrta** cause any problems for them? Why didn't Opu's sister come inside the airport building?*

শুঃ কঃ	–	ডিক্লার করার মতন কিছু আছে?
অঃ	–	না। আমাদের সঙ্গে যা আছে তা শুধুই আমাদের ব্যক্তিগত কাপড়-চোপড় ও আত্মীয়-স্বজনদের জন্য কিছু উপহার।
শুঃ কঃ	–	সিগারেট বা এ্যালকোহল সঙ্গে আছে? থাকলে আমদানী কর দিতে হবে।
অঃ	–	না। না। আমরা মদ-সিগারেট খাই না। তাই ওসব জিনিস আমাদের সঙ্গে নেই।
শুঃ	–	ঠিক আছে। আপানারা যেতে পারেন।
অঃ	–	লীলা, খোকাকে নিয়ে তুমি এখানে অপেক্ষা কর। আমি গিয়ে দেখছি দিদি এলেন কি না।
অঃ	–	এই ট্যাক্সি। যাবে নাকি?
ট্যাক্সিচালক	–	যে বাড়ীতে যাবেন, সে বাড়ীর ঠিকানাটা বলুন।
অঃ	–	দাঁড়ান। ঐতো ভীড়ের মধ্যে আমার দিদি দাঁড়িয়ে আছেন! এই দিদি– এদিকে তাকাও। আমি এখানে- তুমি বাইরে দাঁড়িয়ে কেন?
দিদি	–	ভিতরে লোকজনের ভীড় থাকাতে বাইরে দাঁড়িয়ে অপেক্ষা করছি। লীলা ও খোকাকে দেখছি না যে?
অঃ	–	ওরা ভেতরে আছে। আমি গিয়ে ওদের নিয়ে আসছি।

Vocabulary

Diklar kOra	to declare	**mOd**	booze
...mOton kichu	anything to ... (with verbal noun in possessive form)	**sigareT khawa**	to smoke cigarettes
		Tæksicalok	taxi-driver
kapoR-copoR	clothes and suchlike	**dãRano**	to stand
attio-shOjon	relatives	**dãRan!**	wait!
upohar	present	**oito**	there it/he/she is
amdani	import	**bhiR**	crowd

Grammar point: relative clauses

The following sentence contains a relative clause:

apni je baRite jaben, she baRir ThikanaTa bolun.
Tell me the address of the house that you are going to.

Such clauses are handy devices for packing a lot of information in one sentence. The sentence above literally says:

'to which house (**je baRite**) you are going,
that house's address (**she baRir Thikana**) tell (me)'

The first part of the sentence contains a noun identifying a person or thing ('the house that you are going to'). The noun (**baRi**) is preceded by the relative marker **je**. The second part of the sentence states the main point about that person or thing ('you must tell me its address'). The noun is repeated but now with the demonstrative **she** ('that') in front of it. The result is two linked sentence parts:

... **je baRi** ...   –   ... **she baRi** ...
(information to identify the house)   (main point about that house)

Other relative sentences are formed in the same way:

ora je jinishgulo kineche, she jinishgulo ækebare-i Oproyojonio.
The things that they have bought are completely unnecessary.
(lit.: which things they've bought, those things are completely unnecessary)

apni je shOhore thaken, amar didi-o she shOhore thaken.
My sister lives in the same city you are living in.
(lit.: in which city you live, my sister too lives in that city)

je lokTar shOnge kOtha bolte ce-echilam, she lokTa chilo na.
The person I wanted to talk to was not there.
(lit.: to which person I wanted to talk, that person was not there)

Mini-exercise 2

Say: The house that we have bought is new.
      The language I am learning is easy.
      I will show you the photos that I've taken.

If the repeated noun is very general in meaning (like **je jinishgulo** in the example above), it can be replaced by **ja** 'what'. The second part of the sentence then has **ta** 'that':

ora ja kineche, ta ækebare-i Oproyojonio.
What they have bought is completely unnecessary.

Exercise 5

Complete the dialogue. Use the words in the box:

| dukkhito | na | ni | jhOrer |
| flaiT | ja | din | bekti person |

- je _____ kalke kolkatae jacchen, she bektir shOnge kOtha bolte cai.
- accha - bolun. ami-i shei bekti. kintu _____ bolben, ta kalke bolte parben na? ækhon Onek rat hoe gæche (= *it's very late*).
- sori, sar. kintu apni je flaiT buk korechen, she _____ kænsel hoe gæche.
- she ki? age fon kOren _____ kæno? je _____ buking diechilam, she din apnar shOhokormi (= *colleague*) bolechilen je, 'cinta korben _____ - Dile ba kænsel hObe na.'
- ami khub _____, sar. kintu aj je rOkomer jhOR uTheche, she rOkomer (= *such a*) _____ moddhe biman chaRte parbe na.

Vocabulary point: cause and effect

Here are several useful ways of describing a cause and an effect:
(a) **kamal ei kajTa kOre ni. tai ami dukkho pe-echi.**
    Kamal hasn't done this work. Therefore I am sad.
(b) **ami dukkho pe-echi. karon kamal ei kajTa kOre ni.**
    I am sad because Kamal hasn't done this work.
(c) **kamal ei kajTa kOre ni bole ami dukkho pe-echi.**
    I am sad because Kamal hasn't done this work.
    (lit.: Kamal hasn't done this work - because - I'm sad)
(d) **kamal ei kajTa na kOrate/na kOrae ami dukkho pe-echi.**
    Because Kamal hasn't done this work, I am sad.

Sentence (a) has the word **tai** 'therefore'. Alternatives would be **she jonno** 'because of that' or **she karone** 'for that reason'.
   In sentence (b), **karon** means 'because'. The word **bole** in sentence (c) also means 'because' - but it follows the clause that describes the cause. Sentence (d) has a verbal noun with a locative ending (with **-te/-e**) - this also expresses a cause.

Exercise 6

Yesterday, Arif did not have a good day. Rephrase the sentences below, using the word **bole** to describe the causes of his unhappiness. The first sentence would become:

sharadin brisTi hocchilo bole arifer kharap lagchilo.

1 **sharadin brisTi howate arifer kharap lagchilo.**
2 **frije kono khabar chilo na. she jonno arifer mon kharap chilo.**
3 **khali frij dekhe tar hOtash lagchilo.**
4 **arifer mon kharap lagchilo. karon tar ma ranna kOre ni.**
5 **tar bon pæn-pæn kOrate arifer birokto lagchilo.**
6 **na khe-e skule jete arifer kOsTo lagchilo.** (use **jete hObe**)

Exercise 7

For all the sentences in Exercise 6, ask whether Arif would also have felt like that if the situation had been different. Use past habitual forms. Your first question could be:

brisTi jodi na hoto, taholeo (then too) **arifer kharap lagto?**
(if there had been no rain, would Arif have felt bad then too?)

Reading text – একটু হাসুন।

ছোট মামা সন্টুদের বাড়ীতে বেড়াতে এসে জিজ্ঞেস করলেন-
ছোটমামা – কিরে সন্টু, ফাইনাল পরীক্ষায় অংকে কত নম্বর পেয়েছিস?
সন্টু – দাদার থেকে মাত্র তিন নম্বর কম পেয়েছি, মামা।
ছোটমামা – তোর দাদা কত পেয়েছে?
সন্টু – তিন!
বলুন তো, অংকে সন্টু কত নম্বর পেয়েছে?

$$৩ - ৩ = ?$$

Vocabulary

-re	(expression of affection)	mattro	only
nOmbor	mark	kOm	less

15 নববর্ষে আর কী কী করা হয়?
nObobOrshe ar ki ki kOra hOe?

What else is done on New Year's Day?

In this unit you will learn how to:

- describe Bengali festivities
- describe activities without mentioning the agent
- make complex sentences

Dialogue 1 (Audio 2:54)

*Jenny has met Tipu in the market. Tomorrow is **pOela boishakh**, the first day of the Bengali year and Tipu wants to go to Shahrawardi Uddan, a big park in Dhaka. What are the main attractions of **pOela boishakh**?*

টিপু — আগামীকাল পয়লা বৈশাখ। আপনি আসছেন তো জেনিদি?
জেনি — পয়লা বৈশাখ? সেটা আবার কি?
টিঃ — কী বলছেন আপনি! আপনাকে তো বাংলা মাসের নামগুলি সব শিখিয়েছি! ভুলে গেছেন? বৈশাখ, জ্যৈষ্ঠ্য, আষাঢ় ইত্যাদি? পয়লা বৈশাখ হল বাংলা সনের প্রথম দিন – বাংলা নববর্ষ।

Unit 15: **nObobOrshe ar ki ki kOra hOe?**

জেঃ — হ্যাঁ মনে পড়ছে। আমি অবশ্যই আসবো।
টিঃ — খুব ভোরে আমরা সবাই মিলে সোহরাওয়ার্দী উদ্যানে যাবো। সেখানে প্রতি বছর খুব ঘটা করে নববর্ষ উদ্‌যাপন করা হয়।
জেঃ — নববর্ষে আর কী কী করা হয়?
টিঃ — সর্বত্র মেলা বসে। অনেক কিছু কেনা বেচা হয়। আর বিভিন্ন মঞ্চে চমৎকার সব নাটক মঞ্চস্থ করা হয়। পান্তা ভাতের আয়োজন হয়।
জেঃ — পান্তা-ভাত জিনিসটা আবার কি?
টিঃ — পান্তা-ভাত হল বাসি ভাত। আজকের রাঁধা ভাতে পানি দিয়ে রেখে আগামীকাল ভোরে খাবো। সেই সাথে ইলিশ মাছ ভাজা আর নানা রকমের ভর্তা। খুব ভোরে না আসলে কিন্তু কিছুই ভাগে পাবেন না।
জেঃ — ওমা! তাই নাকি? তাহলে আমি খুব ভোরেই আসবো।

Vocabulary

shOn	year	**naTok**	play
nObobOrsho	New Year	**mOncostho kOra**	to perform
ghOta kore	with great display	**panta bhat**	wet rice
udjapon kOra	to celebrate	**ayojon hOwa**	to be arranged
shOrbottro	everywhere	**bashi**	(left) overnight
mæla	fair	**bhāja**	fries
bOsha	to sit, to be held	**nana rOkomer**	of various types
kena	to buy	**bhOrta**	spicy mash
bæca	to sell	**bhage**	as your share
mOnco	stage		

Vocabulary point: Bengali months

The names of Bengali months are used especially for matters relating to traditional Bengali life and culture, such as **pOela boishakh**. The months span roughly the second half of one Western month and the first half of the following one. Two months together form one season (**ritu**), as follows:

Unit 15: *What else is done on New Year's Day?*

mash	shuru hOe	ritu
boishakh	mid April	grissho
joisTho	mid May	"
ashaRh	mid June	bOrsha
srabon	mid July	"
bhaddro	mid August	shOrot
asshin	mid September	"
kartik	mid October	hemonto
Oggrohayon/Ogghran	mid November	"
poush	mid December	shit
magh	mid January	"
falgun	mid February	bOshonto
coittro	mid March	"

Note the spelling of **ashaRh**: আষাঢ়. The ঢ় (a very rare letter) is pronounced like ড় **R** but followed by aspiration.

The names of the seasons can be followed by **kal** 'time': **grisshokal, bOrshakal** etc.

Specifying dates can be done in the same two ways as with English month names (Unit 12):

joisTher tin tarikh = **teshora joisTho** the 3rd day of **joisTho**
kartiker tæro tarikhe = **tæroi kartike** on the 13th of **kartik**

Exercise 1

Learn the words above and then test your knowledge.

1 apnar jOnmodin kon bangla mashe?
2 põcishe Disembor kon bangla mashe pORe?
3 ashaRh o srabon mashe bangladeshe Onek brisTi hOe – ei ritur nam ki?
4 bOshontokal ingreji kon kon mashe pORe?
5 asshiner age kon mash? o asshiner pOre kon mash?
6 grisshokal shitkaler ce-e gOrom? na shitkal grisshokaler ce-e gOrom?

Grammar point: the passive

In active sentences, the verb describes an action carried out by the subject of the sentence (the agent – underlined here).

shObai khub ghOTa kore nObobOrsho udjapon kOre.
Everyone celebrates New Year's Day with great display.

tara Onek kichu kineche.
They have bought a lot.

However, it is also possible to describe an activity without specifying the agent. This can be done by using a passive sentence, which in Bengali contains a verbal noun followed by a form of **hOwa** 'to be' (in the 3rd person). No agent is represented.

khub ghOTa kore nObobOrsho udjapon kOra hOe.
New Year's Day is celebrated with great display.

Onek kichu kena hoeche.
A lot has been bought.

To grasp this construction, it may initially be helpful to think of **hOwa** in a passive sentence as meaning 'to happen, to take place'. A literal translation of the examples would then be:

'celebrating New Year's Day happens/takes place with great display', and 'buying a lot has happened/taken place'.

Mini-exercise 1

Say: Everything has been bought.
This will be done tomorrow.
It was all eaten yesterday.
Here, New Year is celebrated in April.

If an active sentence has an object, it keeps its object form when the sentence is made passive. This is a big difference from English:

Active	Passive
pulishe take greftar korbe	**take greftar kOra hObe**
The police will arrest him	He will be arrested ('arresting him will happen')
she amake kono Taka dæe ni	**amake kono Taka dewa hOe ni**
He hasn't given me any money	I have not been given any money ('giving me any money has not happened')

Unit 15: *What else is done on New Year's Day?* 195

In the second example, **hOe ni** is used to make a negative perfect, following the general rule for this. Other rules for tense forms in passive sentences are also the same as in active sentences.

Because passive sentences do not specify who carries out the action, they are sometimes used to avoid making direct statements, for example:

> (to someone coming home with two full shopping bags:)
> **Onek kena hoeche, tai na** a lot has been bought, hasn't it?

> (to someone in a queue who inadvertently pushes you:)
> **amake dhakka dewa hocche** I am being pushed

Exercise 2

Ishita's uncle has a garments factory in Narayangonj. Six months ago he started a new fashion line and made a to-do list for this. His secretary now tells him how far they are. What does she say? Her first sentence would be: **shuciTa gOto nobhembor mashe toiri kOra hoeche**.

Original to-do list	*Secretary's update*
1 **shuci toiri kOra** (drawing up a timetable)	drawn up last November
2 **Dijain bibOroni toira kOra** (preparing a prospectus)	500 copies printed in January, 300 extra (= **aro 300**) copies now being printed (print = **chapano**)
3 **bibOroni kretader kache paThano** (sending prospectus to clients)	sent in March
4 **notun garmenTs sromik niyog kOra** (hiring new garment workers)	18 hired last year, 10 to be hired this month
5 **notun than-kapoR ODar dewa** (ordering new fabric)	ordered in December, arrived in February
6 **notun poshak pottrikae biggapon dewa** (advertising new garments in magazines)	advertised last month
7 **bideshi kretader kache ciThi paThano** (sending letter to foreign clients)	not sent yet; to be sent next week

Exercise 3

Here is an announcement taken from a newspaper. Unfortunately, the proofreader failed to notice that the four sentences are in jumbled order. Arrange them in the correct order. There is one verbal noun in the text which has passive meaning but is not accompanied by **hOwa**. Which is it?

এই প্রদর্শনীর জন্য তার কিছু আলোকচিত্রও নির্বাচিত করা হয়েছে। যেমন একটি চিত্রে আঁকা হয়েছে একটি বৃহৎ সাইজের ভাঙা কাপ। এই সব তৈলচিত্রে ও আলোকচিত্রে দেখানো হয়েছে সাধারণ মানুষের জীবনের সংস্কৃতি-সংগ্রামের চিত্র। ১লা বৈশাখে চারুকলা গ্যালারীতে সুমনের তৈলচিত্রের একক প্রদর্শনী করা হবে।

Vocabulary

prodorshoni	exhibition	**manush**	person
cittro	picture	**shOngskriti**	culture
alok-cittro	photo	**shOngram**	struggle
nirbacito kOra	to select	**carukOla**	art
ăka	to draw	**shumon**	Shumon (male name)
brihOt	enormous	**ekOk**	solo
toil-cittro	oil painting		

Grammar point: passives without hOwa

Besides the passive with **hOwa**, there is also a passive formed with **jawa**. This expresses possibility and means: 'something can/could be done'.

mælae Onek kichu kena jae.	In the fair a lot of things can be bought. (lit.: buying a lot of things goes)
oke fon kOra jeto	He could be phoned/We could phone him (lit.: phoning him would go)

You will hear this type of passive very frequently in spoken Bengali, whenever an (im)possibility is expressed. It can even be used with verbs that do not allow a passive in English:

ekhane ghumano jae na	It is impossible to sleep here (lit.: sleeping here does not go)
tar baRite ækbar jawa jeto	We could go to his house some time (lit.: going to his house would go)

# Unit 15: *What else is done on New Year's Day?*

> **Mini-exercise 2**
>
> Say: It can be done.
> We could tell him.
> The letter can be sent now
> It is impossible to say.

Bengali also has passive phrases which are like English 'a broken cup' or 'some rice cooked today'. They are made by simply putting the verbal noun in front of the word that it describes:

ækTa bhanga kap   a broken cup
ajker rādha bhat   rice cooked today (lit.: today's cooked rice)

The agent can be mentioned; it then has the possessive form:

babur lekha ciThi   a letter written by Babu

Exercise 4

Bidisha wants to buy a new phone. What are the questions that she asks Raju, the sales assistant?

raju: ei fonTa-i holo shObce adhunik, didi. ebong dame-o shOsta (= *cheap*).
bidisha: ...
raju: eTa die apni shara prithibite shObaike fon korte parben.
bidisha: ...
raju: pOncash hajar nOmbor memorite rakha jabe.
bidisha: ...
raju: pāc miniTer moddhe carj hoe jae. ebong carj kOra bæTari chOe mash bæbohar kOra jabe.
bidisha: ...
raju: amar kOtha nishcOe-i bisshash korte (= *believe*) paren, didi. karon kasTomarke ami kOkhono mittha kOtha bole ThOkai na.
bidisha: ...
raju: dukkhito, didi. amake khOma korben (= *excuse*). TesT kOrar jonno kretake kOkhono fon dewa hOe na. apnar pOchondo hole jinishTa nie jan. æto cOmotkar fon æto kOm dame apni ar kothae paben, bolun?

Dialogue 2 (Audio 2:57)

Jenny has come to Dipu's parents' home to celebrate Eid-ul-fitr, the Muslim feastday following the thirty-day fast of Ramadan (*rOmjan*). Also there is Anjona, who is a Hindu neighbour. Who has bought new clothes for Eid?

Tipu:	slamalaikum, jenidi. id mobarak.
jeni:	id mobarak, Tipu. ider dine shObai je bhabe notun shaRi pOre, she bhabe ami-o notun shaRi porechi. dekhecho?
Tipu:	hæ̃, kheal korechi. apnake porir mOton shundor lagche. Thik boli nai, Onjona boudi?
Onjona:	hæ̃! shaRite onake cOmotkar lagche! uni tomader shei bideshini otithi, tai na? poricOe korie debe na?
Tipu:	o, sori boudi. ini holen jeni, inglænD theke eshechen. ar jenidi, uni Onjona, amader protibeshi.
Onjona:	nOmoshkar. kæmon achen, didi?
jeni:	bhalo achi. bah apni-o dekhchi notun shaRi porechen!
Onjona:	hæ̃. ami pujar shOmOe jæmon shaRi kini, tæmon ider shOmOe-o kini.
jeni:	besh mOja to! apnar mOton onno shOb hindura-o ki ider shOmOe notun kapoR-copoR kenen?
Onjona:	na. ta nOe. tObe amra shObai mile æke Oporer anondo-utshObe jog di-i.
jeni:	shunte khub bhalo laglo. amader deshe æmonTa hOe na. jOkhon amra bORodin palon kori, tOkhon shudhu poribarer lokjon o khub ghonisTho bondhu-bandhobra ashen.
Tipu:	jenidi, apni ja bollen, ta shudhu iurope-i shOmbhOb. amader dharona jOto beshi lok, tOto beshi anondo.
jeni:	Thik bolecho. ei deshe eshe ami Onek kichu shikhlam.

Vocabulary

id mobarak	happy Eid!	bideshini	foreign (feminine form)
kheal kOra	to notice		
pori	fairy	otithi	guest
shundor lage	to look beautiful (impersonal)	poricOe kOrano	to introduce
		protibeshi	neighbour
boudi	wife of elder brother (or of male friend)	puja	Hindu feast
		æke Oporer	each other's
		utshOb	festivity

Unit 15: *What else is done on New Year's Day?* 199

æmonTa	something like that	lokjon	persons
bORodin	Christmas	ghonisTho	close
palon kOra	to celebrate	bondhu-bandhob	friends

Grammar point: complex sentences

In Unit 14 you learnt how to make relative clauses. The same method is used to form other types of complex sentences consisting of two parts, e.g.:

shObai je bhabe shaRi pOre, she bhabe ami-o shaRi porechi.
I have put on a sari too, just like everyone else puts one on.

jOto beshi lok, tOto beshi anondo.
The more people, the more enjoyment.

The main connecting idea is repeated (**je bhabe** – **she bhabe** and **jOto beshi** – **tOto beshi**) leading to formulations that literally mean:

'the way everyone puts on a sari, that way I too have put on a sari'
'the more a lot of people, the more a lot of enjoyment'

The pair **je** – **she** expresses the same identity (just like in relative sentences) and **jOto** – **tOto** expresses the same amount. These words do not have to come first in their clause. As the following examples show, English would use various different constructions.

je jaegae babul jae, she jaegae polTu jae.
Poltu goes wherever Babul goes.

upol je-i spiDe gaRi calae, she-i spiDe ami calate pari na.
I can't drive a car at such speed as Upol does.

arif jOto biskiT khae, tOto moTa hOe.
The more biscuits Arif eats, the fatter he becomes.

Mini-exercise 3

Say: I will go wherever you go (use **je jaegae**)
I want to play cricket the way you do (use **je bhabe**)
The more people come, the happier I will be.
I can't talk Bengali as well as I can talk English. (use **jOto bhalo bhabe**)

There are also several fixed pairs of words that are often used in this way to connect two clauses in a complex sentence:

jOkhon – tOkhon	when – then
jOtokkhon – tOtokkhon	as long – so long
jekhane – shekhane	where – there
jæmon – tæmon	how – so
jemni – temni	how – so

jOkhon id hOe, tOkhon gorib lokder notun kapoR dewa hOe.
When it is Eid, then poor people are given new clothes.

tumi jOtokkhon caibe, tomar Opekkhae tOtokkhon thakbo.
I'll wait for you as long as you want.

shaRiTa dekhte jæmon shundor, tæmon damTa-o cORa.
The sari is as beautiful to look at as its price is high.

This method of making complex sentences means that in Bengali, it is very easy to express correlations, where something happens in the same place, or at the same time or in the same manner as something else.

Exercise 5

Here are some Bengali proverbs and fixed sayings. Can you guess their meanings?

1 **jOtokkhon shash** (= breath), **tOtokkhon ash** (= hope).
2 **jOto gOrje** (= it thunders), **tOto bOrshe** (= it rains) **na**.
3 **jæmon gach, tæmon fOl**.
4 **je machTa palae** (= escapes), **sheTa bORo**.
5 **jemni bOla, temni kOra**.

jOto gOrje, tOto bOrshe na

Exercise 6

Match the sentence parts.

amra asha kori je (= we hope that)

1 jeni jOtokkhon bangladeshe thakbe
2 arif jekhane jabe
3 shonTu jOto beshi Onko shikhbe
4 rina je bhabe chattro-chattrider poRieche
5 rajkumar jOkhon tushar-kOnake cuma debe
6 apni amader shOnge bangla shikhe

a tOto beshi nOmbor pabe.
b she bhabe she bhobisshote-o pORabe.
c tOtokkhon anondo pabe.
d she tOkhon ghum theke jege uThbe (jaga = wake up).
e shekhane mOjar khabar thakbe.
f anondo pe-echen.

Reading text

Read the following newspaper review of a play performed on পয়লা বৈশাখ.

- Is the critic's final verdict positive or negative?

গতকালকে সুমন্ত রায়ের প্রথম লেখা নাটক 'ঐ দিনগুলি' মঞ্চস্থ করলো 'সুসময়' নাট্যগোষ্ঠী। নাটকের পাত্র-পাত্রীরা সবাই ভালো অভিনয় করেছেন। মঞ্চ সজ্জা ছিল মনোমুগ্ধকর। মঞ্চের একপাশে ছিল একটি ব্যস্ত মেলার দৃশ্য, অন্য পাশে ছিল একটা নিরিবিলি ঘর। কিন্তু, নাটকের নামকরণ যত সহজ, গল্প তত জটিল। যখন দর্শক মনে মনে ভাবছেন যে তারা গল্পটা বুঝতে পারছেন, ঠিক তখনই আবার অজানা অতীত থেকে নতুন চরিত্ররা উঠে আসছে। এর ফলে, নাট্যকারের বক্তব্য ঠিক বোঝা যায় নি। যাই হোক নব্য নাট্যকারের ভাষা, সংলাপ ও শব্দ চয়ন ছিল উপভোগ্য। পরিচালককে ধন্যবাদ দিতে হয় তার পরিচ্ছন্ন পরিচালনার জন্য। নাট্যশালায় প্রচণ্ড গরম থাকা সত্ত্বেও, দর্শকরা নাটকটি উপভোগ করেছেন।

Vocabulary

| naTTogosThi | acting company | obhinOe kOra | to act |
| pattro-pattri | actor and actress | mOnco shOjja | stage decoration |

monomugdhokor	very pleasing	jai hok	anyway, nevertheless
drissho	sight, scene		
niribili	quiet	nobbo	new
namkOron	title	shOnglap	dialogue
shOhoj	simple	shObdo cOyon	choice of words
joTil	complicated		
dOrshok	spectator	upobhoggo	enjoyable
Ojana	unknown	poricalok	director
otit	the past	poricchonno	neat, clean
coritro	character	poricalona	directing
fOle	as a result of (with possessive)	naTToshala	theatre
		shOtte-o	in spite of (with basic form)
naTTokar	playwright	upobhog kOra	to enjoy
bOktobbo	intention		

Transliterations of Bengali-script texts

Bengali script

Exercise 3

1 amar bon 2 amar pa 3 tomar bon 4 tomar mukh 5 or mukh 6 or bon 7 ma-baba 8 amma-abba

Exercise 6

tomar baba: ami anar khabo.
tomar ma: ami anar khabo na. ami am khabo.
æni: ami apel khabo.
tomar bon: ami anar khabo na. ami am khabo na. ami kOla khabo.
tumi: ...

Unit 1

Exercise 7

1 caci.
2 ekhane.
3 bormira.
4 tomar dada.
5 apnar chele.
6 ækTa nepali boi.
7 apnara kæmon achen?
8 amra khub bhalo achi.
9 tomar didi ki ekhane?
10 na. amar didi ækhon bharote.

Unit 2

Exercise 4

era, apnar, oke, tui, take, o, apnara, eke, tomake.

Exercise 9

bulbul: adab khalu. kæmon achen?
khalu: adab. ami bhalo achi. tumi kæmon acho?
bulbul: bhalo achi. khala kothae?
khalu: tomar khala baRite. tomar bhai bonra kothae?
bulbul: ora baire. amma-abba o baire gæchen.
khalu: accha. tahole ami ækhon jai. khoda hafej.
bulbul: khoda hafej.

Exercise 10

- ei chele, duiTa shOrbonamer udahOron dao.
- ke? ami?
- bah bah. khub bhalo to!

Unit 3

Exercise 8

1 tumi kothae thako?
2 Thik ache?
3 tomar baba ki ekhane?
4 ami ækhon jai?
5 uni ki khaben?
6 tomar kOeTa dokan ache?
7 kOejOn kOrmocari tomar dokane kaj kOre?

a hæ̃, tumi ækhon jao.
b amar nOeTa dokan ache.
c uni æk gelash pani (= waTar) khaben.
d ponero jOn kOrmocari kaj kOre.
e ami Dhakae thaki.
f na. uni baire.
g hæ̃, Thik ache.

Unit 4

Exercise 8

shangbadik: apni ki apnar deshke (= deshTa) bhalobashen?
rajnitibid: hæ̃. Obossho-i bhalobashi.

Transliterations of Bengali-script texts

shangbadik: tahole apnar Taka-pOesha shOb bideshi bænke rakhen kæno?
rajnitibid: na! na! apnar dharona Thik nOe. deshi bænke rakhi.
shangbadik: bah. apnar kOeTa ækaunT ache?
rajnitibid: chOeTa ækaunT ache. proti ækaunTe Onek Taka ache.
shangbadik: dhonnobad. desher jOnogOn poRe khushi hObe.

Unit 5

Reading text

gOto porshu amra Dhaka theke cOTTogram eshechi. amra base coRe eshechi. ekhane dui din beRiechi. gOtokalke amra gaRite coRe rangamaTi giechi. rangamaTi pahaRi elaka ebong dekhte khubi shundor. shekhane Onek upojatio lokjon bash kOre. elakaTa bangladesher ækebare purbo dike. amra rangamaTite eshe hatir piThe coRechi. amra kaptai lek dekhechi. shekhane amra Onek chobi tule-chi ebong Onek mOja korechi. tarpOre amra shondha-bælae cOTTograme fire eshechi.

Unit 6

Exercise 7

1 apnar amma ki bhalo ranna kOren? ar apnar abba?
2 apnar ki bacca ache?
3 apni ki kOkhono dilli ba cOTTograme giechen?
4 apni ki bangla nije nije shekhen? naki kono shikkhOker kache shekhen?
5 apni ækhon 'Dhaka' bolun. ebare 'dhakka' bolun. pãc miniT pOre abar bolben.

Unit 7

Exercise 8

    shukno bORa   æk rupi
    Dal-ruTi   tin rupi
    niramish poroTa   car rupi

khicuRi   aRai rupi
bhãja mach   tin rupi
TOk doi   deR rupi
guR ca   pOncash pOesha

Unit 8

Dialogue 1

dokandar: apnader ki cai?
kakima: adha keji holdi, æksho geram jira, ar æk poa gũRa dhonia din. bhalo shukna moric ache?
dokandar: hæ̃, ache. dækhen.
kakima: accha. shoa keji din.
dokandar: ar kichu lagbe?
kakima: hæ̃, ækhon mone poRche. shorishar tel lagbe. æk liTar din.
dokandar: ar kichu cacchen apnara?
kakima: narikeler dOrkar chilo. kintu–na. thak. amar bhai gram theke paThabe.
rifat: bashae kOla nei, kakima. amaderke æk dOjon kOla din.
dokandar: æk hali shagor kOlar dam tirish Taka. shOb milie aTsho collish Taka ar ashi pOesha din. dhonnobad. abar ashben.

Exercise 3

1 apni _____ bajare jaben, kakima? – ekTu pOre jabo.
2 bajare _____ kinben?   – cal-Dal ada-roshun kinbo.
3 ami ashbo? naki _____?   – tumi ekhane thako.
4 ekhane _____ korbo?   – tumi Tebil banio. chOeTae mehman ashbe.
5 tai naki? _____ dawat diechen?   – tomar mama-mami, khala-khalu, bondulabhai ashben.

Exercise 4

ækTa boi o ækTa khata nin. khataTa boier nice rakhun. boier upore ækTa kOlom rakhun. ar ækTa boi nin. ækhon khataTa boigulor majhkhane rakhun. ar ækTa kOlom nin. oi kOlomTa khatar upore

Transliterations of Bengali-script texts

rakhun. ækhon apni ghOrer baire jan. dOsh sekenD pOre abar ghOrer bhitore ashben. ækhon bolun: khataTa o boiguli kothae?

Exercise 6

1 lungi – nil 20Ta, shobuj 10Ta.
2 shaRi – shobuj 8Ta, badami 5Ta, lal 3Ta, golapi 4Ta.
3 salwar kamij – shada 4 seT, nil 3 seT.
4 sharT – shada 11Ta, nil 7Ta, shobuj 9Ta.

Reading texts

dudhwala: ami khoriddar ThOkai na. dudhe pani mishai Thik-i, kintu mape kOm dei na.
cal bikkreta: ami-o na. tin poa cale æk poa kãkor mishale, æk sher hOe kina, tumi-i bOlo, bhai?

shangbadik: mæDam, apnar bOyosh koto?
naika: dukkhito. ami shOb shOmOe-e aenar dike takai. kælenDarer dike na.

Unit 9

Reading text

projojok: amra shudhu namkOra lekhok cai. notun lekhok nei na.
lekhok: Thik ache. tahole amar chOddonamTa bæbohar korun.
projojok: apnar chOddonamTa ki?
lekhok: robindronath Thakur.

Unit 10

Reading text

gOtokal shondha shaRe shatTae narayongOnje ækTa bhOeabOho bhumikOmpo hoeche. bhOe-e bohu mohila o shishura Oggæn hoe gæche. tarpOr-i shuru holo procOnDo jhOR-brisTi. ThanDae bohulok Oshushto hoe poReche. kichu kichu rasta-ghaT bhenge gæche. aj dupure Tæksite coRe Disi shaheber stri ghOTonasthOle eshechilen. tini Olpo kichu shahajjo diechen. bohu mulloban sthapotto nOsto hoe gieche. æmon bhumikOmpo loke age kOkhono dækhe ni.

Unit 11

Exercise 4

gOtolkalke rOmnae ækTa bikkhobh michil chilo. michile onnanno dOsh-baroTa dOl jog dilo. pãcjOn neta netritto dilen. tãder pechone hajar hajar lokjon chilo. shObai slogan dite dite pres-klaber shamne elo. shekhane eshe tara netader boktrita shunlo. tarpOre bibhinno dOler kormira presiDenT-bhObone jete sthir korlo. kintu pOthe pulish kormider badha dilo. tOkhon pulish o michilkarider moddhe shOngghOrsho shuru holo. ebong kOe-ækjOn netake greftar korlo. shondhar dike pulish shOb rasta theke michilkarider shorie dilo.

Reading text

borgi elo deshe

khoka ghumalo, paRa juRalo.
borgi elo deshe.
bulbulite dhan khe-eche.
khajna debo? ki she!
dhan furalo, pan furalo.
khajnar upae ki?
ar kOTa din shobur koro.
roshun bunechi.

Unit 12

Exercise 7

1 æk miniTe kOe sekenD?
2 shaRe tin ghOnTae kOe miniT?
3 æk dOshoke kOe mash?
4 æk shoTabdite kOe dOshok?
5 Disembor masher koto tarikhe krismas?
6 kon tarikhTa age? OkToborer cobbish tarikh? na chabbishe OkTobor?
7 kon tarikhTa age? me masher couddo tarikh? na couTha me?

Reading text

sobhiet rashiyar amole ækjOn markin shikkhOk rashiyar kono ekTi skule Onko kOraten. ækdin klashe Onko bojhate gie tini jiggesh korlen:

ns of Bengali-script texts

shikkhOk: bOlo to, pãc rubole ækjoRa moja kine jodi ami bish rubole bikkri kori, tObe ami ki pabo?
chattro: saiberiyae shat bOchor!

Unit 13

Reading text

nirbacone jOe labh kOrar pOre prodhanmontrir shakkhatkar nite elen shangbadikra.

shangbadik: montri porishOd gOThon kOrar age nishcOe-i karo pOramOrsho neben?
prodhanmontri: Obossho-i! kintu amar strike abar er moddhe Tene anchen kæno?

Unit 14

Dialogue 1

opu: hælo. ami opu ganguli bolchi. ami apnader kompanir bimane agamikalker flaiTe kolkata jacchi.
shOhokari: ji, bolun.
opu: shunechi idaning antorjatik flaiTe nirapOttar karone Onek cek hOe. flaiT dOshTae chaRle kOTae riporT korte hObe?
shOhokari: Diparcarer aRai ghOnTa age riporT korben. shOmOe mOton jodi põuchate paren, tahole cintar kichu nei.
opu: inTarneTer maddhome cek-in kOrar cesTa korechilam. kintu borDing-pasTa prinT korte pari ni.
shOhokari: sori sar. ei muhurte amader websaiTe ekTu DisTarb ache. jodi aj cek-in korte na pere thaken, tahole kalke bimanbOndore korte parben.
opu: accha. infOrmeshon debar jonno dhonnobad.
shOhokari: apnake-o dhonnobad. bimanbOndore shOmosshae poRle, amader ofishe jogajog korben.

Dialogue 3

shulko kOrmokOrta: Diklar kOrar mOton kichu ache?
opu: na. amader shOnge ja ache, ta shudhu-i amader bektigOto kapoR-copoR o attio-shOjonder jonno kichu upohar.

shulko
kOrmokOrta: sigareT ba ælkohol shOnge ache? thakle amdani kOr dite hObe.
opu: na, na. amra mOd-sigareT khai na. tai oshOb jinish amader shOnge nei.
shulko
kOrmokOrta: Thik ache. apnara jete paren.
opu: lila, khokake nie tumi ekhane Opekkha kOro. ami gie dekhchi didi elen ki na.

---

opu: ei Tæksi. jabe naki?
Tæksicalok: je baRite jaben, she baRir ThikanaTa bolun.
opu: dãRan. oito bhiRer moddhe amar didi dãRie achen! ei didi – edike takao. ami ekhane. tumi baire dãRie kæno?
didi: bhitore lokjoner bhiR thakate baire dãRie Opekkha korchi. lila o khokake dekhchi na je?
opu: ora bhitore ache. ami gie oder nie ashchi.

Reading text

choTo mama shonTuder baRite bæRate eshe jiggesh korlen:

choTomama: kire shonTu, fainal porikkhae Ongke koto nOmbor pe-echish?
shonTu: dadar theke mattro tin nOmbor kOm pe-echi, mama.
choTotmama: tor dada koto pe-eche?
shonTu: tin.

bolun to, Ongke shonTu koto nOmbor pe-eche?

Unit 15

Dialogue 1

Tipu: agamikal pOela boishakh. apni ashchen to, jenidi?
jeni: pOela boishakh? sheTa abar ki?
Tipu: ki bolchen apni! apnake to bangla masher namguli shOb shikhiechi! bhule gæchen? boishakh, joisTho, ashaRh, ittadi? pOela boishakh holo bangla shOner prothom din – bangla nObobOrsho.
jeni: hæ̃, mone poRche. ami Obossho-i ashbo.

Transliterations of Bengali-script texts

Tipu: khub bhore amra shObai mile shohrawardi uddane jabo. shekhane proti bOchor khub ghoTa kore nObobOrsho udjapon kOra hOe.
jeni: nObobOrshe ar ki ki kOra hOe?
Tipu: shOrbottro mæla bOshe. Onek kichu kena bæca hOe. ar bibhinno mOnce cOmotkar shOb naTok mOncostho kOra hOe. panta bhater ayojon hOe.
jeni: panta-bhat jinishTa abar ki?
Tipu: panta-bhat holo bashi bhat. ajker rãdha bhate pani die rekhe agamikal bhore khabo. shei shathe ilish mach bhãja ar nana rOkomer bhOrta. khub bhore na ashle kintu kichu-i bhage paben na.
jeni: oma! tai naki? tahole ami khub bhore-i ashbo.

Exercise 3

ei prodorshonir jonno tar kichu alokcittro-o nirbacito kOra hoeche. jæmon ekTi cittre ãka hoeche ekTi brihOt saijer bhanga kap. ei shOb toilcittre o alokcittre dækhano hoeche shadharon manusher jiboner shOngskriti-shOngramer cittro. pOela boishakhe carukOla gælarite shumoner toilcittrer ekOk prodorshoni kOra hObe.

Reading text

gOtokalke shumonto rae-er prothom lækha naTok 'oi dinguli' mOncostho korlo 'shushOmOe' naTTogosThi. naToker pattropattrira shObai bhalo obhinOe korechen. mOnco shOjja chilo monomugdhokor. mOncer ækpashe chilo ekTi bæsto mælar drissho, onno pashe chilo ækTa niribili ghOr. kintu naToker namkOron jOto shOhoj, gOlpo tOto joTil. jOkhon dOrshok mone mone bhabchen je tara gOlpoTa bujhte parchen, Thik tOkhon-i abar Ojana otit theke notun coritrora uThe ashche. er fOle naTTokarer bOktobbo Thik bojha jae ni. jai hok, nobbo naTTokarer bhasha, shOnglap, o shObdo cOyon chilo upobhoggo. poricalokke dhonnobad dite hOe tar poricchonno poricalonar jonno. naTToshalae procOnDo gOrom thaka shOtte-o dOrshokra naTokTi upobhog korechen.

Bengali script – summary

Vowels

Spelling after consonant	Spelling elsewhere	Sound
া	আ	a
ি	ই	i
ী	ঈ	i
ু	উ	u
ূ	ঊ	u
ো	ও	o
not written	অ	O (but sometimes o)
ৈ	ঐ	oi
ৌ	ঔ	ou
ে	এ	e (but sometimes æ)
া/য	এ্যা	æ

Consonants

ক	k	খ	kh	গ	g	ঘ	gh	ঙ/ং	ng
চ	c	ছ	ch	জ	j	ঝ	jh		
ত/ৎ	t	থ	th	দ	d	ধ	dh	ন	n
প	p	ফ	f	ব	b	ভ	bh	ম	m
ট	T	ঠ	Th	ড	D	ঢ	Dh	ণ	n
হ	h	ল	l	য	j				
র	r	ড়	R	ঢ়	Rh				
শ	sh	স	sh	ষ	sh				
য়	e/y								

্র	r (after consonant)	ঁ	(written above a vowel to indicate that the vowel is nasalised)
র্	r (before consonant)		
ঋ	ri (word-initial)	এঁ	(written before a vowel to indicate that the vowel is nasalised)
ৃ	ri (after consonant)		

Bengali script – summary

Conjunct consonants

ক + ক = ক্ক	kk
চ + চ = চ্চ	cc
জ + জ = জ্জ	jj
ট + ট = ট্ট	TT
ড + ড = ড্ড	DD
ত + ত = ত্ত	tt
দ + দ = দ্দ	dd
ন + ন = ন্ন	nn
প + প = প্প	pp
ব + ব = ব্ব	bb
ম + ম = ম্ম	mm
ল + ল = ল্ল	ll
গ + ু = গু	gu
শ + ু = শু	shu
হ + ু = হু	hu
র + ু = রু	ru
র + ৃ = রৃ	ru
হ + ৃ = হৃ	hri
ক + ল = ক্ল	kl
প + ল = প্ল	pl
ম + ল = ম্ল	ml
গ + ন = গ্ন	gn
ত + ন = ত্ন	tn
ধ + ব = ধ্ব	dh
জ + ব = জ্ব	j
স + ব = স্ব	sh (word-initial)
	ssh (word-medial)
হ + ব = হ্ব	bb
শ + ম = শ্ম	sh
দ + ম = দ্ম	dd plus nasal vowel
ন + ম = ন্ম	nm
ক + ত = ক্ত	kt
ন + ত = ন্ত	nt
স + ত = স্ত	st
ত + থ = ত্থ	tth
ন + থ = ন্থ	nth
স + থ = স্থ	sth
ন + দ = ন্দ	nd

Bengali script – summary

ব + দ = ব্দ	bd
দ + ধ = দ্ধ	ddh
ন + ধ = ন্ধ	ndh
ব + ধ = ব্ধ	bdh
ত + ্র = ত্র	tr
ক + ্র = ক্র	kr
চ + ছ = চ্ছ	cch
স + প = স্প	shp
ক + স = ক্স	ksh
খ + ষ = ক্ষ	kkh (but **kh** word-initially)
ষ + ক = ষ্ক	shk
ষ + ট = ষ্ট	sT
ষ + ণ = ষ্ণ	shn
ল + প = ল্প	lp
ল + ট = ল্ট	lT
ম + প = ম্প	mp
ম + ভ = ম্ভ	mbh
ন + ত = ন্ত	nt
ণ + ট = ণ্ট	nT
ণ + ঠ = ণ্ঠ	nTh
ণ + ড = ণ্ড	nD
ঙ + গ = ঙ্গ	ng
জ + ঞ = জ্ঞ	gg
জ্ঞা	gæ̃
ঞ + চ = ঞ্চ	nc
ঞ + জ = ঞ্জ	nj
ত + র + ু = ত্রু	tru
দ + র + ু = দ্রু	dru
ভ + র + ু = ভ্রু	bhru
শ + র + ু = শ্রু	sru
ন + ত + র = ন্ত্র	ntr
ষ + ট + র = ষ্ট্র	str
স + ত + র = স্ত্র	str
জ + জ + ব = জ্জ্ব	jj
ত + ত + ব = ত্ত্ব	tt
ন + দ + ব = ন্দ্ব	nd

Bengali script – summary

Special sign	Name	Meaning
্য	jO-fOla	preceding consonant is long
্	hOshonto	preceding consonant is not followed by inherent vowel
।	dāRi	full stop

Numbers

Cardinal numbers

When they are part of an ordinary sentence, the cardinal numbers of Bengali are usually followed by **-Ta** or **-Ti** (but **-jOn** for people):

duiTa boi	**tinTi puTul**	**dOshjOn chattro**
two books	three dolls	ten students

0	০	shunno	শূন্য
1	১	æk	এক
2	২	dui	দুই
3	৩	tin	তিন
4	৪	car	চার
5	৫	pãc	পাঁচ
6	৬	chOe	ছয়
7	৭	shaT	সাত
8	৮	aT	আট
9	৯	nOe	নয়
10	১০	dOsh	দশ
11	১১	ægaro	এগারো
12	১২	baro	বারো
13	১৩	tæro	তের
14	১৪	couddo	চৌদ্দ
15	১৫	ponero/ponoro	পনের/পনর
16	১৬	sholo	ষোল
17	১৭	shOtero/shOtoro	সতের/সতর
18	১৮	aTharo	আঠারো
19	১৯	unish	উনিশ
20	২০	bish/kuRi	বিশ/কুড়ি
21	২১	ekush	একুশ
22	২২	baish	বাইশ
23	২৩	teish	তেইশ

Numbers

24	২৪	cobbish	চব্বিশ
25	২৫	põcish	পঁচিশ
26	২৬	chabbish	ছাব্বিশ
27	২৭	shatash	সাতাশ
28	২৮	aTash	আটাশ
29	২৯	untrish	উনত্রিশ
30	৩০	tirish/trish	তিরিশ/ত্রিশ
31	৩১	æktrish	একত্রিশ
32	৩২	bottrish	বত্রিশ
33	৩৩	tettrish	তেত্রিশ
34	৩৪	coutrish	চৌত্রিশ
35	৩৫	põetrish	পঁয়ত্রিশ
36	৩৬	chOttrish	ছত্রিশ
37	৩৭	shãitrish/shattrish (E)	সাঁইত্রিশ/সাতত্রিশ
38	৩৮	aTtrish	আটত্রিশ
39	৩৯	unocollish	উনচল্লিশ
40	৪০	collish	চল্লিশ
41	৪১	ækcollish	একচল্লিশ
42	৪২	biallish	বিয়াল্লিশ
43	৪৩	tetallish	তেতাল্লিশ
44	৪৪	cuallish	চুয়াল্লিশ
45	৪৫	põetallish	পঁয়তাল্লিশ
46	৪৬	checollish	ছেচল্লিশ
47	৪৭	shatcollish	সাতচল্লিশ
48	৪৮	aTcollish	আটচল্লিশ
49	৪৯	unopOncash	উনপঞ্চাশ
50	৫০	pOncash	পঞ্চাশ
51	৫১	ækanno	একান্ন
52	৫২	bahanno	বাহান্ন
53	৫৩	tepanno	তেপান্ন
54	৫৪	cuanno	চুয়ান্ন
55	৫৫	pOncanno	পঞ্চান্ন
56	৫৬	chappanno	ছাপ্পান্ন
57	৫৭	shatanno	সাতান্ন
58	৫৮	aTanno	আটান্ন
59	৫৯	unoshaT	উনষাট
60	৬০	shaT (or shaiT E)	ষাট
61	৬১	ækshoTTi	একষট্টি
62	৬২	bashoTTi	বাষট্টি
63	৬৩	teshoTTi	তেষট্টি
64	৬৪	coushoTTi	চৌষট্টি

65	৬৫	põeshoTTi	পঁয়ষট্টি
66	৬৬	cheshoTTi	ছেষট্টি
67	৬৭	shatshoTTi	সাতষট্টি
68	৬৮	aTshoTTi	আটষট্টি
69	৬৯	unoshOttor	ঊনসত্তর
70	৭০	shOttor	সত্তর
71	৭১	ækattor	একাত্তর
72	৭২	bahattor	বাহাত্তর
73	৭৩	teattor/tiattor	তেয়াত্তর/তিয়াত্তর
74	৭৪	cuattor	চুয়াত্তর
75	৭৫	põcattor	পঁচাত্তর
76	৭৬	chiattor	ছিয়াত্তর
77	৭৭	shatattor	সাতাত্তর
78	৭৮	aTattor	আটাত্তর
79	৭৯	uno-ashi	ঊনআশি
80	৮০	ashi	আশি
81	৮১	ækashi	একাশি
82	৮২	birashi	বিরাশি
83	৮৩	tirashi	তিরাশি
84	৮৪	curashi	চুরাশি
85	৮৫	põcashi	পঁচাশি
86	৮৬	chiashi	ছিয়াশি
87	৮৭	shatashi	সাতাশি
88	৮৮	OsTashi/aTashi (E)	অষ্টাশি/আটাশি
89	৮৯	unonobboi	ঊননব্বই
90	৯০	nobboi	নব্বই
91	৯১	ækanobboi	একানব্বই
92	৯২	biranobboi	বিরানব্বই
93	৯৩	tiranobboi	তিরানব্বই
94	৯৪	curanobboi	চুরানব্বই
95	৯৫	põcanobboi	পঁচানব্বই
96	৯৬	chianobboi	ছিয়ানব্বই
97	৯৭	shatanobboi	সাতানব্বই
98	৯৮	aTanobboi	আটানব্বই
99	৯৯	niranobboi	নিরানব্বই
100	১০০	æk shOto/æksho	একশত/একশ
1,000	১,০০০	æk hajar	এক হাজার
100,000	১,০০,০০০	æk lakh/æk lokkho	এক লাখ/এক লক্ষ
10,000,000	১,০০,০০,০০০	æk koTi	এক কোটি

Ordinal numbers

For the ordinal numbers used in dates (e.g. 1st of May **pOela me**, 16th of December **sholoi Disembor**), see Unit 12.

Outside dates, another set of ordinals is used. Some examples are:

tritio din	**shOptom srenite**	**ekobingshotitOmo shOtabdi**
the third day	in the seventh class	the 21st century

This set has the following words for 1st to 25th:

1st	১ম	prothom	প্রথম
2nd	২য়	ditio	দ্বিতীয়
3rd	৩য়	tritio	তৃতিয়
4th	৪র্থ	coturtho	চতুর্থ
5th	৫ম	pOncom	পঞ্চম
6th	৬ষ্ঠ	shOsTho	ষষ্ঠ
7th	৭ম	shOptom	সপ্তম
8th	৮ম	OsTom	অষ্টম
9th	৯ম	nObom	নবম
10th	১০ম	dOshom	দশম
11th	১১শ	ækadOsh	একাদশ
12th	১২শ	dadOsh	দ্বাদশ
13th	১৩শ	trOyodOsh	ত্রয়োদশ
14th	১৪শ	coturdOsh	চতুর্দশ
15th	১৫শ	pOncodOsh	পঞ্চদশ
16th	১৬শ	shoRosh	ষোড়শ
17th	১৭শ	shOptodOsh	সপ্তদশ
18th	১৮শ	OsTadOsh	অষ্টাদশ
19th	১৯শ	unobingsho	ঊনবিংশ
20th	২০শ	bingsho	বিংশ
21th	২১তম	ekobingshotitOmo	একবিংশতিতম
22th	২২তম	dabingshotitOmo	দ্বাবিংশতিতম
23th	২৩তম	trOyobingshotitOmo	ত্রয়োবিংশতিতম
24th	২৪তম	coturbingshotitOmo	চতুর্বিংশতিতম
25th	২৫তম	pOncobingshotitOmo	পঞ্চবিংশতিতম

Another common method for expressing ordinals is to use the cardinal number followed by the word **nOmbor**:

car nOmbor dokane	**tar baro nOmbor chele**	**bish nOmbor gaRi**
in the fourth shop	her twelfth son	the twentieth car

Fractions

¼	১/৮	shiki	সিকি
½	১/২	adha/Ordhek	আধা/অর্ধেক
¾	৩/৮	poune æk	পৌনে এক
1¼	১ ১/৮	shoa æk	সোয়া এক
1½	১ ১/২	deR	দেড়
1¾	১ ৩/৮	poune dui	পৌনে দুই
2¼	২ ১/৮	shoa dui	সোয়া দুই
2½	২ ১/২	aRai	আড়াই
3½	৩ ১/২	shaRe tin	সাড়ে তিন
4½	৪ ১/২	shaRe car	সাড়ে চার
	etc.		

Bengali grammar – summary

Personal pronouns

	Subject	Possessive	Object
sing. 'I'	ami	amar	amake
'you' (familiar)	tumi	tomar	tomake
'you' (polite)	apni	apnar	apnake
'you' (intimate)	tui	tor	toke
'he/she' (close by)	e	er	eke
'he/she' (far off)	o	or	oke
'he/she' (other)	she	tar	take
plur. 'we'	amra	amader	amader
'you' (familiar)	tomra	tomader	tomader
'you' (polite)	apnara	apnader	apnader
'you' (intimate)	tora	toder	toder
'they' (close by)	era	eder	eder
'they' (far off)	ora	oder	oder
'they' (other)	tara	tader	tader

	Subject	Possessive	Object
polite sing.			
'he/she' (close by)	ini	enar/ẽr	enake/ẽke
'he/she' (far off)	uni	onar/õr	onake/õke
'he/she' (other)	tini	tãr	tãke
polite plur.			
'they' (close by)	enara/ẽra	enader/ẽder	enader/ẽder
'they' (far off)	onara/õra	onader/õder	onader/õder
'they' (other)	tãra	tãder	tãder

Interrogative pronoun 'who'

	Subject	Possessive	Object
singular	ke	kar	kake
plural	kara	kader	kader

Indefinite pronoun 'anybody'

Subject	Possessive	Object
keu	karo/karur	kauke/kakeo

Reflexive pronoun 'myself/yourself/himself' etc.

	Subject	Possessive	Object
singular	nije	nijer	nijeke
plural	nijera	nijeder	nijeder(ke)

Inanimate nouns

a(n)	ækTa, ækTi
the	-Ta/-Ti (singular)
	-gulo/-guli/-gula (E) (plural)
's/of	-er/-r (possessive)
in, at, on, to	-e/-te (locative)

Bengali grammar – summary

Personal nouns

a(n) ækjOn

	Subject	Possessive	Object
singular	bon 'sister'	boner	bonke
plural	bonra	bonder	bonder(ke)

Verbs

Verbal noun

Consists of verb stem plus **-a** (**-wa** if stem ends in a vowel) or **-ano**:

kOr-a 'do', **dho-wa** 'wash', **ghum-ano** (also: **ghumono** W) 'sleep'.

Possessive ends in **-r**:

kOra-r, dhowa-r, ghumano-r

Locative ends in **-e** or **-te**; verbs like **ghumano** use past participle plus **thaka**:

kOrae/kOrate, dhowae/dhowate, ghumie thakae/ghumie thakate

Simple present tense

ami/amra   kori
tumi/tomra   kOro
tui/tora   korish
e/o/she/era/ora/tara   kOre
apni/ini/uni/tini/
apnara/ẽra/enara/õra/onara/tãra   kOren

Stem vowel changes: **O** becomes **o**
                        o becomes **u**
                        æ becomes **e**
                        e becomes **i**.

In the simple present, these changes take place only in the **ami** and **tui** forms.

If the stem ends in a vowel, **-ish** is reduced to **-sh** and **-en** to **-n**:

tui dhush, apni dhon.

Irregular simple present tense of **newa** 'take' (and **dewa** 'give'):

ami	ni-i, nei (E)
tumi	nao
tui	nish
she	næe
apni	næn

Present progressive tense

ami	korchi
tumi	korcho
tui	korchish
she	korche
apni	korchen

Vowel changes: O > o, o > u, æ > e, e > i (but a remains)

If the stem ends in a vowel, the ending has **-cch-**:

ami dhucchi, tumi dhuccho, tui dhucchish, she dhucche, apni dhucchen

Simple past tense

ami	korlam (also **korlum** W)
tumi	korle (also **korla** colloquial E)
tui	korli
she	korlo
apni	korlen

The stem vowel changes: O>o, o>u, æ>e, e>i

Stem vowel **a** changes to **e** only if the stem ends in **a** (e.g. **khawa** 'eat'):

khelam

But **gawa** and **cawa** add **i**:

gailam, cailam

Verbs in **-ano**:

> **ami ghumalam, tumi ghumale, tui ghumali, she ghumalo, apni ghumalen**

Irregular simple past tense of **jawa** 'go' and **asha** 'come':

> **ami gelam, tumi gele, tui geli, she gælo, apni gelen.**
> **ami elam, tumi ele, tui eli, she elo, apni elen** (but in E also **ashlam, ashle**, etc.)

Past progressive tense

ami	korchilam (also korchilum W)
tumi	korchile (also korchila colloquial E)
tui	korchili
she	korchilo
apni	korchilen

Vowel changes: **O > o, o > u, æ > e, e > i** (but **a** remains)

If stem ends in a vowel, ending has **-cch-**:

> **ami dhucchilam, tumi dhucchile, tui dhucchili, she dhucchilo, apni dhucchilen**

Past habitual tense

ami	kortam (also kortum W)
tumi	korte (also korta colloquial E)
tui	korti
she	korto
apni	korten

The stem vowel changes: **O>o, o>u, æ>e, e>i**

Stem vowel **a** changes to **e** only if the stem ends in **a** (e.g. **khawa** 'eat'):

> **khetam**

But **gawa** and **cawa** add **i**:

> **gaitam, caitam**

Verbs in **-ano**:

> ami ghumatam, tumi ghumate, tui ghumati, she ghumato, apni ghumaten

Present perfect tense

> ami korechi
> tumi korecho
> tui korechish
> she koreche
> apni korechen

Stem vowel changes: **a > e, O > o, o > u, æ > e, e > i**

Irregular present perfect tense of **jawa** 'go':

> ami giechi, tumi giecho, tui giechish, she gieche, apni giechen. (colloquially: **ami gechi, tumi gæcho, she gæche, tui gechish, apni gæchen**)

Verbs ending in **-ano**:

> ami ghumiechi, tumi ghumiecho, tui ghumiechish, she ghumieche, apni ghumiechen

In first syllable of such verbs: **e>i, O>o**:

> **ami shikhiechi** etc. (from **shekhano**), **ami poRiechi** (from **pORano**)

Past perfect tense

> ami korechilam (also **korchilum** W)
> tumi korechile (also **korechila** colloquial E)
> tui korechili
> she korechilo
> apni korechilen

All the forms are identical to the first person of the present perfect (**korechi**) with the following endings added: **-lam, -le, -li, -lo, -len**.

Future tense

ami korbo
tumi korbe
tui korbi
she korbe
apni korben

Stem vowel changes: **O** > **o**, **o** > **u**, **æ** > **e**, **e** > **i** (but stem vowel **a** remains)

Future tense of **gawa** 'sing' and **cawa** 'want':
ami gaibo, tumi gaibe, tui gaibi, she gaibe, apni gaiben
ami caibo, tumi caibe, tui caibi, she caibe, apni caiben

Imperative

Present imperative (for commands meant to be carried out immediately):

(tumi/tomra) kOro!
(tui/tora) kOr!
(apni/apnara) korun! (E also: kOren!)
(she/tara) koruk!

Vowel change before **-un** and **-uk**: **O**>**o**, **æ**>**e**, **e**>**i**, **o**>**u**.

If the stem ends in a vowel, **-un** is reduced to **-n** (without vowel change) and **-uk** to **-k** (with vowel change).

Irregular present imperative of **asha** 'come':

(tumi) esho! (E also asho!)
(tui) ae!
(apni) ashun! (E also ashen!)
(she) ashuk!

Future imperative (for commands meant to be carried out at a later point):

(tumi) koro (with vowel change: **a**>**e**, **O**>**o**, **o**>**u**, **æ**>**e**, **e**>**i**)
(tui) korish (**O**>**o**, **o**>**u**, **æ**>**e** and **e**>**i**, but stem vowel **a** remains; after a vowel, **-ish** is reduced to **-sh**)
(apni) korben (identical to polite form of future tense)

The future imperative is made negative by adding **na**. The present imperative cannot be made negative.

Infinitive

korte

The stem vowel changes: **O>o, o>u, æ>e, e>i**

Stem vowel **a** changes to **e** only if the stem ends in **a** (e.g. **khawa** 'eat'):

khete

But **gawa** and **cawa** add **i**:

gaite, caite

Past participle

kore

Identical to present perfect tense, but with **-chi/-cho/-chish/-che/-chen** removed.

Conditional participle

korle

Identical to the **tumi/tomra** form of the simple past tense.

Adverbs

kore or **bhabe** are added to an adjective (e.g. **shundor** 'beautiful') to make an adverb: **shundor kore/bhabe** 'beautifully'.

Some adjectives (e.g. **shabdhan** 'careful', **deri** 'late') add **-e** (after a consonant) or **-te** (after a vowel) to make an adverb: **shabdhane** 'carefully', **derite** 'late' (adv.).

Word order

The most neutral word order has the verb at the end of the clause:

ami take kalke okhane dekhechi.

But the simple past tense of **hOwa**, when used in the meaning 'is, are', is never in final position:

> she holo amar skuler bondhu.

Words starting with **j-** (e.g. **jodi, jOkhon, jOto, je bhabe** etc.) can be initial in the clause but are more usually in second position or later:

> jodi tumi cao, ...
> tumi jodi cao, ...
> tumi cao jodi, ...

Questions words (e.g. **ke, ki, kObe, kothae** etc.) can also be initial but it is more usual for them to be in medial position:

> tumi kothae jaccho?

The words **kina** 'whether' and **bole** 'that; because' come at the end of their clause; that clause as a whole usually comes at the beginning of the sentence:

> tomra okhane jabe kina amake bOlo.
> she ashbe bole ghoshona koreche.
> shOmOe chilo na bole ashlam na.

An adjective can come before the indefinite article:

> bhalo ækTa boi

Negation

The word **na** usually comes after the verb:

> amra ar okhane jabo na.

In a clause with **jodi, na** comes in front of the verb:

> tumi okhane jodi na jao

To make a present perfect or past perfect tense form negative, the present tense plus **ni** (or **nai**, colloquial E) is used:

> ami kori ni, tumi kOro ni, tui korish ni, she kOre ni, apni kOren ni

The future imperative is made negative by adding **na**. The present imperative cannot be made negative.

The negative of **ache** is **nei** or **nai** (E).

Bengali often omits the verb 'am/is/are':

    she ækhon lOnDone   **tumi moTa**
    he is now in London   you are fat

When such a sentence specifies a location, it is made negative by inserting **nei** (colloquial E. **nai**):

    she ækhon lOnDone nei   he is not in London now

When it does not specify a location but some other property, it is made negative by inserting one of the following forms:

    ami noi, tumi nOo, tui nosh, she nOe, apni nOn

    tumi moTa nOo   you are not fat

E. Bengali often uses just **na** in these cases:

    tumi moTa na   you are not fat

Translation of reading texts

Unit 5

The day before yesterday, we came to Chittagong from Dhaka. We came by bus. We have come for a visit of two days. Yesterday we went to Rangamati by car. Rangamati is a hilly region and it is very beautiful to see. A lot of indigenous people live there. The region is towards the very eastern part of Bangladesh. After coming to Rangamati, we rode on the back of an elephant. We saw Lake Kaptai. We took a lot of photos there and had a lot of fun. After that, in the evening, we came back to Chittagong.

Unit 8

MILKMAN: I don't cheat customers. I mix water with the milk, certainly, but I don't give less as far as the measurement is concerned.
RICE-SELLER: I don't either. If I mix three weight units of rice with one weight unit of grit, you say, friend, whether that makes four weight units?

JOURNALIST: Madam, how old are you?
ACTRESS: I'm sorry. I always look in the mirror, not at the calendar.

Unit 9

DIRECTOR: We only want famous writers. We don't take new writers.
WRITER: That's OK. Then use my pseudonym.
DIRECTOR: What is your pseudonym?
WRITER: Rabindranath Tagore.

Unit 10

Reading text 1

Yesterday, policemen arrested and took away my friend. He is a student leader and had joined and led a demonstration without police permission. This morning, I went to a lawyer with my friend's father. We explained the whole incident to the lawyer. But the lawyer said that my friend will not be released quickly. The police have brought a bomb case against him. We went to the court and gave quite a few officials a bribe. But in spite of taking the money nobody has given us any help. My friend is still detained in prison.

Reading text 2

Yesterday, at half past seven in the evening, a horrific earthquake took place in Narayangonj. Many women and children fainted with fright. Afterwards, a violent storm and rain started. Many people have fallen ill because of the cold. Several roads and streets have been damaged. This afternoon, the wife of the District Commissioner came to the site of the incident by taxi. She has given a small amount of help. Many valuable monuments have been destroyed. People have never seen such an earthquake before.

Unit 11

Pirates have come to our country

The little boy slept, the neigbourhood was quiet.
Pirates have come to our country.
The small nightingales have eaten the paddy.
Should I give 'tax'? What is that?
The paddy is finished; the crop is finished.
What to do about tax?
Wait a few days,
For the garlic I have sown.

Unit 12

In the time of the Soviet Union, an American teacher used to teach arithmetic in a school in Russia. One day, as he was explaining arithmetic in class, he asked:

Translation of reading texts 233

TEACHER: Tell me, if I buy a pair of socks for five rubles and sell them for twenty rubles, then what do I get?
STUDENT: Seven years in Siberia!

Unit 13

After winning in the election, journalists came to do an interview with the Prime Minister.

JOURNALIST: Before forming a cabinet, you will no doubt take somebody's advice?
PRIME MINISTER: Of course! But why are you dragging my wife into this now?

Unit 14

His youngest uncle had come to the house of Shontu's family for a visit and asked:

YOUNGEST UNCLE: Well, Shontu, what mark did you get for arithmetic in your final exam?
SHONTU: I got only three marks less than my brother, uncle.
YOUNGEST UNCLE: How much did your brother get?
SHONTU: A three.

Now say: what mark did Shontu get in arithmetic?

Unit 15

Yesterday the acting group 'Good Times' performed 'Those Days', the first play written by Shumonto Ray. The actors and actresses in the play all acted well. The stage decorations were very pleasing. On one side of the stage was a scene of a busy fair, on the other side was a quiet room. But the storyline of the play was as complicated as its title was simple. Just when the spectators are thinking that they understand the story, new characters pop up again from an unknown past. As a result of this, it is not possible to understand precisely the playwright's intention. Nevertheless, the new playwright's language, dialogue and choice of words were enjoyable. The director should be thanked for his clean directing. In spite of it being terribly hot in the theatre, the spectators enjoyed the play.

Key to exercises

The sounds of Bengali

Exercise 2
æk, dui, tin, car, pãc, chOe, shat, aT, nOe, dOsh.

Exercise 4
matha 'head'; kOpal 'forehead'; bhru 'eyebrow'; kan 'ear'; gal 'cheek'; thutni 'chin'; kãdh 'shoulder'; kobji 'wrist'; hat 'hand'; anggul 'finger/toe'; nOkh (W nokh) 'nail'; pa 'foot'

Exercise 5
ma 'mother'; amma (E) 'mother'; baba 'father'; abba (E) 'father'; bon 'sister'; didi 'elder sister'; stri 'wife'; me-e 'girl/daughter'; chele 'boy, son'

Exercise 6
ekhane – okhane; keu – kichu; ke – ki; amar – tomar; chele – me-e; bhai – bon; ma – baba; amma – abba (E); hat – pa; gOrom – ThanDa; khola – bOndho; ciThi – kham; megh – akash; nodi – nao; Dan – bã; hæ̃ – na

The Bengali script

Exercise 1

আ	া	ই	ি	উ	ু	ও	ো
a	a	i	i	u	u	o	o

ক	খ	ম	ল	র
k	kh	m	l	r

Key to exercises

Exercise 2

(a) khal, khil, khuli, khola; (b) ami, amar, amar ma, amar mukh; (c) am, lau, lal alu; (d) ami, khai, ami am khai

Exercise 3

1g, 2c, 3d, 4b, 5h, 6f, 7a/e, 8a/e
8 amma-abba: this is Eastern Bengali; 7 is in general use.

Exercise 4

1h, 2c, 3i, 4g, 5f, 6a, 7d, 8b, 9j, 10e

Exercise 5

anar; lau; am; lal-alu; tel; nun; apel; kopi; mula; kOla

Exercise 6

father: pomegranate; mother: mango; Annie: apple; sister: banana; tumi: ami am khabo (if, indeed, you want to eat mango).

Exercise 7

1 bOr, bou 2 nebo, nebe 3 era, ora 4 bOkbOk, pænpæn 5 prem, pret 6 alu, alo 7 ain, ukil 8 boi, koi 9 akar, bæpar

Unit 1

Plural forms

amra bhalo achi 'We are fine'

Exercise 1

1 and 2 Three speakers: two young boys (bahar and shonTu) and a lady (whom they address as kaki 'aunt').

Exercise 4

1 apnar me-e ekhane? 2 apni kæmon achen? 3 tumi ki bangla jano? 4 ækTa prosno korte pari? apnar nam ki? 5 amra ki am khabo? 6 ækTa prosno korte pari? apni kothae thaken?

Exercise 6

1b, 2a, 3a, 4a, 5b, 6b

Exercise 7

1 aunt 2 here 3 Burmese people 4 your elder brother 5 your son 6 a Nepali book 7 How are you (polite plural)? 8 We are very well. 9 Is your elder sister here? 10 No, my elder sister is now in India.

Unit 2

Exercise 1

Bijoy – 6 (at least); Kumkum – 5 (at least).

Exercise 3

1 chele 2 baba 3 khala 4 apa 5 cacato bon 6 mami 7 caci 8 choTo bon 9 kaki 10 khalu. Male – 1, 2, 10; female – the others.

Exercise 4

1 tomake 2 era 3 apnar 4 take 5 o 6 eke, oke (or: oke, eke) 7 tui 8 apnara.

Exercise 5

1 hæ̃, eTa amar saikel. 2 she lOnDone thake. 3 na, she hindi jane na kintu she bangla jane. 4 na, ami tomake bhalobashi na. 5 na, she kOla pOchondo kOre na kintu she am pOchondo kOre. 6 na, ami tar khalato bhai; amar ma tar khala o tar ma amar khala.

Exercise 6

1 ækTa notun bangali resTurenT ache. 2 rannaghOre khabar ache. 3 kono jaega nei. 4 amar pOkeTe kono Taka nei. 5 am ache o anarOsh ache. 6 apel nei o kOla nei.

Exercise 7

2 amar Dan hate kono Taka nei. 3 anarOsh nei. 4 DakTikiT nei. 5 kono kagOj nei. 6 amar pleTe kono bhat nei.

Key to exercises

Exercise 8

চ	c	ছ	ch	জ	j	ঝ	jh
ত	t	থ	th	দ	d	ধ	dh	ন	n
প	p	ফ	f	ব	b	ভ	bh	ম	m
ট	T	র	r	ল	l	ঁ	nasalised vowel

Exercise 9

হ h; khala: his wife; bulbuler bhai: his nephew; bulbuler bon: his niece; bulbuler amma: his sister-in-law; bulbuler abba: his sister-in-law's husband

Exercise 10

who; I.

Unit 3

Exercise 2

1 uni ke? tãr/onar nam ki? 2 uni ki tãr/onar stri? 3 enara kara? enader nam ki? 4 era ki enader chele-me-e? tumi ki tader ceno? 5 tomar ma-baba kothae? ishita ki tãder dawat koreche?

Exercise 3

1 ami ækjOn shangbadik. 2 uni ækjOn ukil. 3 amar bORo bhai ækjOn injiniar. 4 na, amar kaka ækjOn shikkhOk. 5 amar baba draibhar chilen.

Exercise 4

amar mone hOe she ækjOn dhopa – tar hate ækTa shaban ache.
... she ækjOn cashi – tar hate ækTa kodal ache.
... she ækjOn kaTh-mistri – tar hate ækTa hatuRi ache.
... she ækjOn dokandar – tar hate kichu khucra Taka ache.
... she ækjOn pulish – tar hate ækTa laThi ache.
... she ækjOn cakor – tar hate ækTa jhaRu ache.

Exercise 6

2 khaled dhoni kintu tãr baba gorib chilen. 3 amar bhagne boka kintu amar bhagni buddhiman. 4 ei bæbshayi kutshit kintu tãr stri shundori. 5 tomar cakor moTa kintu amar cakor patla. (You may have given the various people other characteristics, but the sentence pattern should be the same in each case.)

Exercise 7

amader couddoTa gaRi ache. amader duiTa jip ache. amar æksho shaRi ache. amader aTharojOn cakOr ache.

Exercise 8

1e, 2g, 3f, 4a, 5c, 6b, 7d

Unit 4

Exercise 1

dure; kache-i; shoja; ghurun; mathae; hate; kothae; dækhar

Exercise 2

2 oiTa ribhar sTriT. 3 oigulo dokan. 4 ei bhobon ækTa jadughOr. 5 moshjidTa khub ækTa dure nOe – oi rastar shes mathae. 6 bajarTa khub ækTa kache-i nOe. oi dike bish miniT hãTun. ækTa shetu dekhte paben. okhane Dane ghurun.

Mini-exercise

jadughOrTa khola. kintu dokanTa bOndho. mondirgulo kache-i. okhane ækTa durgo-o ache. sheTa khub bORo.

Exercise 3

There are shops and homes. There is a small temple at the end.

Exercise 4

2 mita: pærise ækTa shundor nodi ache. upol: kintu pæriser rastae kono bhalo riksha nei. 3 mita: æmsTarDæme Onek shetu ache. upol: kintu oi shOhorer rastagulo khub shoru. 4 mita: florense shundor bhObon ache. upol: kintu florens iTalir rajdhani na. 5 mita: barline Onek cOoRa rasta ache. upol: kintu barline kono bhalo dewal nei.

Exercise 6

1 thaki 2 bhaben 3 mare; mari 4 hashe; kãde 5 hãTe 6 janen; jani 7 thake; jano; thake.

Key to exercises

Exercise 7

2 apnar bOro mama kæmon achen? uni bhalo achen. 3 apnar choTo bhai kæmon ache? she khub ækTa bhalo nei. 4 apni kæmon achen? ami khubi bhalo achi. 5 apnara kæmon achen? amra bhalo achi.

Exercise 8

The politican has revealed that he has a lot of money.

Unit 5

Dialogue 1

Yes he is; Proshun is going to play the **tObla**.

Exercise 2

2 ami shuni. 3 ami baje kOtha boli na. 4 ami aje-baje khabar kini na. 5 ami fOrashi shikhi. 6 ami boi likhi.

Exercise 3

2 apni-o ki protidin car ghOnTa tObla prakTis kOren? 3 apnio ki bikale daba khælen? 4 apni-o ki protidin apnar i-mel pORen o uttor lekhen? 5 apni-o ki protidin dOshTa shOngskrito shObdo shekhen? 6 apni-o ki shondha-bælae apnar make fon kOren?

Exercise 4

1 dhui 2 khai 3 bajai 4 jai 5 pORan 6 pai.

Exercise 5

2 she protidin car ghOnTa tObla prakTis kOre. 3 bikale she daba khæle. 4 protidin she tar i-mel pORe o uttor lekhe. 5 protidin she dOshTa shOngskrito shObdo shekhe. 6 shondha-bælae she apnake fon kOre.

1 shOkale she prothome tar hat-mukh dhoe. 2 tarpOr jOl-khabar khae. 3 tarpOr dui ghOnTa tObla bajae. 4 nOeTae she o tar bondhura skule jae. 5 baroTa porjonto tader shikkhOk taderke ingreji o shOngskrito bhasha pORan. 6 tara æk ghOnTa lanc-brek pae.

Dialogue 2

No – that would have meant going by elephant.

Exercise 7

2 hæ̃, tãke ciThi likhechi. 3 hæ̃, boiTa poRechi. 4 hæ̃, shOb bujhechi. 5 hæ̃, daba khelechi. 6 hæ̃, she gOtokalke esheche.

Exercise 8

2 tarpOr jOl-khabar khe-echi. 3 tarpOr dui ghOnTa tObla bajiechi. 4 nOeTae ami o amar bondhura skule gechi. 5 baroTa porjonto amader shikkhOk amaderke ingreji o shOngskrito bhasha poRiechen. 6 amra æk ghOnTa lanc-brek pe-echi.

2 'apni aj car ghOnTa tObla prakTis kOrechen?' 'na, aj ami tObla prakTis kori ni.' 3 'apni aj bikale daba khelechen?' 'na, ami aj bikale daba kheli ni.' 4 'apni aj apnar i-mel poRechen o uttor likhechen?' 'na, ami aj amar i-mel poRi ni o uttor likhi ni.' 5 'apni aj dOshTa shOngskrito shObdo shikhechen?' 'na, ami aj kono shOngskrito shObdo shikhi ni.' 6 'apni aj shondha-bælae make fon korechen?' 'na, ami aj tãke fon kori ni.'

Dialogue 3

He waited 4 hours and got his mobile phone and money stolen. His bike was also stolen. He had no money for the bus.

Exercise 9

2 – apnara ki bhabe ekhane eshechen?
   – amra gaRite coRe eshechi.
3 – apni ki bhabe ekhane eshechen?
   – ami lOnce ekhane eshechi.
4 – apni ki bhabe ekhane eshechen? lOnce?
   – ami lOnce coRe ashi ni, saikele eshechi.
5 – apnara ki bhabe ekhane eshechen?
   – amra hẽTe hẽTe eshechi.
6 – apni ki bhabe ekhane eshechen? hẽTe hẽTe?
   – ami hẽTe ashi ni, hatite coRe eshechi.

Reading text

In the Eastern part of Bangladesh; Lake Kaptai.

Key to exercises 241

Unit 6

Dialogue 1

Sumita; mango (and later rice with hilsha-fish).

Exercise 1

2 – apni ki kãThal pOchondo kOren? – hæ̃, kãThal khub pOchondo kori. 3 – apnar shami ki jhal khabar pOchondo kOren? – hæ̃, jhal khabar khub pOchondo kOren. 4 – apnar chele-me-e ki shak pOchondo kOre? – hæ̃, shak pOchondo kOre. 5 – apnara ki protidin bhat khan? – hæ̃, amra protidin bhat khai. 6 – apnar me-e ki mach pOchondo kOre? – hæ̃, she mach khub pOchondo kOre.

1 shumita: tumi ki rui mach pOchondo kOro? dipti: hæ̃, rui mach khub pOchondo kori. 2 shumita: tumi ki kãThal pOchondo kOro? dipti: hæ̃, kãThal khub pOchondo kori. 3 shumita: tomar shami ki jhal khabar pOchondo kOre? dipti: hæ̃, jhal khabar pOchondo kOre. 4 shumita: tomar chele-me-e ki shak pOchondo kOre? dipti: hæ̃, shak pOchondo kOre. 5 shumita: tomra ki protidin bhat khao? dipti: hæ̃, amra protidin bhat khai. 6 shumita: tomar me-e ki mach pOchondo kOre? dipti: hæ̃, she mach khub pOchondo kOre.

Exercise 3

bajabo; shunbo; bajaben; gaibo; gaiben; gaibo; korben; Dakbo; shunben; bajaben; gaibo; shunben.

Exercise 4

to Bimola: esho! (asho! E); bOsho!; dækho!; shono!
to Shujon: ashun!; boshun!; dekhun!; shunun!
to Moyna: ae!; bOsh!; dækh!; shon!
about Diya: ashuk!; boshuk!; dekhuk!; shunuk!; kintu kono shObdo na!

Dialogue 3

To take it easy and watch a Hindi film.

Exercise 5

1d, 2c, 3f, 4a, 5g, 6b, 7e.

Kajol:
1 cup koro na! 2 bosho na! 3 tomar kaj koro na! 4 tomar khataTa tãke dio na! 5 kOlom die likho na! 6 baire jeo na! 7 ækshathe khelo na! a khataTa bæger moddhe rakho! b bhitore thako! c ce-ar theke oTho! d golmal kOro! e jhOgRa kOro! f ishitar shOnge kOtha bOlo! g pensil die lekho.

Exercise 6

oTho! tomader dãt majo! tomader mukh dho-o! jOl-khabar khao! golmal koro na! ækhon skule jao! skule jhOgRa koro na! mon ide poRo! kOlom die likho! hasha-hashi koro na! carTae bashae esho!

Exercise 7

1 hæ̃, amar amma bhalo ranna kOren. amar abba kintu khub ækTa bhalo ranna kOren na. 2 amar ækTa chele ache. 3 ami cOTTograme gechi kintu dillite jai ni. 4 ami nije nije bangla shikhi. 5 'Dhaka'; tarpOre 'dhakka'

Of course your answers may be different (but not to question 5, we hope).

Unit 7

Dialogue 1

Ingredients: kãca moric, dhonia pata, pẽaj, roshun, Dal, holdi (o tel o lObon)

Exercise 1

2 bhalo bhabe khao! 3 tarpOre taRa-taRi kore skule jeo! 4 shabdhane rasta par ho-o! 5 skul theke derite bashae esho na! 6 tarpOre nirObe tomar dadar shOnge daba khelo!

Exercise 3

1 balbul pẽaj kaTche. 2 saiful dhonia dhucche. 3 onup bashae gæche. 4 Onadi okhane; she mach bhãjche. 5 polTu Dal naRche. 6 shunan ashe nai. she bashae poRche. 7 hæ̃, she bhat khacche. 8 ami take bhat dicchi.

Key to exercises

Dialogue 2

She doesn't like spicy food and is allergic to nuts.

Exercise 4

2 'palong shakTa apnar kæmon lagche?' 'palong shakTa bhalo lagche.' (or: 'amar bhalo lagche.') 3 'DalTa apnar kæmon lagche?' 'DalTa bhalo lagche.' 4 'shimTa apnar kæmon lagche?' 'shimTa bhalo lagche.' 5 'alu-bhOrtaTa apnar kæmon lagche?' 'alu-bhOrtaTa bhalo lagche.' 6 'doiTa apnar kæmon lagche?' 'doiTa bhalo lagche.'

2 'palong shakTa apnar cheler kæmon lagche?' 'tar bhalo lagche' (or: 'bhalo lagche') 3 'DalTa apnar cheler kæmon lagche?' 'tar bhalo lagche' etc.

2 'palong shakTa apnar maer kæmon legeche?' 'onar bhalo legeche' (or: 'bhalo legeche') 3 'DalTa apnar maer kæmon legeche?' 'onar bhalo legeche' etc.

Exercise 5

2 tahole apnar khub pipasha lagbe, didi. 3 tahole apnar khub ghum lagbe, didi. 4 tahole apnar khub ThanDa lagbe, didi. 5 tahole apnar khub klanto lagbe, didi. 6 tahole apnar Oshustho lagbe, didi.

Dialogue 3

Shumi is not well. Ishita suggests taking a paracetamol, eating an apple or orange, taking some rest or calling the doctor.

Exercise 6

kothae; khide; ami-i; pOchondo; bhalo; kOro; ami.

Exercise 7

2 na, amar ghum-Tum lagche na. 3 ji, ami mangsho-Tangsho keTechi. 4 na, weTar bhat-Tat khae ni. 5 na, ami shak-Tak dhui ni. 6 hæ̃, kababe lObon-TObon diechi.

Exercise 8

1 The fish.

Unit 8

Dialogue 1

They buy ½ kilo turmeric, 100 gram cumin, 230 gram coriander powder, 1¼ kilo dry chilli, 1 litre mustard oil and a dozen bananas.

Exercise 1

deR keji lal alu; shaRe tin liTar tel; tirish geram jira; shoa dui sho geram dhonia gũRa; unish keji/adha mOn polao cal.

Exercise 2

A bit more than 5½ kilo.

car sho bish Taka din.

Mini-exercise

kObe ekhane eshechen? kæno ekhane eshechen? kotodin thakben? pOre kothae jaben?

Exercise 3

1 kOkhon; 2 ki ki; 3 ekhane thakbo; 4 ki; 5 kader

Dialogue 2

She buys a silk salwar-kameez.

Exercise 4

From the top, there will be: pen, book, pen, notebook, book, in that order.

Exercise 5

2 na, baroTar pOre fire eshechi. 3 na, gaRiTa baRir pechone rekhechi. 4 na, frijer baire rekhechi. 5 na, kOlagulo Tebiler upore rekhechi. 6 na, boiTa apnar jonno kinechi.

Exercise 6

2 amar aTTa shobuj shaRi, pãcTa badami shaRi, tinTa lal shaRi o carTa golapi shaRi chai. apnar kache ache na ki? 3 amar car seT shada salwar kamij o tin seT nil salwar kamij cai. 4 amar ægaroTa shada sharT, shatTa nil sharT o nOeTa shobuj sharT cai.

Key to exercises

Dialogue 3
A newspaper and a women's magazine.

Exercise 7
1d, 2c, 3b, 4e, 5a.

Unit 9

Dialogue 1
300 taka; it contains foodstuff, which is forbidden.

Exercise 1
1e, 2d, 3c, 4b, 5a.

Exercise 2
– walaikum-salam. ei ciThi dite bhule gechi. – kolkatae paThate cai.
– ami banglate likhte shikhechi. – lekhen. dhonnobad.

Exercise 3
Sending e-mail; playing chess; watching TV.

Exercise 4
2 haRiTa bhalo bhabe dhue cular upore rakho. 3 pẽ-ajTa keTe amake dao. 4 Dal ranna kore bhat ranna koro. 5 bhat na khe-e bashae jeo na. 6 agami kalke abar eshe mach ranna korbe.

Exercise 5
2 A: kaj shesh korbe. tarpOr ekhane esho. B: na, kaj shesh korbo. tarpOre ami bashae jabo. 3 A: tomaderke dekhbe. she ki bolbe? B: ki bolbe? amaderke dekhbe. khushi hObe. 4 A: arif fon koreche. boleche, 'bashae khabar nei'. B: ami bashae jabo. take dhOmok debo.

Dialogue 3
Yes. The money has come into his account, he can open a savings account and he can cash his cheque.

Exercise 6

2 hæ̃, kine niechi. 3 nai. dudhTa shes kore felechi. 4 na, bhule gechi.
5 hæ̃, amar shOb i-mel poRe felechi. 6 hæ̃, she baroTae eshe poReche.

Unit 10

Dialogue 1

He wants to watch TV, finds the arithmetic work difficult and English unpleasant.

Mini-exercise 1

põetallish miniT; pOncanno miniT; unoshaT miniT; tettrish miniT; põcish miniT

Mini-exercise 2

– shaRe dOshTa baje? – na, shaRe ægaroTa baje. – poune pãcTa baje? – na, shoa pãcTa baje.

Exercise 1

1 'mOnco kOtha' shuru hOe duiTa collishe. 2 'shOngbad' ponero miniT colbe. 3 'uDi uDpekar' shes hOe shaRe tinTae. 4 'shukhi poribar' shaRe tinTae shuru hObe. 5 'muktir pOthe' duiTa collishe shes hObe.

Exercise 2

1 she adha ghOnTa Tibhi dekheche. 2 chOeTa collishe she bhat khabe. 3 she tar choTo bhai o boner shOnge bhat khabe. 4 she tar babar kache Ongko shikhbe. 5 pial nOeTae ghumate jabe.

Exercise 3

1 ækhon nOeTa baje. 2 ami tirish miniT dhore bangla poRchi. 3 ami protidin shaRe aTTa theke shaRe nOeTa porjonto bangla poRi. 4 ami aj shatTae ghum theke uThechi. 5 ami goto kalke shaRe ægaroTae ghumate gechi. (Your answers may of course be different.)

Exercise 4

almari – shobarghOr; sofa – bOsharghOr; cula – rannaghOr; caer kap – khabarghOr; gach – bagan; shaban – gosholkhana/snanghOr

Key to exercises

Exercise 5

2 jodi kichu ghOTe. 3 jodi karo shOnge tader bashae jai. 4 jodi fon kOre. 5 jodi onno keu fon kOre. 6 jodi brisTi pORe.

Exercise 6

2. tara kOkhono ashbe na. 3 tara amar jonno kono upohar nie ashbe na. 4 taderke kichu-i khawabo na. 5 na, ami kono sinema dekhte cai na. 6 amar mon kharap hOe nai.

Reading text 1

He was in a demonstration that did not have police permission; his prospects are not good.

Mini-exercise 3

tomar boner fon nOmbor ki? eTa tomar bonke dio. amar bonra dillite thaken. aj rattre amar bonder fon korbo.

Exercise 7

1 tusharkOnar ma mara gæchen. 2 tusharkOna bamonder baRite esheche. 3 bamonra tusharkOnake tader baRite thakte dieche. 4 ækdin dusTo rani apel nie esheche. 5 dusto rani tusharkOnake apel dieche. 6 apel khe-e tusharkOna ghumie poReche. 7 Onek bOchor pOre ækjOn rajkumar põuche gæche. 8 rajkumar tusharkOnake cuma dieche.

Exercise 9

1l, 2d, 3e, 4m, 5n, 6f, 7h, 8j, 9b, 10a, 11c, 12g, 13i, 14k.

Reading text 2

An earthquake in Narayangonj; the D.C.'s wife has distributed some relief.

Unit 11

Dialogue 1

They held a press conference on Tuesday and demonstrated on Wednesday; they will ask the PM to hand over power to a caretaker government and, if necessary, will call a general strike.

Exercise 1

hOrtal; michil; dabi; protibad; birodhi dOl (opposition) prodhan-montri; khOmota; shOrkar; shOrkari dOl; protarona kOra (government)

Exercise 2

nirbacon; shOngshOd; prodhan montri; birodhi; protibad; michil; hOrtal.

Exercise 3

ami dekhlam/shunlam/nilam/korlam/holam/shulam; tumi dekhle/ shunle/nile/korle/hole/shule; tui dekhli/shunli/nili/korli/holi/shuli; she dekhlo/shunlo/nilo/korlo/holo/shulo; apni dekhlen/shunlen/nilen/ korlen/holen/shulen

Exercise 4

10–12 parties; they marched to the press club, listened to speeches, started marching to the presidential building and clashed with the police.

Mini-exercise

tushar kOna gOto shombare elo. mongolbare she baRiTa porishkar korlo. budhbare she bajar korlo. brihOshpotibare she bhat ranna korlo. shukrobare she ækTa apel khelo o ghumie poRlo. shonibare bamonra kãdlo. robibare ækjOn rajkumar elo ebong take cuma dilo.

Exercise 5

carTae uni tãr choTo me-er jonno shoping korlen. rat shaRe aTTae tãr me-er jOnmodiner parTi shuru holo. mongolbar nOeTae uni tãr boktrita cek korlen. dupur ækTa theke tinTa porjonto uni dOler kormider shOnge alocona korlen. tinTae theke uni ciThipOttro poRlen. rat aTTae uni tãr strir shOnge mondire gelen. budhbar ægaroTae uni chattro-chattrider jonno boktrita dilen. dupur ækTae uni sromik netader shOnge alocona korlen. bikal duiTae uni shangbadikder shakkhatkar dilen. shondha pãcTae uni em-pi-der shathe ca khelen.

Dialogue 2

There may have been among the people watching a magician's performance in the field by the roadside.

Key to exercises

Exercise 6

1 ami ca banachilam. 2 ami amar bondhur shathe kOtha bolchilam. 3 amra ranna ghOre kap dhucchilam. 4 ami amar ca khacchilam. 5 ami amar mobaile kOtha bolchilam.

Exercise 7

2 she pokeT marte cesTa korchilo. 3 she jal Taka chapate cesTa korchilo. 4 she kalo bajare jinishgulo bikkri korte cesTa korchilo. 5 she cãdabaji korte cesTa korchilo. 6 she ækjOn mohilar bæg chintai korte cesTa korchilo.

2 ami pokeTmar noi. konodin pokeT mari ni. 3 ami jaliat noi. konodin jal Taka chapai ni. 4 ami kalobajari noi. konodin kalo bajare jinishgulo bikkri kori ni. 5 ami cãdabaj noi. konodin cãdabaji kori ni. 6 ami chintaikari noi. konodin chintai kori ni.

Exercise 8

1 ami amar nijer gaRi meramot korte pari. 2 ami nijeke khub bhalo bhabe bojhate pari. 3 ami nijeke bhalobaste pari. 4 ami shObshOmOe nijer bæpare kOtha bolte cai. 5 ami nijeke aenae dekhe khushi hoi.

Unit 12

Dialogue 1

The school used to be under a big tree; they would get beaten whenever they hadn't learned things by heart properly.

Exercise 1

2 age Onek piTuni khetam. 3 age pOchondo kortam. 4 age jeto. 5 age bhalo bhabe fuTbOl khelte partam. 6 age mohilader shathe gOlpo korte amar Onek bhalo lagto. 7 age robindro-shongit gaitam.

Exercise 2

1 madaripure thaktam. 2 'Donovan' skule poRtam. 3 rikshae coRe skule jetam. 4 ami bædminTon khelte pOchondo kortam. 5 chuTite amra grame jetam. 6 amar ma amar jonno ilish mach ranna korten. khub-i bhalo lagto. (Your answers may of course be somewhat different.)

Dialogue 2

Eating mango, catching fish, seeing the Kohinoor.

Exercise 3

Fruit shop; fish shop; sweet shop; clothes shop.

Exercise 4

hoeche; thakten; eshechen; hoechilen; can ni; ashlen; korechen.

Mini-exercise

aj julaier æk tarikh. amra aTharoi june lOnDon theke fire eshechilam. julaier dOsh tarikhe skul shuru hObe. bishe julaie amader dadabhai ashbe. Disembor mashe amra abar lOnDone jabo.

Exercise 5

carTae ami ninar jonno shoping korechilam. rat shaRe aTTae ninar jOnmodiner parTite gechilam. unishe OkTobor shOkal nOeTae ami amar boktrita cek korechilam. dupur ækTa theke tinTa porjonto dOler kormider shOnge alocona korechilam. tinTa theke ciThipOttro poRechilam. rat aTTae amar strir shOnge mondire gechilam. bishe OkTobor shOkal ægaroTae ami chattro-chattrider jonno boktrita diechilam. dupur ækTae sromik netader shOnge alocona korechilam. bikal duiTae ami shangbadikder shakkhatkar diechilam. shondha pãcTae em-pi-der shathe ca khe-echilam.

Exercise 7

1 shaT sekenD. 2 duisho dOsh miniT. 3 æksho bish mash. 4 dOsh dOshok. 5 põcish tarikhe. 6 OkToborer cobbish tarikh. 7 couTha me.

Dialogue 3

He doesn't feel like sitting in more classes today.

Exercise 8

1 sar, ami baRite jete cai. jete onumoti din. 2 na, baRite jete parbe na. tomake jete debo na. 3 ma, poRte amar iccha hOe na. Ti-bhi dekhte pari? 4 prodhan montri, amra cai na je pOela januari nirbacon hok. 5 malik, onurodh korchi je dOya kore amaderke shahajjo korun.

Key to exercises 251

Exercise 9

2 ami apnaderke bolchi je ami shObshOmOe apnader jonno porissrom korechi, shObshOmOe apnader jonno porissrom kori o bhobisshote-o apnader jonno porissrom korbo. 3 ami apnaderke bolchi je ami konodin mittha kOtha boli ni, konodin mittha kOtha boli na, o bhobisshote-o mittha kOtha bolbo na. 4 ami apnaderke bolchi je ami shObshOmOe amar deshTake bhalobeshechi, shObshOmOe amar deshTake bhalobashi o bhobisshote-o amar deshTake bhalobashbo. 5 ami apnaderke bolchi je ami konodin ghush khai ni, konodin ghush khai na o bhobisshote-o ghush khabo na. 6 ami apnaderke bolchi je ami nirbaconer shOmOe apnaderke Taka diechi, nirbaconer shOmOe apnaderke Taka dei o bhobisshote-o nirbaconer shOmOe apnaderke Taka debo.

2 ami apnaderke bolchi je amar protipOkkho apnader jonno konodin porissrom kOre ni, apnader jonno konodin porissrom kOre na o bhobisshote-o apnader jonno porissrom korbe na. 3 ami apnaderke bolchi je amar protipOkkho mittha kOtha boleche, mittha kOtha bOle, o bhobisshote-o mittha kOtha bolbe. 4 ami apnaderke bolchi je amar protipOkkho tar deshTake bhalobashe ni, bhalobashe na o bhobisshote-o bhalobashbe na. 5 ami apnaderke bolchi je amar protipOkkho shObshOmOe ghush khe-eche, shObshOmOe ghush khae o bhobisshote-o ghush khabe. 6 ami apnaderke bolchi je amar protipOkkho apnaderke konodin nirbaconer shOmOe Taka dæe ni, apnaderke konodin Taka dæe na o bhobisshote-o kono Taka debe na.

Unit 13

Dialogue 1

She thinks it was dangerous for Jenny to go onto the river in a boat.

Exercise 1

1 miT-miTe 2 bhOn-bhOn 3 khiT-khiT, bOkor-bOkor 4 jhOk-jhOk

Exercise 2

2 shurjasto dekhte cOmotkar lagchilo. 3 taragulo jhOk-jhOk korchilo. 4 Tipu amar kOtha shune Obak holo. 5 gram theke cole gie amar dukkho lagchilo. 6 agami mashe abar okhane jabo.

Dialogue 2

He lost his chickens and ducks in the flood. It was also very hard to feed his cows and goats.

Exercise 3

1 amar dharona tar Onek jomi nei. 2 tar kono TrækTor nei. 3 hæ̃, chilo. 4 cashir stri hãsh-murgi palato. 5 hal-cash korte hOe, fOshol fOlate hOe o kOr dite hOe.

Exercise 4

2 noukae oThar shOmOe-e brisTi shuru holo. 3 nodite ghorar pOre gramTa dekhechi. 4 brisTir fOle onno gramgulite jawa shOmbhOb chilo na. 5 ghash-kuTa kenar jonno cashike kichu Taka diechi. 6 fupur shOnge chade ca khabar age goshol korechi.

Exercise 5

2 tahole ca bananor dOrkar. 3 tahole tomar shamir kena ucit. 4 tahole take Taka dewar proyojon. 5 tahole amar Onek kOmla khawar dOrkar. 6 tahole amar jonno bhat ranna korte hObe.

Dialogue 3

The farmer's wife is more optimistic.

Exercise 6

2 tara noukae coRe nodite ghureche bole jeni bollo. 3 jenir gramTa dekhte kæmon legeche, fupu jiggesh korlen. 4 jeni dekhlo je akashe taraguli jhOk-jhOk korche. 5 Tipu jenike jiggesh korlo lOnDoner akashe-o cãd oThe ki na. 6 fupu bollen je tini can na je Tipu baje kOtha boluk.

Exercise 7

1f, 2a, 3h, 4c, 5d, 6b, 7g, 8e.

Unit 14

Dialogue 1

The website is having a technical problem.

Key to exercises

Exercise 1

2 apni jodi shOmOe mOton aste paren, tahole kono shOmossha hObe na. 3 apni amar kOtha jodi na bojhen, tahole bolben. 4 apnar jodi pasporT thake, tahole kono cintar karon nei. 5 apni jodi dilli hoe kolkatae jete can, tahole dillite kanekTing flaiT nite hObe. 6 apnar stri jodi apnar shOnge jae, tahole amader janaben.

Mini-exercise 1

amar shOmOe thakle, jabo. tumi gele, ami-o jabo. arif caile, she-o aste parbe. tar khide lagle, amra ækTa resTurenTe jabo.

Exercise 2

2 bimaner TikeT jodi kinte pari (or: TikeT kinte parle), jabo. 3 amar jodi Taka thakto (or: amar Taka thakle), tomake ditam. 4 tumi jodi Onko na bojho (or: na bujhle), tomake shahajjo korbo. 5 tomar homwark jodi shesh kore thako (or: homwark shesh kore thakle), Tibhi dekhte paro. 6 tumi jodi ilish-mach khete cao (or: tumi khete caile), amra aj khabo.

Dialogue 2

No, there is some turbulence and the food will be given later. Lila's blanket.

Exercise 3

1 shujon Tipur ce-e bORo. 2 opu kamaler ce lOmba. 3 kamal shObce bORo. 4 shujon kamaler theke tirish senTimiTar beshi lOmba. 5 opu o Tipu æki shOman lOmba.

Exercise 4

2 banglar abohawa amader desher abohawar ce gOrom. 3 banglar gachguli amader desher gachgulir ce lOmba. 4 bangali rajnitibidra o amader desher rajnitibidra æki rOkom buddhiman. 5 bangali khabar amader desher khabarer ce jhal. 6 bangla bhasha amader desher bhashar ce shoja.

Dialogue 3

No. It was too crowded.

Mini-exercise 2

amra je baRiTa kinechi, she baRiTa notun. ami je bhashaTa shikhchi, she bhashaTa shoja. ami je chobigulo tulechi, she chobigulo tomake dækhabo.

Exercise 5

1 bekti 2 ja 3 flaiT 4 ni; din; na 5 dukkhito; jhORer

Exercise 6

2 frije kono khabar chilo na bole arifer mon kharap chilo. 3 khali frij dekhlo bole tar hOtash lagchilo. 4 arifer ma ranna kOre ni bole tar mon kharap lagchilo. 5 tar bon pæn-pæn korchilo bole arifer birokto lagchilo. 6 na khe-e skule jete hObe bole arifer kOsTo lagchilo.

Exercise 7

2 frije jodi khabar thakto, taholeo arifer mon kharap thakto? 3 khali frij jodi na dekhto, taholeo arifer hOtash lagto? 4 arifer ma jodi ranna korto, taholeo arifer mon kharap lagto? 5 arifer bon jodi pæn-pæn na korto, taholeo arifer birokto lagto? 6 arifer jodi na khe-e skule jete na hoto, taholeo tar kOsto lagto?

Unit 15

Dialogue 1

There are fairs to go to, things to buy, plays to watch, and **panta-bhat** to eat.

Exercise 1

1 amar jOnmodin coittro mashe. 2 pŏcishe Disembor poush mashe pORe. 3 ei ritur nam bOrshakal. 4 bOshontokal februari, marc, epril mashe pORe. 5 asshiner age bhaddro o asshiner pOre kartik. 6 grisshokal shitkaler ce-e gOrom.

Mini-exercise 1

shOb kichu kena hoeche. eTa kalke kOra hObe. gOtokalke shOb khawa hoeche. ekhane, nObobOrsho epril mashe udjapon kOra hOe.

Key to exercises

Exercise 2

2 januari mashe Dijain bibOronir pãcsho kopi chapano hoeche. aro tinsho kopi ækhon chapano hocche. 3 bibOroniTa marc mashe kretader kache paThano hoeche. 4 gOto bOchore aTharojOn sromik niyog kOra hoeche. e mashe aro dOshjOn niyog kOra hObe. 5 notun than-kapoR Disembor mashe ODar dewa hoeche. februari mashe põucheche. 6 notun poshak gOto mashe pottrikae biggapon dewa hoeche. 7 bideshi kretader kache ækhono ciThi paThano hOe ni. agami shOptae paThano hObe.

Exercise 3

The correct order is: 4th sentence, 1st sentence, 3rd sentence, 2nd sentence. The verbal noun with passive meaning not followed by **hOwa** is found in the phrase **ekTi bhanga kap** (a broken cup).

Mini-exercise 2

eTa kOra jae. oke bOla jeto. ciThiTa ækhon paThano jae. eTa bOla jae na.

Exercise 4

– ei fonTa die shara bharoter moddhe fon kOra jae? – kOTa nOmbor memorite rakha jabe? – bæTari carj hote kotokkhon lagbe? o tarpOre kotodin bæbohar kOra jabe? – apnar kOtha ki bisshash korte pari? – TesT kOrar jonno amake fonTa dewa jabe?

Dialogue 2

Jenny, all Muslims and many Hindus (including Anjona).

Mini-exercise 3

tumi je jaegae jabe, ami-o she jaegae jabo. tumi je bhabe krikeT khælo, she bhabe ami-o khelte cai. jOto lok ashe, ami tOto khushi hObo. ami jOto bhalo bhabe ingreji bolte pari, tOto bhalo bhabe bangla bolte pari na.

Exercise 5

1 As long as there is life (breath), there is hope. 2 Things may look frightening, but that doesn't mean they will really happen. 3 The fruit is just like the tree it came from; like father/mother, like son/

daughter. 4 Whenever we can't get a thing, we want it more and more. 5 It was done the way it had been said (and without delay).

Exercise 6

1c, 2e, 3a, 4b, 5d, 6f.

Reading text

The final verdict is positive (but the play's exact intention is hard to understand).

Bengali–English glossary

In this glossary, nasalised vowels (e.g. ã and õ) are given immediately after the ordinary vowels (e.g. **a** and **o**). The letter **æ** comes after **a**; **O** after **o**; **D** after **d**; and **T** after **t**.

a

abar	আবার	again, then
abba	আব্বা	father (E)
accha	আচ্ছা	OK/all right, I see
ada	আদা	ginger
adab	আদাব	hello, goodbye
aena	আয়না	mirror
agami	আগামী	coming, next
age	আগে	before, in the past
aj	আজ	today
ajkal	আজকাল	nowadays
akash	আকাশ	sky
alap kOra	আলাপ করা	to consult
almari	আলমারী	wardrobe
alo	আলো	light
alu	আলু	potato
am	আম	mango
amma	আম্মা	mother (E)
amol	আমল	time, days
ana	আনা	to fetch, bring
anggul	আঙ্গুল	finger, toe
anondo	আনন্দ	pleasure, joy
anondo laga	আনন্দ লাগা	to feel happy
anondo pawa	আনন্দ পাওয়া	to feel happy
antorjatik	আন্তর্জাতিক	international
apa	আপা	elder sister (E)

ar	আর	more; and
ar kichu	আর কিছু	anything else
aram	আরাম	ease, comfort
are!	আরে!	my goodness!
asha	আসা	to come
ashol	আসল	real
aste aste	আস্তে আস্তে	slowly
attio-shOjon	আত্মীয়-স্বজন	relatives
ãc	আঁচ	heat
ãka	আঁকা	to draw

æ

æk	এক	one
æka æka	একা একা	alone
ækbar	একবার	once
æke Oporer	একে অপরের	each other's
ækebare	একেবারে	totally
ækhon	এখন	now
ækhono	এখনো	still
æki	একই	same
æki rOkom	একই রকম	equally
ækjoRa	একজোড়া	a(n), a pair
ækshathe	একসাথে	together (E)
æto	এত	so
æto Tuku	এতটুকু	so little

b

baba	বাবা	father
bacca	বাচ্চা	child
bachur	বাছুর	calf
badam	বাদাম	nut
badami	বাদামি	brown
badha dewa	বাধা দেওয়া	to stop, prevent
bagan	বাগান	garden
bah	বাহ্	well, well!
baire	বাইরে	outside
baja	বাজা	to strike
bajano	বাজানো	to play
bajar	বাজার	market
baki	বাকি	left over

Bengali–English glossary

banano	বানানো	to make
bandhobi	বান্ধবী	friend (female)
bangla	বাঙ্গলা	Bengali
bap-re bap!	বাপ্-রে-বাপ্!	my goodness!
barma	বার্মা	Burma
baRano	বাড়ানো	to increase
baRi	বাড়ী	house
bash kOra	বাস করা	to live
basha	বাসা	house (E)
bati	বাতি	lamp
bā	বাঁ	left(hand)
bādha	বাঁধা	to bind, fasten
bæbohar kOra	ব্যবহার করা	to use
bæbshayi	ব্যবসায়ী	businessman
bæca	বেচা	to sell
bæla	বেলা	time period
bæpar	ব্যাপার	thing, matter
bæRano	বেড়ানো	to come out, be published, go for a trip
bæsto	ব্যস্ত	busy
bætha	ব্যথা	pain
bebi-Tæksi	বেবী-ট্যাক্সি	tuk-tuk
begun	বেগুন	aubergine
besh	বেশ	quite
besh kOejOn	বেশ কয়জন	quite a few
besh to	বেশ তো	yes, sure
beshi	বেশি	much, more
bhaba	ভাবা	to think, worry
bhag	ভাগ	part
bhaggo	ভাগ্য	fortune
bhagne	ভাগ্নে	sister's son
bhagni	ভাগ্নি	sister's daughter
bhai	ভাই	brother
bhaijhi	ভাইঝি	brother's daughter
bhaipo	ভাইপো	brother's son
bhaiya	ভাইয়া	elder brother (E)
bhalo	ভালো	good
bhalo bhabe	ভালো ভাবে	well
bhalobasha	ভালোবাসা	to love, like
bharot	ভারত	India
bharotio	ভারতীয়	Indian
bhasha	ভাসা	to float

bhasha	ভাষা	language
bhat	ভাত	(cooked) rice
bhãj kOra	ভাঁজ করা	to fold (up)
bhãja	ভাঁজা	to fry
bhiR	ভিড়	crowd
bhitore	ভিতরে	in
bhobisshot	ভবিষ্যত	future
bhor	ভোর	early morning
bhObon	ভবন	building
bhOddrolok	ভদ্রলোক	gentleman
bhOe	ভয়	fear
bhOn-bhOn kOra	ভন্‌ভন্‌ করা	to buzz
bhOra	ভরা	to fill
bhOrta	ভর্তা	spicy mash
bhugol	ভূগোল	geography
bhule jawa	ভুলে যাওয়া	to forget
bibhinno	বিভিন্ন	different
bijli	বিজলি	electricity
bikal	বিকাল	late afternoon
bikkri kOra	বিক্রি করা	to sell
bilat	বিলাত	England
biman	বিমান	aeroplane
bimanbOndor	বিমানবন্দর	airport
birodhi dOl	বিরোধী দল	opposition party
birokto laga	বিরক্ত লাগা	to feel irritated
biruddhe	বিরুদ্ধে	against
bisshito	বিস্মিত	amazed
bissho-biddalOe	বিশ্ববিদ্যালয়	university
bisshudbar	বিস্যুদবার	Thursday
bissram	বিশ্রাম	rest
bodh hOe	বোধ হয়	it seems
bodh hOwa	বোধ হওয়া	to feel
bohu	বহু	many
boi	বই	book
bojha	বোঝা	to understand
bojhano	বোঝানো	to explain
boka	বোকা	stupid
boktrita	বক্তৃতা	speech
bon	বোন	sister
bondhu	বন্ধু	friend (male)
bondhu-bandhob	বন্ধু-বান্ধব	friends
bonna	বন্যা	flood

Bengali–English glossary

bormi	বর্মী	Burmese
bou	বউ/বৌ	bride
boudi	বৌদি	wife of elder brother (or of male friend)
bOchor	বছর	year
bOka	বকা	to scold
bOkor-bOkor kOra	বকর-বকর করা	to chatter
bOktobbo	বক্তব্য	intention
bOla	বলা	to say
bOndho	বন্ধ	closed
bORo	বড়	big
bORodin	বড়দিন	Christmas
bOsha	বসা	to sit down
bOwa	বওয়া	to blow
bOyosh	বয়স	age
brihOshpotibar	বৃহস্পতিবার	Thursday
buddhiman	বুদ্ধিমান	clever
budhbar	বুধবার	Wednesday
buking dewa	বুকিং দেওয়া	to make a booking

c

ca	চা	tea
cabi	চাবি	key
caca	চাচা	father's brother (E)
caci	চাচী	wife of father's brother (E)
cakor	চাকর	servant
cakri	চাকরি	job
cal	চাল	rice
camoc	চামচ	spoon
caridike	চারিদিকে	on all sides
cash	চাষ	farming
cash-bash kOra	চাষবাস করা	to farm
cashi	চাষি	farmer
cawa	চাওয়া	to want; to look
cãd	চাঁদ	moon
ce-e, ce	চেয়ে/চে'	than
cehara	চেহারা	face
cena	চেনা	to know
cesTa kOra	চেষ্টা করা	to try
chad	ছাদ	roof
chaRa	ছাড়া	without, except

chaRano	ছাড়ানো	to free, release
chattri	ছাত্রী	student (female)
chattro	ছাত্র	student (male)
chele	ছেলে	boy, son
cheRe dewa	ছেড়ে দেওয়া	to let go
chintai	ছিনতাই	mugging
chintaikari	ছিনতাইকারী	mugger
chobi tola	ছবি তোলা	take pictures
choTo	ছোট	little, young
chuTi	ছুটি	holiday, day off
cin	চীন	China
cina	চীনা	Chinese
cinta	চিন্তা	thought; worry
cinta kOra	চিন্তা করা	to worry
cittro	চিত্র	picture
ciThi	চিঠি	letter
ciThi-pOttro	চিঠি-পত্র	letter
coinik	চৈনিক	Chinese
cor	চোর	thief
coritro	চরিত্র	character
coRe	চড়ে	by, in
cOlo	চলো	let's
cOmotkar	চমৎকার	wonderful
cOoRa	চওড়া	broad
cORa	চড়া	to ride, drive
cula	চুলা	fire (of cooker)
cuma	চুমা	kiss
curi hoe jawa	চুরি হয়ে যাওয়া	to get stolen
curi kOra	চুরি করা	to steal

d

daba	দাবা	chess
dabi	দাবি/দাবী	demand
dada	দাদা	elder brother
daitto	দায়িত্ব	duty
dam	দাম	price
dawat kOra	দাওয়াত করা	to invite
dãRano	দাঁড়ানো	to stand
dãt	দাঁত	tooth
dækha	দেখা	to see
dækha hObe	দেখা হবে	till later

dækhano	দেখানো	to show
dækhar mOton	দেখার মতন	worth seeing
deri	দেরি/দেরী	late
desh	দেশ	country
dewa	দেওয়া	to give; to let; to allow
dhan	ধান	paddy, rice
dharona	ধারণা	idea, impression
dhone	ধনে	coriander (W)
dhoni	ধনী	rich
dhonia	ধনিয়া	coriander (E)
dhonnobad	ধন্যবাদ	thanks, thank you
dhore	ধরে	for, during
dhowa	ধোয়া	to wash
didi	দিদি	elder sister
die	দিয়ে	with (the use of)
dik	দিক্	direction
dike	দিকে	towards
din	দিন	day
ditio	দ্বিতীয়	second
doi	দই/দে	yoghurt
dokan	দোকান	shop
dokandar	দোকানদার	shopkeeper
dOya kore	দয়া করে	please
dOrja	দরজা	door
dOrkar	দরকার	need
dOrshok	দর্শক	spectator
drissho	দৃশ্য	sight, scene
dudh	দুধ	milk
dudhwala	দুধওয়ালা	milkman
dukkhito	দুঃখিত	sad, sorry
dukkho	দুঃখ	sadness
dupur	দুপুর	early afternoon
dur	দূর	far, distant

D

Dak	ডাক	post
Daka	ডাকা	to call
Dakat	ডাকাত	robber
DakTikiT	ডাকটিকিট	stamp
Dal	ডাল	lentils
Dan	ডান	right(hand)

Dhala	ঢালা	to pour
Dhoka	ঢোকা	to enter

e

e	এ	this
ebong	এবং	and
ei je	এই যে	hey!
eibar(e)	এইবার/এইবারে	this time
eibhabe	এইভাবে	in this way
eimattro	এইমাত্র	just now
eirOkom	এইরকম	such (a)
ekhane	এখানে	here
ekTu	একটু	a little, a bit
elaka	এলাকা	area

f

farshi	ফারসি/ফার্সি	Farsi
fæla	ফেলা	to throw (away)
fera	ফেরা	to return
fOl	ফল	fruit
fOle	ফলে	as a result of
fOrashi	ফরাসী	French
fupa	ফুপা	husband of father's sister (E)
fupu	ফুপু	father's sister (E)
furano	ফুরানো	to be finished

g

gal	গাল	cheek
gaRi	গাড়ি/গাড়ী	car
ghash	ঘাস	grass
ghonisTho	ঘনিষ্ঠ	close
ghora	ঘোরা	turn, go
ghoshona dewa	ঘোষণা দেওয়া	to announce
ghOnTa	ঘণ্টা	hour
ghOr	ঘর	room (E and W); house, home (W)
ghOta	ঘটা	to happen
ghOtona	ঘটনা	event, incident
ghum	ঘুম	sleep
ghumano	ঘুমানো	to sleep

Bengali–English glossary

ghush	ঘুষ	bribe
ghush khawa	ঘুষ খাওয়া	to take bribes
golapi	গোলাপি	pink
gorib	গরিব/গরীব	poor
goru	গরু	cow
gosholkhana	গোসলখানা	bathroom (E)
gOenagãti	গয়নাগাঁটি	jewellery
gOlpo	গল্প	story
gOrom	গরম	warm
gOto	গত	last, past
gram	গ্রাম	village
greftar kOra	গ্রেফতার করা	to arrest
grihini	গৃহিণী	housewife

h

hal dewa	হাল দেওয়া	to plough
haRi	হাড়ি	pan
hasha	হাসা	to laugh
hat	হাত	hand
hati	হাতি/হাতী	elephant
haT	হাট	market
hãsh	হাঁস	duck
hãTa	হাঁটা	walk
hæ̃	হ্যাঁ	yes
hingsha	হিংসা	jealousy
hira	হীরা	diamond
hishab	হিসাব	account
hoe	হয়ে	via
holdi	হলুদি	turmeric
holud	হলুদ	yellow
hote pare	হতে পারে	perhaps
hOrtal	হরতাল	general strike
hOtash	হতাশ	dejected
hOwa	হওয়া	to be(come); to happen; have to

i

iccha kOra	ইচ্ছা করা	to want
icche kOra	ইচ্ছে করা	to want (W)
id	ঈদ	Eid
id mobarak	ঈদ মোবারাক	happy Eid!

idaning	ইদানীং	recently
ilish	ইলিশ	hilsha
ingrej	ইংরেজ	English
inshallah	ইনশাল্লাহ্	God willing (Muslim)
itihash	ইতিহাস	history
ittadi	ইত্যাদি	etc.

j

ja	যা	what
jadughOr	জাদুঘর	museum
jaega	জায়গা	room, space
jai hok	যাই হোক	anyway, nevertheless
jal Taka	জাল টাকা	counterfeit money
jana	জানা	to know
janala	জানালা	window
janano	জানানো	to let know
jawa	যাওয়া	to go
jæmon	যেমন	such as, for example
je	যে	that
jela	জেলা	district
jhal	ঝাল	hot, spicy
jhOk-jhOk kOra	ঝক্-ঝক্ করা	to shine
jhOR	ঝড়	storm
ji	জি	yes (E)
jib-jontu	জীব-জন্তু	animal
jiggesh kOra	জিজ্ঞেস করা	to ask
jinish	জিনিস	thing
jinishpOttro	জিনিসপত্র	things
jira	জিরা	cumin (E)
jire	জিরে	cumin (W)
jodi	যদি	if
jogajog kOra	যোগাযোগ করা	to contact
jomi	জমি	land
jonno	জন্য	for
joTil	জটিল	complicated
jOkhon	যখন	when, while
jOl	জল	water (W)
jOla	জ্বলা	to burn
jOl-khabar	জল-খাবার	breakfast (W)
jOma hOwa	জমা হওয়া	to be credited
jOma rakha	জমা রাখা	to deposit

Bengali–English glossary

jOnmodin	জন্মদিন	birthday
jOnogOn	জনগণ	people
jOr	জ্বর	fever
jOr uTheche	জ্বর উঠেছে	.... has a fever
jOtno kOra	যত্ন করা	to take care of
jukto-rajjo	যুক্তরাজ্য	UK
jukto-rastro	যুক্তরাষ্ট্র	US

k

kache	কাছে	near, with
kaj	কাজ	work
kaj kOra	কাজ করা	to work
kaje-i	কাজেই	therefore
kaka	কাকা	father's brother
kaki	কাকি	wife of father's brother
kal(ke)	কাল/কালকে	tomorrow, yesterday
kalo	কালো	black
kalobajari	কালোবাজারী	black marketeer
kan	কান	ear
kapoR-copoR	কাপড়-চোপড়	clothes and suchlike
karjalOe	কার্যালয়	office
karon	কারণ	reason; because
karone	কারণে	because of
kaTa	কাটা	to cut
kaTh-mistri	কাঠ-মিস্ত্রি	carpenter
kãci	কাঁচি	scissors
kãda	কাঁদা	to cry
kãpa	কাঁপা	to shake
kæmne	কেমনে	how
kæmon	কেমন	how
kæno	কেন	why
kæsh kOra	ক্যাশ করা	to cash
ke	কে	who
keci	কেচি	scissors (E)
kena	কেনা	to buy
kerani	কেরানী/কেরানি	official
khabar	খাবার	food
khabar-dabar	খাবার-দাবার	food and things
khæla	খেলা	to play
khajna	খাজনা	tax
khala	খালা	mother's sister (E)

khali	খালি	empty
khalu	খালু	husband of mother's sister (E)
kham	খাম	envelope
khashi	খাসি	goat
khata	খাতা	notebook
khawa	খাওয়া	to eat
kheal kOra	খেয়াল করা	to notice
kheal rakha	খেয়াল রাখা	to keep an eye on
khicuRi	খিচুড়ি	rice with lentils and vegetables
khide/khuda	খিদে/খুদা	hunger
khiT-khiT kOra	খিট-খিট্ করা	to fret, grumble
khoda-hafez	খোদা-হাফেজ	goodbye (Muslim leave-taking)
khoka	খোকা	little boy
khola	খোলা	open
khola	খোলা	to open
khoriddar	খরিদ্দার	customer
khoti	ক্ষতি	damage
khõj kOra	খোঁজ করা	to seek out, enquire
khõja	খোঁজা	to look for
khObor	খবর	news
khOborer kagoj	খবরের কাগজ	newspaper
khOmota	ক্ষমতা	power
khub beshi	খুব বেশী	a lot
khub	খুব	very, very much
khun kOra	খুন করা	to murder
khuni	খুনি/খুনী	murderer
khushi	খুশি/খুশী	glad
ki	কি/কী	what
ki bhabe	কি ভাবে	how, what way
ki kore	কি করে	how
ki na	কী না	whether
ki shOrbonash	কী সর্বনাশ!	how terrible!
kichu	কিছু	something
kichu kichu	কিছু কিছু	several
kichudin	কিছু দিন	a couple of days
kisher jonno	কিসের জন্য	for what?
klanto	ক্লান্ত	tired
kobji	কজি	wrist
kon	কোন	which
kono	কোনো	any

Bengali–English glossary

kono ækTa	কোনো একটা	a, some
konodin	কোনোদিন	ever
korma	কোরমা/কোর্মা	rice with yoghurt, coconut-milk, nuts, meat
kormi	কর্মী	worker
kothae	কোথায়	where
kothao	কোথাও	anywhere
kotodin	কতদিন	how many days
kotokkhon	কতক্ষন	how long
koThin	কঠিন	difficult
kObe	কবে	when, on which day
kOe-ækTa	কয়েকটা	a couple
kOkhon	কখন	when
kOkhono	কখনো	ever, at any time
kOl	কল	watertap
kOla	কলা	banana
kOlom	কলম	pen
kOm	কম	little, less
kOmbol	কম্বল	blanket
kOmla	কমলা	orange
kOr	কর	tax
kOra	করা	to do
kOrmocari	কর্মচারী	clerk
kOrta	কর্তা	boss
kOsTo	কষ্ট	trouble, difficulty
kOsTo kOra	কষ্ট করা	to take trouble
kOtha	কথা	words, what is said
kuci-kuci kore	কুচি-কুচি করে	in small pieces

l

labh	লাভ	use, benefit
lal	লাল	red
lau	লাউ	gourd
lebu	লেবু	lemon
lekha	লেখা	to write
lekhok	লেখক	writer
lok	লোক	person
lokjon	লোকজন	persons, people
lOmba	লম্বা	tall, long
lOnka	লঙ্কা/লংকা	chilli (W)

m

ma	মা	mother
mach	মাছ	fish
maddhome	মাধ্যমে	through
majhe majhe	মাঝে মাঝে	regularly
majhkhane	মাঝখানে	between
makhano	মাখানো	to mix
mal-pOttro	মাল-পত্র	luggage
mama	মামা	mother's brother
mami	মামি	wife of mother's brother
mangsho	মাংস	meat
manush	মানুষ	person
mara	মারা	to hit, beat
markin	মার্কিন	American
mash	মাস	month
mashi	মাসি	mother's sister (W)
matha	মাথা	head
matha dhoreche	মাথা ধরেছে	...has a headache
mattro	মাত্র	only
maTh	মাঠ	field
maya	মায়া	pity
mæla	মেলা	fair
me-e	মেয়ে	girl, daughter
megh	মেঘ	cloud
mesho	মেসো	husband of mother's sister (W)
michil	মিছিল	demonstration
michilkari	মিছিলকারী	demonstrator
mile	মিলে	together
mishano	মিশানো	to mix
mish-mishe kalo	মিসমিশে কালো	pitch-black
mishOr	মিশর	Egypt
misTi	মিষ্টি	sweet
mittha kOtha	মিথ্যা কথা	lies
miTi-miTi	মিটিমিটি	twinkling
miT-miTe shOetan	মিটমিটে শয়তান	a deceitful devil
moddhe	মধ্যে	in
mohila	মহিলা	lady
moja	মোজা	sock
mon	মন	mind
mon cae	মন চায়	I want

Bengali–English glossary

mondir	মন্দির	temple
mone ache	মনে আছে	I remember
mone hOe	মনে হয়	I think, it seems
mone poRche	মনে পড়ছে	I remember
mongolbar	মঙ্গলবার	Tuesday
montri	মন্ত্রী	minister
montri porishOd	মন্ত্রী-পরিষদ	cabinet
moric	মরিচ	chilli (E)
mote-i na	মোটেই না	not at all
moTa	মোটা	fat
mOd	মদ	booze
mOja	মজা	pleasure, fun
mOja pawa	মজা পাওয়া	to enjoy oneself
mOn	মণ	c. 37.5 kg (40 **sher**)
mOnco	মঞ্চ	stage, theatre
mOncostho kOra	মঞ্চস্থ করা	to perform
mOshae	মশায়	sir, Mr
mOton	মতন	like
mukh	মুখ	mouth
mukhostho kOra	মুখস্থ করা	to learn by heart
murgi	মুরগি/মুরগী/মুর্গি	chicken

n

nagorik	নাগরিক	citizen
naika	নায়িকা	actress
nak	নাক	nose
naki	নাকি	or
nam	নাম	name
namkOra	নামকরা	famous
nao	নাঁও	boat
naRa	নাড়া	to stir
nasta	নাস্তা	breakfast (E)
naTok	নাটক	play
neta	নেতা	leader
netritto dewa	নেতৃত্ব দেওয়া	to lead
newa	নেওয়া	to take
nice	নিচে	under; down
nie	নিয়ে	about; with (the use of)
nil	নীল	blue
nirbacon	নির্বাচন	election
niribili	নিরিবিলি	quiet

nirOb	নীরব	silent
nirObe	নীরবে	silently
nishcOe	নিশ্চয়	certainly
nishedh	নিষেধ	forbidden
nishedh kOra	নিষেধ করা	to forbid
nobbo	নব্য	new
nodi	নদী	river
nObobOrsho	নববর্ষ	New Year
nOmbor	নম্বর	mark
nOmoshkar	নমস্কার	hello
nun	নুন	salt (W)

o

o	ও	also; and
o ma!	ওহ্ মা!	oh my!
obhinOe kOra	অভিনয় করা	to act
oitihashik	ঐতিহাসিক	historical
okhane	ওখানে	there
onnanno	অন্যান্য	other, different
onno	অন্য	other
onuggrohopurbok	অনুগ্রহপূর্বক	please
onumoti	অনুমতি	permission
onurodh kOra	অনুরোধ করা	to request
otit	অতীত	the past
oTha	ওঠা	to go up, to get up, to board

O

Obak hOwa	অবাক হওয়া	to be surprised
Obak kOra	অবাক করা	to surprise
Obak laga	অবাক লাগা	to be surprised
Obhab	অভাব	lack
Obossho-i	অবশ্যই	certainly
Ojana	অজানা	unknown
Olpo ekTu	অল্প একটু	a little
Onek	অনেক	much, many
Oneke-i	অনেকেই	many people
Opekkha kOra	অপেক্ষা করা	to wait
Opurbo shundor	অপূর্ব সুন্দর	extremely beautiful
Oshustho	অসুস্থ	unwell

Bengali–English glossary

p

pa	পা	foot
pæn-pæn kOra	প্যানপ্যান করা	to nag
pala	পালা	to keep, tend
palon kOra	পালন করা	to celebrate
pani	পানি	water (E)
para	পারা	can, be allowed
parOssho	পারস্য	Iran
parshi	পারসী	Iranian
paRa	পাড়া	neighbourhood
pashe	পাশে	next to
pasher	পাশের	next, adjoining
pata	পাতা	to extend, spread
patla	পাতলা	thin
paThano	পাঠানো	to send
pawa	পাওয়া	to get, receive
pechone	পেছনে	behind
peT	পেট	stomach
peTuk	পেটুক	gluttonous, glutton
pẽaj	পেঁয়াজ	onion
piric	পিরিচ	saucer
pishe	পিসে	husband of father's sister (W)
pishi	পিসি	father's sister (W)
piTh	পিঠ	back
poa	পোয়া	c. 230 grams
pokeTmar	পকেটমার	pickpocket
polao	পোলাও	pilau
ponDit	পণ্ডিত	pundit, teacher
poricOe kOrano	পরিচয় করানো	to introduce
porikkha	পরীক্ষা	examination
porjonto	পর্যন্ত	until
poroTa	পরোটা	paratha
porshu	পরশু	day before yesterday/after tomorrow
pottrika	পত্রিকা	magazine
pouro shObha	পৌরসভা	local council
põuchano	পৌঁছানো	to arrive
pOchondo kOra	পছন্দ করা	to like
pOhela/pOela	পহেলা/পয়লা	first
pOra	পরা	to put on (clothes)
pOramOrsho	পরামর্শ	advice

pOre	পরে	later, after
pOrer din	পরের দিন	the next day
pORa	পড়া	to study, read; fall
pORano	পড়ানো	teach
pOth	পথ	path, way
põca	পঁচা	rotten
põca lage	পঁচা লাগে	it is unpleasant
prakTis kOra	প্র্যাকটিস করা	to practise
prio	প্রিয়	favourite
prithibi	পৃথিবী	world
procOnDo	প্রচণ্ড	severe, violent
prodhan	প্রধান	main, head
prodhan-montri	প্রধান-মন্ত্রী	prime minister
prodorshoni	প্রদর্শনী	exhibition
prosno	প্রশ্ন	question
protarona kOra	প্রতারণা করা	to cheat
prothom(e)	প্রথম/প্রথমে	(at) first
proti	প্রতি	each
protibad	প্রতিবাদ	protest
protibeshi	প্রতিবেশী	neighbour
proyojon	প্রয়োজন	need
puja	পূজা	Hindu feast
pukur	পুকুর	pond
pulish	পুলিশ	policeman
purano	পুরানো	old
purbo	পূর্ব	east
puron kOra	পূরণ করা	to complete

r

rajkumar	রাজকুমার	prince
rajnitibid	রাজনীতিবিদ	politician
rakha	রাখা	to put, place
ranna kOra	রান্না করা	to cook
rannaghOr	রান্নাঘর	kitchen
rasta	রাস্তা	street
rastar shesh mathae	রাস্তার শেষ মাথায়	at the end of the street
rat	রাত	night
rãdha	রাঁধা	to cook
robibar	রবিবার	Sunday
roshun	রসুন	garlic
rOng	রং	colour

Bengali–English glossary

rOsh	রস	juice
ruTi	রুটি	roti

s

salwar-kamij	সালোয়ার-কামিজ	salwar kameez
shabdhan	সাবধান	careful
shabdhane	সাবধানে	carefully
shada	সাদা	white
shadharon	সাধারণ	ordinary
shadhin	স্বাধীন	free
shagor kOla	সাগর কলা	large-size banana
shahajjo kOra	সাহায্য করা	to help
shaheb	সাহেব	mister, sir (Muslim term of respect)
shak	শাক	leafy greens
shakkhatkar	সাক্ষাৎকার	interview
shal	সাল	calendar year
shami	স্বামী	husband
shamne	সামনে	in front of
shangbadik	সাংবাদিক	journalist
shara	সারা	whole, all
shaRi	শাড়ি	sari
shathe	সাথে	with (E)
shãtar	সাঁতার	swimming
shebika	সেবিকা	nurse
shekha	শেখা	to learn
shekhane	সেখানে	there
shekhano	শেখানো	to teach
sher	সের	c 0.9 kg
shes hOwa	শেষ হওয়া	to be finished
shes kOra	শেষ করা	to finish
sheTu	সেতু	bridge
shigghro	শীঘ্র	quickly
shikkhika	শিক্ষিকা	teacher (female)
shikkhOk	শিক্ষক	teacher (male)
shim	শিম	broad beans
shishu	শিশু	baby
shobar ghOr	শোবার ঘর	bedroom
shobji	সব্জি/সব্জী	vegetable
shobuj	সবুজ	green
shoja	সোজা	straight, easy

shombar	সোমবার	Monday
shona	শোনা	to hear, listen
shondha	সন্ধ্যা	evening
shonibar	শনিবার	Saturday
shorie dewa	সরিয়ে দেওয়া	to remove
shorisha	সরিষা	mustard (E)
shorshe	সর্ষে	mustard (W)
shoru	সরু	narrow
shotti kOtha	সত্যি কথা	truth
showa	শোয়া	to lie down
shOb	সব	all
shOb kichu	সব কিছু	everything
shOb milie	সব মিলিয়ে	altogether
shObai	সবাই	all, everyone
shObdo	শব্দ	word, sound
shObshOmOe	সবসময়	always
shOhoj	সহজ	simple
shOhokari	সহকারী	assistant
shOhor	শহর	town
shOhosha	সহসা	quickly
shOkal	সকাল	morning
shOman	সমান	equally
shOmossha	সমস্যা	problem
shOmosshae pORa	সমস্যায় পড়া	to run into problems
shOmOe	সময়	time
shOmOe mOton	সময় মতন	in good time
shOncoyi hishab	সঞ্চয়ী হিসাব	savings account
shOngbad	সংবাদ	news
shOngbad shOmmelon	সংবাদ সম্মেলন	press conference
shOnge	সঙ্গে	with
shOnglap	সংলাপ	dialogue
shOngram	সংগ্রাম	struggle
shOngshOd	সংসদ	parliament
shOngskriti	সংস্কৃতি	culture
shOngskrito	সংস্কৃত	Sanskrit
shOpta	সপ্তাহ	week
shOrbottro	সর্বত্র	everywhere
shOrkar	সরকার	government
shOtteo	সত্ত্বেও	in spite of
shuci	সূচি	timetable
shudhu	শুধু	only

Bengali–English glossary

shudhumattro	শুধুমাত্র	only
shukh	সুখ	happiness
shukhi	সুখী	happy
shukna	শুকনা	dry (E)
shukno	শুকনো	dry (W)
shukrobar	শুক্রবার	Friday
shundor	সুন্দর	beautiful
shundor laga	সুন্দর লাগা	to look beautiful
shuru hOwa	শুরু হওয়া	to begin
shuru kOra	শুরু করা	to begin
shustho	সুস্থ	well, healthy
sinema	সিনেমা	cinema; film
slamalaikum	স্লামালাইকুম	hello (Muslim greeting)
snan-ghOr	স্নানঘর	bathroom (W)
stri	স্ত্রী	wife

t

ta hole	তাহলে	then
ta(i)	তা/তাই	that
tachaRa(-o)	তাছাড়া/তাছাড়াও	besides
tai	তাই	therefore
tai na ki?	তাই নাকি?	is that so?
takano	তাকানো	to look
tar mane	তার মানে	its meaning is, this means that
tara	তারা	star
tarikh	তারিখ	date
tarpOr(e)	তারপর/তারপরে	after that
taRa-taRi	তাড়াতাড়ি	quickly
teji	তেজী	strong
tel	তেল	oil
thaka	থাকা	to live, stay
thana	থানা	police station
theke	থেকে	from, out of; than
to	তো	really, indeed, actually
tObe	তবে	but
tObla	তবলা	small drum
tOkhon	তখন	then
tOktOk	তকতক্	sparkling clean
tOk-tOk kOra	তকতক্ করা	to sparkle
tOttabodhayok	তত্ত্বাবধায়ক	caretaker, interim
tritio	তৃতীয়	third

tushar kOna	তুষারকণা	Snow White

T

Taka	টাকা	taka, money
Taka-pOesha	টাকা-পয়সা	money
Tana	টানা	to pull, drag
Tæksicalok	ট্যাক্সিচালক	taxi-driver
ThanDa	ঠাণ্ডা	cold
Thik	ঠিক	right, OK, correct
Thikana	ঠিকানা	address
Thik-i	ঠিকই	indeed
ThOkano	ঠকানো	to cheat
TOk	টক	sour

u

ucit	উচিৎ	necessary
udjapon kOra	উদ্‌যাপন করা	to celebrate
ukil	উকিল	lawyer
upobhog kOra	উপভোগ করা	to enjoy
upohar	উপহার	present
upojatio	উপজাতীয়	indigenous
upore	উপরে	on, over, above
utshOb	উৎসব	festivity
uttor dewa	উত্তর দেওয়া	to answer
ũcu	উঁচু	high

w

walaikum-salam	ওয়ালাইকুম-সালাম	hello (Muslim greeting)

Index

Using this index, you can find discussion of particular topics easily. The numbers refer to the relevant units.

Grammar index

For quick reference, you can also look in the Grammar summary. **Bengali** words are in **bold** type, *English* words are in *italics*.

a and *the* 4
ache, nei, thaka 2, 11
adverbs 7

bhalo lage 7
bole 13, 14

comparative sentences 14
complex sentences 15
compound words 7
conditional clauses 14
conditional participle 14

demonstratives 4
doubling of adjectives 12

echo words 7

future 6

habitual past 12
holo 11
human nouns 10

-i 7
imperative 6
impersonal construction 7
indefinite pronoun 10
infinitive 9
interrogative pronoun 8

leaving out pronouns 8
locative of nouns 4

negative sentences 1, 4, 5, 6, 12
numerals 3, 8, 10

passive clauses 15
past participle 9
past perfect 12
past progressive 11
personal pronouns 1, 2, 3
possessive of nouns 4
postpositions 8
present perfect 5
present progressive 7
present tense 4, 5

Index

questions 1, 8, 13

reflexive pronoun 11
relative clauses 14
'repeating' words 13

simple past 11

-Ta/-Ti 4

verbal noun 13

word order 1, 13, 14

Topics

amounts and weights 8

clothes 8
colours 8
cooking 7
crime 11

dates 12, 15
days and their parts 10, 11

family 2
farming 13
feast days 15
food 6, 7, 8

homes 10

illness 7

jobs 3

music 5

nationalities 1

personal characteristics 3
politics 11
post and bank services 9

towns 4
transport 5
travel 5, 9, 14
TV programmes 10

village life 13

Functions

addressing people 1

buying things 8

counting 3, 8

describing a sequence of actions 9
describing locations 4
describing people 3
describing the old days 12

emphasising 7
expressing a cause 14
expressing existence 2
expressing feelings 7, 13
expressing likes and dislikes 6, 7
expressing possession 3
expressing possibility 15

giving directions 4
giving orders and suggestions 6
giving permission 12
giving personal information 1
greetings 1

making a comparison 14

ordering food and drink 7

reporting speech 13
requesting 9, 12

stating a condition 14
stating an obligation 13

telling the time 10

Related titles from Routledge

Colloquial Urdu

Tej K. Bhatia and Ashok Koul

Colloquial Urdu is easy to use and completely up to date! Written by experienced teachers for self-study or class use, the course offers you a step-by-step approach to written and spoken Urdu. No prior knowledge of the language is required.

What makes *Colloquial Urdu* your best choice in personal language learning?

- interactive – lots of exercises for regular practice
- clear – concise grammar notes
- practical – useful vocabulary and pronunciation guide
- complete – including answer key and special reference section

By the end of this rewarding course you will be able to communicate confidently and effectively in Urdu in a broad range of everyday situations.

ISBN13: 978-0-415-13540-5 (pbk)
ISBN13: 978-0-415-28950-4 (audio CDs)
ISBN13: 978-0-415-44539-9 (pack)
ISBN13: 978-0-203-97730-9 (ebk)
ISBN13: 978-0-415-47058-2 (MP3)

Available at all good bookshops
For ordering and further information please visit:
www.routledge.com

Related titles from Routledge

Colloquial Hindi

Tej K. Bhatia

Colloquial Hindi is easy to use and completely up to date! Written by an experienced teacher for self-study or class use, the course offers you a step-by-step approach to written and spoken Hindi. No prior knowledge of the language is required. What makes *Colloquial Hindi* your best choice in personal language learning?

- interactive – lots of exercises for regular practice
- clear – concise grammar notes
- practical – useful vocabulary and pronunciation guide
- complete – including answer key and special reference section

By the end of this rewarding course you will be able to communicate confidently and effectively in Hindi in a broad range of everyday situations.

ISBN13: 978-0-415-41956-7 (pbk)
ISBN13: 978-0-415-39527-4 (audio CDs)
ISBN13: 978-0-415-39527-4 (pack)
ISBN13: 978-0-415-43152-8 (ebk)
ISBN13: 978-0-415-49823-4 (MP3)

Available at all good bookshops
For ordering and further information please visit:
www.routledge.com